# THE AESTHETES

## A SOURCEBOOK

# THE AESTHETES

## A SOURCEBOOK

EDITED BY

## IAN SMALL

*Department of English Language and Literature*
*University of Birmingham*

ROUTLEDGE & KEGAN PAUL
LONDON, BOSTON AND HENLEY

First published in 1979
by Routledge & Kegan Paul Ltd

39 Store Street,
London WC1E 7DD,

Broadway House,
Newtown Road,
Henley-on-Thames,
Oxon RG9 1EN and

9 Park Street,
Boston, Mass. 02108, USA

Set in Monotype Baskerville 169, 10/12
and printed and bound in Great Britain at
The Camelot Press Ltd, Southampton

British Library Cataloguing in Publication Data

The Aesthetes.
1. Arts, European – History – Addresses, essays,
lectures 2. English literature – 19th century
3. Aesthetic movement (British Art) – Addresses,
essays, lectures
I. Small, Ian
700'.94    NX542    79–40247

ISBN 0 7100 0145 2
ISBN 0 7100 0146 0 Pbk

# CONTENTS

## Part III REACTIONS TO AESTHETICISM

# PLATES

*between pages 96 and 97*

George Du Maurier's cartoons

# ACKNOWLEDGMENTS

Acknowledgment is gratefully made to the following publishers for permission to reprint material: to William Blackwood & Sons Ltd for *Miss Brown*; to The Bodley Head for material from *Works* by Max Beerbohm; and to Macmillan Ltd, publishers of Alfred Tennyson. George Du Maurier's work is reproduced by permission of *Punch*. I should like to thank both my colleagues at Birmingham University for answering numerous queries and Dr Ian Ross of Trinity College Dublin for help in assembling material. Thanks are also due to the many people who helped with proofs, particularly Miss Christine Thomas and Mr Toby English.

Ian Small
University of Birmingham

# Introduction

Art for Art's sake! Hail, truest Lord of Hell!
Hail Genius, Master of the Moral Will!
'The filthiest of all paintings painted well
Is mightier than the purest painted ill!'
Yes, mightier than the purest painted well,
So prone are we toward the broad way to Hell.

(*Tennyson*)

The Aesthetic movement, or Art for Art's Sake movement, which in England flourished from the late 1860s until the early 1890s, was one rooted in a series of paradoxes. The profoundest of these paradoxes involves the question whether it is indeed possible for art to exist for its own sake and thus whether the description 'Art for Art's Sake' finally has any real meaning. It was a question which most of the apologists of Aestheticism failed to answer properly and the conviction that the artist was responsible not simply to his art lay behind most of the hostile reactions to the movement.

The first problem though, for the literary critic, is to define historically the Aesthetic movement. Aestheticism pretended both a philosophy of life and a philosophy of art, and so the Aesthetic movement was both a literary and a social phenomenon. In his social guise the aesthete was – and still is – immediately recognisable. A series of fashions for extravagant dress, exaggerated poses, for the cultivation of the beautiful in so diverse a range of objects as wallpapers, flowers and blue china were the most immediately recognisable characteristics of a social cult. All these fashions were modelled upon the example of figures in the literary and artistic world of the 1870s and 1880s, and they created, particularly in London and Oxford, a readily identifiable social phenomenon that was a clearly defined and obvious target for the social satirists of the time. Aestheticism, in one way or another, figured as one of the butts of the precise satire of W. H. Mallock in *The New Republic* in 1877, of the waspish and caustic wit of George Du Maurier's cartoons a few years later in *Punch* and of the affable exaggerations of W. S. Gilbert's libretto for *Patience* in 1881. And yet the literary movement which generated those absurd fashions for knee-breeches, peacocks' feathers, sunflowers and blue china stubbornly resists precise definition. The Aesthetic movement was in no way a school like the Pre-Raphaelite Brotherhood, a group of like-minded artists, their unity publicly advertised by a manifesto and a common signature to their works; but contemporary critics failed to distinguish between Pre-Raphaelitism and Aestheticism, and even now, given the perspective of a hundred years, it is not easy to see what actually united so diverse a group of personalities as Walter Pater, Oscar Wilde, Algernon Swinburne and James Abbott McNeill Whistler as a movement, far less what connected them to Pre-Raphaelitism. But to contemporaries the later movement appeared to be only a development of the former, and so Rossetti and the other Pre-Raphaelites became included in generalisations about Aestheticism. And as the origins of Aestheticism are confused, so too is its demise. At some point in the early 1890s, as the cultivation of the beautiful experience for its own sake was replaced as an artistic credo by the cultivation of *any* experience for its own sake, Aestheticism modulated into that movement which we now call Decadence.

None the less, the one leading characteristic that did unify the work of all the main writers (and artists) associated with Aestheticism was their fixed determination to value art far more highly than Victorian literary and art-criticism had hitherto done. The primacy not only of the creation of art, but particularly of the experience of it was the affront to Victorian sensibility that Aestheticism perpetrated. The experience of art was held to be not only equal in value to the experiences of life, but in some cases even capable of transcending them. 'To experience life in the manner of art' was the definition of spiritual success in the terms of Aestheticism: and it is precisely this fundamental revaluation of the relationship between art and life which is the key concern of all Aesthetic criticism and which allows the modern reader a way of exploring the revolutionary nature of the movement.

The first serious claim during the course of the nineteenth century that aesthetics and ethics were entirely separable categories of thought, that art should suffer no incursions from the moral sphere, was made by the French poet and novelist Théophile Gautier in the preface to his novel *Mademoiselle de Maupin* in 1835. Gautier contrasted beauty with utility and declared unequivocally that beauty in nature or in art could have no end other than itself. Two decades later those and similar sentiments had crossed the Channel and become crucial elements in Algernon Swinburne's poetry and criticism. In *Poems and Ballads* (1866) he took what had hitherto been forbidden topics as the subject for poetry: illicit kinds of love, blasphemy and indulgent sensuality figured prominently in Swinburne's lyrics. The events that followed the publication of the book formed a pattern that typified responses to the other allegedly scurrilous works produced under the influence of the leading ideas of Aestheticism. Press reviews accused Swinburne of sordidness and depravity and mention was persistently made of his allusions to sexual unnaturalness. *Punch* gave him licence to change his name to its proper form, 'Swineborne'. The immediate consequence was that the book was withdrawn by its original publishers, Edward Moxon, a distinguished house who numbered Tennyson among their authors. Swinburne succeeded in placing it with John Camden Hotten, a publisher with a rather compromised reputation and who quickly urged him to compose and publish a pamphlet, *Notes on Poems and Reviews*, as a defence against the chorus of condemnation that *Poems and Ballads* had encountered. Swinburne's essay was naturally highly polemical. Its concluding paragraphs contained the first sustained plea in English literature for the freedom of art from any limitations imposed by moral considerations. A more closely reasoned, deliberate and certainly more persuasive elaboration of Swinburne's account of what formed the proper relationship between art and morality followed soon afterwards in his study *William Blake*. Swinburne found in Blake, as he had in Gautier and Baudelaire, a precursor of Aestheticism and in his essay he maintained unequivocally that the morality of any work of art was an incidental effect and its formal accomplishment a central one. The argument that art reflected life in such a way as to allow the audience, reader or spectator to make observations about man's moral nature was of course firmly entrenched in Victorian culture: so much so that to call the validity of it into question was tantamount to uttering heresy. Indeed the dominant view in aesthetics, from Plato's *Republic* onwards, is that any experience of art is intrinsically involved with ethics. The prolonged and bitter criticism that Aestheticism was to encounter during the 1870s and 1880s was not directed so much against particular artifacts – although they were ridiculed – but against the basic formalism of the Aesthetic movement, the assertion that art and literature could, in some way, be morally neutral.

The most sustained, profound, and – in terms of English literature – most influential Aesthetic critic to question prevailing Victorian critical orthodoxies was Walter Pater. Pater was a retiring Oxford don. He was elected to a fellowship at Brasenose College in the late 1860s and lived a life in London and Oxford that was marked by its quietness. Although he was almost painfully shy, his career was crowded with the acquaintance of eminent figures or men who were destined to achieve fame or notoriety. He taught Gerard Manley Hopkins, and, later, Oscar Wilde, over whom his influence was complete. He also taught Lionel Johnson and influenced Arthur Symons, George Moore and W. B. Yeats. His most stimulating and certainly his most notorious work was his first, *Studies in the History of the Renaissance* (1873). Indeed the rest of his career can be seen as a deliberate elaboration and clarification of the propositions he advanced there. None the less, Pater's importance for the subsequent development of Aestheticism is difficult to overestimate for he was the first serious and forthright English critic to maintain that aesthetics, far from being implicated in cultural and moral issues, could, and should, exist freed from those contexts. This claim for the relative autonomy of aesthetics and ethics implied, on Pater's part, certain presuppositions about the nature of perception and strong convictions about the relative status and function of art and criticism, all of which were transmitted as aphorisms to the Aesthetic movement generally, and in particular to Oscar Wilde.

During the late 1850s and 1860s a group of British psychologists, amongst whom Herbert Spencer, Alexander Bain and James Sully were the most eminent, had conducted a systematic investigation into the nature of perception and cognition. Developing some leading eighteenth-century ideas, they proposed that the mind perceives the exterior world by a series of impressions of it. (The term 'impression' was one that reverberated through both psychological speculation and literary and art criticism until the turn of the century.) It was the nature of the individual mind to dwell upon the uniqueness of an impression, upon what differentiated it qualitatively from the multitudes preceding or following it. This same group of psychologists also attempted to analyse in what ways aesthetic responses would prove amenable to psychological investigation. They maintained that all human activities were capable of being divided into two broad categories: those that were fundamentally life-enhancing and those that were undertaken for their own sake. It was in this latter category that they located man's prototypical aesthetic impulses. The extent of man's civilisation was determined by his ability to discriminate between the pleasures given by this sort of activity. Art represented simply the highest conceivable quality and quantity of human pleasure; it was vouchsafed to the spectator in terms of an impression and was therefore relative to the individual receiver of that impression. In the 1850s and 1860s, then, there was a body of new scientific opinion prepared to treat aesthetic response entirely in isolation from any other consideration – ethical or perceptual.

Now it seems that Pater was broadly aware of the extent and nature of this debate on the psychology of aesthetics simply because the closely related set of terms or jargon – *impression, discrimination, relative* and *pleasure* – that had been generated by it was appropriated in its entirety by him into his two most polemical early essays, the preface and the conclusion to *The Renaissance*. In his preface Pater began by revising Arnold's famous dictum (taken from his lecture, delivered in 1861, 'On Translating Homer') that the critic must 'see the object as in itself it really is'. Pater focused attention away from the object of contemplation and on to the contemplating mind. Arnold's injunction seemed to ignore the large and pertinent question of the nature of individual responses to a work of art – what Pater called the critic's 'impression' of it. The business of the aesthetic critic was therefore to discriminate his impressions of the object under contemplation. But as impressions were always relative to the individual spectator, so the ability to discriminate fully and finely his impressions of art defined the successful critic. As a consequence the practice of criticism moved away from the sphere of aesthetics – general or abstract questions about the nature of the beautiful – and became concerned with concrete and specific examples of beauty. Now Pater's thesis that a work of art can be perceived only by means of the individual impression of the spectator was pursued in the book's conclusion, which he had published as part of a long periodical essay on William Morris in 1868. Knowledge and experience of the world – perception generally, Pater maintained – are only a succession or series of impressions of it. The simple phenomenological proposition behind Pater's work is that the perceiver is certain of only his *own* impressions, and the individual, although celebrating his individuality, is consequently isolated in the 'chamber' of his own mind, a victim of his own impressions of the world beyond. And to overcome this isolation, success in life became, in Pater's eyes, defined in terms of the heterogeneity of experience: of controlling one's life in such a way as to ensure as many pleasurable experiences as possible – in Pater's famous phrase, burning with a 'hard gem-like flame'. At this point the experience of art becomes of paramount importance because it is both more intense and more reliable than the day-to-day experiences of life. Experience of art thus transcends, or improves upon, the experiences of life.

In one of his autobiographies, *The Trembling of the Veil*, W. B. Yeats reported how on an evening soon after he had made Oscar Wilde's acquaintance, he saw Wilde conspicuously flourishing a copy of *The Renaissance*:[1]

> 'It is my golden book; I never travel anywhere without it, but it is the very flower of decadence: the last trumpet should have sounded the moment it was written.' 'But', said the dull man, 'would you not have given us time to read it?' 'O no,' was the retort, 'there would have been plenty of time afterwards – in either world.'

The view that Pater's work was amoral was quite a widely held one. He omitted the conclusion from the second edition of *The Renaissance* in 1877 because he 'conceived it might possibly mislead some of those young men into whose hands it might fall'. Indeed there is evidence that in the mid 1870s Pater acquired a reputation at Oxford as a teacher who was exerting a dubious influence upon undergraduates. He appeared as a thinly disguised character – Mr Rose – in W. H. Mallock's *The New Republic* (1877), a broadly satirical book about Oxford in the 1870s which caricatured for the most part the more eminent figures of Matthew Arnold, John Ruskin, Benjamin Jowett and T. H. Huxley. The portrait of Mr Rose struck some contemporary reviewers as an unnecessarily caustic one and in places it is indeed unpleasant. But the image of Pater that the book offered was quite widespread – particularly in Oxford. Pater was denounced in a sermon by the Bishop of Oxford, passed over for a junior proctorship in the university in 1874, and when in 1876 he announced his candidature for the election of the Professor of Poetry his action was greeted with a chorus of either derision or bitter contempt. His critics and opponents maintained that *The Renaissance* was an

1 W. B. Yeats, *Autobiographies* (1955), 130.

unhealthy book and Pater quickly acquired a reputation as the prototypical aesthete. The hostility to his work culminated in a series of scornful attacks in *The Oxford and Cambridge Undergraduates' Journal* in 1877. As Pater had appeared to endorse the idea of experience for its own sake, so his work quickly acquired overtones of decadence. The reaction to *The Renaissance* repeated the equally hostile, but much more public, response to *Poems and Ballads* a few years earlier. Later in his life Pater confessed to the critic and poet Edmund Gosse that he disliked the name of 'hedonist' for it created 'such a bad effect on the minds of people who don't know Greek'. Pater was complaining about the way in which his scrupulously precise and rather moral epicureanism – epitomised, for example, by the ascetic hero of his novel, *Marius the Epicurean* (1885) – had been taken as the theoretical justification for the excesses of Aestheticism. But the pejorative overtones of the term 'hedonist' were in a sense quite understandable, because as Pater had recommended art for art's sake and then experience for experience's sake, so his programme for individual aesthetic discrimination *could* modulate into a programme for decadence: experience for its own sake could very easily become (as in the case of Dorian Gray and his creator) *illicit* experience for its own sake.

Initially, however, what caught the public's imagination and then the eye of the famous cartoonist George Du Maurier was something much more harmless: the absurd, but finally inconsequential series of fads that those who professed Aestheticism seemed intent upon pursuing: the fashion for blue china that Dante Gabriel Rossetti and James Abbott McNeill Whistler had begun and Oscar Wilde had taken up; the knee-breeches that Wilde had popularised as an Aesthetic 'costume'; and in particular the inordinately high value placed upon the sunflower and the lily. Du Maurier's cartoons appeared in *Punch* in the late 1870s and the early 1880s and they probably did as much to familiarise a large readership with what was basically a metropolitan movement as any of its authentic products. But they would have been impossible without the very public figure of Wilde to focus upon. Indeed on several occasions he *appears* to be the specific target of Du Maurier's cartoons (although Du Maurier claimed to be caricaturing the type rather than the individual). In one cartoon which appeared in 1881 Maudle (which, with Postle-thwaite, was Du Maurier's name for the archetypal aesthete) a figure with Wilde's heavy face, figure and flowing hair, is seen leaning with his head on his hands towards a Mrs Brown. In his caption Du Maurier gives Maudle Wilde-like epigrams:[1]

> *Maudle.* 'How *consummately* lovely your son is, Mrs Brown!'
> *Mrs Brown (a Philistine from the country).* '*What*? He's a *nice, manly* boy, if you mean *that*, Mr Maudle. He has just left school, you know, and wishes to be an artist.'
> *Maudle.* '*Why* should he be an artist?'
> *Mrs Brown.* 'Well, he must be *something*!'
> *Maudle.* 'Why should he *be* anything? Why not let him remain for ever content to *exist beautifully*?'
> [*Mrs Brown determines that at all events her Son shall not study Art under Maudle.*]

Late in the preceding year Du Maurier had drawn attention to another characteristic of Aestheticism: its propensity to exclusiveness and élitism. The object of satire on this occasion was the reverence for flowers. In *Punch*, Postlethwaite was made to recite a Christmas story, 'Fleur des Alpes', in which his admiration for the edelweiss above the sunflower and lily conferred upon him social distinction.[2]

> The Aesthetic Young Man rose languidly from his seat, and leaning against a bookcase, with the Lily in his hand, and the Peacock's Feather in his hair, he read aloud . . .
> 'You have never heard of MAUDLE and Mrs CIMABUE BROWN? I dare say not. To know them is a Joy, and the privilege of a select and chosen few; for they are simply Perfect. Yet in their respective perfection, they differentiate from each other with a quite ineffably subtle exquisiteness.
> For *She* is Supremely Consummate – whereas *He* is Consummately Supreme. I constantly tell them so, and they agree with me.
> I also make a point of telling everybody else.
> My modesty prevents me from revealing to you all they tell me (and everybody else) about myself, beyond the mere fact that they consider me alone to combine, in my own mind and person, Supreme Consummateness with Consummate Supremacy – and I agree with them. We get on uncommonly well together, I can tell you.'

The exclusiveness that the Aesthetes professed was maintained by a jargon, an exclusive language, which formed the subject of many of

---

1 George Du Maurier, 'Maudle on the Choice of a Profession' *Punch*, vol. LXXX, 12 February 1881. See plate no. 6.
2 George Du Maurier, 'Fleur des Alpes', *Punch*, vol. LXXIX, 25 December 1880. See p. 174 below.

Du Maurier's jokes about them, especially their excessive use of superlatives. 'Consummate', 'blessed', 'precious' and in particular, 'utter' are the characteristic exclamations of his Aesthetes. The use of a precious and archaic diction, that basic Pre-Raphaelite and Aesthetic literary furniture, was another target for Du Maurier:[1]

> Glad lady mine, that glitterest,
> In shimmah of summah athwart the lawn,
> Canst tell me which is bitterest,
> The glammah of Eve, or the glimmah of dawn?

In fact preciousness and élitism were not by any means charges restricted to Aestheticsm. They had been levelled in the early 1860s against the intellectual culture that Matthew Arnold had advocated and against some of the tendencies of Pre-Raphaelitism. But when the accusation was made against Aestheticism it was related to that other charge of amorality. The Aesthetic movement seemed not only to court exclusiveness and obscurity but actually to claim that they were positive virtues.

It was an issue that once again Pater was deeply involved in as a source. The obscurity of art, above all of some modern English poetry, was a topical subject in the 1880s. To some members of the late Victorian reading public the achievement of their major poets, particularly Robert Browning and Dante Gabriel Rossetti, was compromised by the apparent obscurity of some passages in their work. To some of their critics obscurity in poetry seemed to deny what they took to be one of the central functions of language – that of communication. Their argument can be summarised by a quotation from Benjamin Jowett, the liberal theologian, enormously influential Master of Balliol College, Oxford and reputedly one of Pater's sternest critics. Jowett compared the apparently *necessary* obscurity of dead languages – in some Greek poetry, for instance – with what he saw as the *avoidable* obscurity of some recent English Poetry:[2]

> There are many passages in some of our greatest modern poets which are far too obscure; in which there is no proportion between style and subject; in which any half-expressed figure, any harsh construction, any distorted collocation of words, any remote sequence of ideas is admitted [. . . .] The obscurities of early Greek poets arose

1 George Du Maurier, 'Vers de Société', *Punch*, vol. LXXII, 13 January 1877.
2 Benjamin Jowett, *The Republic of Plato* (1876), 1.

*xix*

necessarily out of the state of language and logic which existed in their age [. . . .] For us the use of language ought in every generation to become clearer and clearer.

What Jowett was taking to be the pre-eminent characteristic of language was its social function. But to Pater the obscurity of both Browning and Rossetti had a further dimension, one involving artistic integrity. Pater emphasised the very centrality of obscurity or complexity in any modern work because those qualities became a necessary consequence of the problems involved in artistic creation. It was in precisely these terms that Pater described Rossetti's work:[1]

> His own meaning was always personal, and even recondite, in a certain sense measured and casuistical, sometimes complex and obscure: but the term was always, one could see, deliberately chosen from many competitors as the *just* transcript of that peculiar phase of soul, which he alone knew, precisely as he alone knew it.

In Pater's eyes, that is, a poem quite simply expresses the poet, and therefore obscurity (for the potential reader) is an almost inevitable consequence of the artist's fidelity to his own feelings and becomes evidence of the difference that exists between his sensibility and that of ordinary humanity. The assertion that the soul or sensibility of the artist is, by definition, of a different kind from that of most of his audience was broadly a late Romantic commonplace, and one that was central to the 1890s – and in particular to W. B. Yeats's – conception of what it meant to be an artist. (Indeed the image of the estranged, alienated artist is one of the traditions of the nineteenth century most freely drawn upon by the twentieth.) For Pater, though, there was a further and equally important point. The measure of an artist's fidelity to felt experience was to be found in his style, and style in art or literature or music became the signature of the *man* in his work. Now Pater's concept of style was in fact one which in critical terms turns out to be both restricted and unhelpful. It ignored, for example, the idea of a style based upon the common features of an age, of a nationality, or of a school. Rigorously and consistently employed, that is, his usage precludes the important senses of the term that are alluded to in names like *baroque, eighteenth-century* or *Impressionist*. Style was, in Pater's eyes, despite his reservations, above all else a hallmark of individuality.

But – to return to his example of Rossetti's verse – Pater's advocacy

---

1 Walter Pater, 'Dante Gabriel Rossetti' in *Appreciations* (1889), 207.

of a poet's right to create an individual style, if only as a consequence of the uniqueness of his sensibility, courted those very dangers of obscurity and élitism that Du Maurier had dwelt upon in his *Punch* cartoons. It was tantamount to constructing a *private* language. Moreover as the only morality which Aesthetic writers claimed to observe was that involved in the processes of creating art (that is the perfection of a work of art within its own terms), so their artistic conscience was aroused by the differences that existed not between moral and immoral art but between well-executed and ill-executed art. Within the terms of the expressive aesthetic that Pater had claimed for the modern poet, the formal characteristics of art, because they stood as a sign of the artist's individuality, became paramount. And in its expressive and formal qualities it was music, in Pater's famous definition, which became the model of all the other arts because in that art form the division between content and form can have no meaning.

However Pater had cleverly – and presumably quite deliberately – all but avoided a key issue, that of the way in which works of literature are received by the reader. (The topic is in fact briefly alluded to in the last paragraph of his essay 'Style'.) Contemporary critics had of course objected – and quite correctly so – that an expressive aesthetic such as Pater (and, later, Wilde and Whistler) had proposed, failed to account for the fact that art also has a public dimension: that is, that art has an audience. This expressive aesthetic seemed to explain perfectly the motives of an artist like Rossetti, who was reluctant to exhibit his pictures. However, some of the artists more closely associated with Aestheticism were of an altogether different disposition. Indeed of all the famous figures associated with the movement, Pater was probably the most retiring and least self-assured, in no sense a public figure. But most of the famous writers who were identified with the Aesthetic movement took great pains not only to address an audience but actually to exist in the public gaze. A figure like Wilde, for example, seemed to *need* a public response, to live as a celebrity – and finally as a scapegoat: all of which, of course, was quite inconsistent with a purely Aesthetic point of view because it made the argument that art was above all else personal, expressive and private impossible to sustain with any plausibility.

The two most public figures involved with the Aesthetic movement were James Abbott McNeill Whistler and Oscar Wilde. Although to a contemporary public they were represented as proclaiming the same views about art, Whistler's actual commitment to Aesthetic doctrines was in fact rather limited. It would be much more accurate to describe the aims revealed in *The Gentle Art of Making Enemies* (1890) as having their origins in Impressionism. Historically, however, the relationship between Aestheticism and Impressionism is a very complicated one. The history of the early reception in England of Impressionist work and Impressionist aspirations for art is extremely involved, mainly because of the partiality of its propagandists. What is certain, however, is that to contemporary eyes Impressionism became confused with Aestheticism, for their aims were broadly comparable and the 'impression' was a concept central to both movements. None the less Whistler was important for Aestheticism for two reasons. In the first place his case for libel against Ruskin was a confrontation between naturalism or realism (other terms particularly difficult to define accurately during this period) and Whistler's argument that art works by compositional values that have nothing to do with what is 'represented' was a proposition broadly in sympathy with Aesthetic ideas. In 1877 Whistler had exhibited at the first Grosvenor Gallery Exhibition, and John Ruskin, perhaps the most influential English art-critic and art historian of the nineteenth century, his reputation at this time undiminished, berated him as a 'coxcomb' who had 'flung a pot of paint into the public's face'. Whistler sued Ruskin for libel in 1878. The resulting case was a confrontation of a series of issues: newness in art confronting authority; the foreign – French models for art – confronting English traditions; but most significantly, realism, and thus artistic conscientiousness, confronting the dilettantism of art for art's sake. Whistler won the case, but only nominally, for he was awarded only a farthing damages. The moral victory belonged to Ruskin.

The second reason for Whistler's importance to the Aesthetic movement was really epitomised by the Ruskin case. Whistler's evidence was basically a public performance. He existed – thrived – in the public gaze, as a carefully stylised personality. The idea of a cultivated and artificial public personality was a quality of which he was very aware. In *The Gentle Art of Making Enemies* he reported how he met both George Du Maurier and Oscar Wilde at the first exhibition of his Venice etchings, 'brought them face to face, and taking each by the arm, enquired, "I say, which one of you two invented the other, eh?" ' And Whistler's most famous literary work, his

'Ten O'Clock' lecture, delivered first in 1885, is both studiedly theatrical and provocatively witty. It sets out the case for the freedom of the artist from any moral or social responsibilities by a series of quite deliberately hyperbolic and epigrammatic statements, the effect of which was to present a histrionically artificial and provocative pose. This cultivation of an artificial, public persona or mask, was perfectly consistent with some of the leading ideas of Aestheticism, particularly as they had been developed by Wilde.

Oscar Wilde is the most famous, although certainly not the most original, writer associated with Aestheticism. Indeed, as even contemporary historians like Walter Hamilton pointed out, without the figure of Wilde to act as a focus for public attention, the Aesthetic movement would have been an altogether more low-key affair. Wilde came from Trinity College, Dublin, to Oxford where he encountered the leading critical voices of the last half of the century – John Ruskin, Matthew Arnold and, most importantly, Walter Pater. After leaving Oxford Wilde settled in London. His flamboyance, paradoxical wit and audacious dress soon turned him into a celebrity, a process hastened by Du Maurier and W. S. Gilbert. His first book of verse, *Poems* (1881), published at his own expense, and his lengthy lecture tours of both the USA and England settled him even more firmly as a public figure. He edited *Woman's World* for a short period and in the last half of the 1880s wrote the plays, a novel (*The Picture of Dorian Gray* (1891)) and the critical essays – collected as *Intentions* in 1891 – that won him more substantial fame.

Initially Wilde was content in his critical work to follow Pater's example. His leading ideas, phrases, and even Pater's pronounced verbal mannerisms all found their way into Wilde's early work. But Wilde was a public and controversial Pater. As *The Renaissance* had proposed that the experience of art presented experience in its most intense, and thus most valuable, moments, so Wilde translated this notion into a cult of artificiality. For Wilde the first requirement in life was to be 'as artificial as possible'. Truth – Pater's invocation of truth to a 'personal sense of fact' in his 'Style' essay – Wilde replaced with lies and masks. And so, because aesthetics and ethics in Wilde's works are proposed as completely independent modes of thought, art, by cultivating the artificial, becomes removed from experience and therefore characterised by its unreality. The main paradox that most of Wilde's critical writing poses, then, is that art is not concerned with imitating the phenomena of life, but of improving upon life by providing a superior model for it. And so art has no use: its function therefore is to offer a momentary, unreal perfection amid the banal or sordid experiences of life. Indeed life can in consequence appear as an inferior, and so less satisfying, version of artistic experience. For example, Wilde could claim quite seriously – although, of course, paradoxically – that a landscape in nature 'is a second-rate Turner, with all the artist's faults exaggerated'. Consequently (as Gautier half a century beforehand had claimed), art finds its own perfection within itself; and as Gilbert in 'The Critic as Artist' in *Intentions* argues 'through Art, and through Art only, can we shield ourselves from the sordid perils of actual existence'. Here the careful reader immediately encounters one of the many difficulties inherent in Wilde's case. To claim, as Whistler had done, that a picture, for example, is *no more* than simply an arrangement of colours or shapes is to assert that the art-object has an ontological status finally no different from that of the other objects of the world. But Wilde's argument was not as simply formalist as this. To propose that there is a relationship between a landscape in nature and a landscape in art – even an inverted one – is to endorse the proposition that there is a difference between the status of art-objects and other objects. What is confusing among Aesthetic writers is that both arguments are freely drawn upon. But for the practising critic the most important implication of a total inversion of the assumed relationship between art and life was simple but dramatic. Criticism could become analogous with creation for it was a creative process that took its material from art instead of life. So by emphasising the subjectivity of criticism in actively *constructing* the aesthetic experience, Wilde all but exonerated the critic from the need to say anything about the work of art allegedly under discussion. The critic merely took that work as a starting point for a second creation – his own.

Now for Wilde's *oeuvre* and career there were two vital consequences of this elevation of the function of the critic. One was the resulting emphasis upon the critic's sensibility. As art is a refuge from the banality of life, what distinguishes the artist-critic from the world that he inhabits is the quality of his feelings. Wilde's critical dialogue, 'The Critic as Artist', establishes the primacy of sensibility in the contemplation of the work of art. In two other works by Wilde this idea is also central. In *The Picture of Dorian Gray* the histrionic aesthete, the character who treats life in the spirit of art by the cultivation of the fine nuances of feeling, is Lord Henry Wotton: partly a mask, one feels, for Wilde himself. Lord Henry defines what distinguishes him from the ordinary society of men in terms of the quality of his sensibility, for it alone provides the justification for the artist-critic to experience everything. Ultimately, therefore, it also defines his alienation from society in terms of ordinary, received morality. The topic had been broached earlier by Wilde in 'The Critic as Artist':[1]

> The artistic critic, like the mystic, is an antinomian always. To be good, according to the vulgar standard of goodness, is obviously quite easy. It merely requires a certain amount of sordid terror, a certain lack of imaginative thought, and a certain low passion for middle-class respectability. Aesthetics are higher than ethics. They belong to a more spiritual sphere. To discern the beauty of a thing is the finest point to which we can arrive. Even a colour-sense is more important, in the development of the individual, than a sense of right and wrong. Aesthetics, in fact, are to Ethics in the sphere of conscious civilization, what, in the sphere of the external world, sexual is to natural selection. Ethics, like natural selection, make existence possible. Aesthetics, like sexual selection, make life lovely and wonderful, fill it with new forms, and give it progress, and variety and change. And when we reach the true culture that is our aim, we attain to that perfection of which the saints have dreamed, the perfection of those to whom sin is impossible, not because they make the renunciations of the ascetic, but because they can do everything they wish without hurt to the soul, and can wish for nothing that can do the soul harm, the soul being an entity so divine that it is able to transform into elements of a richer experience, or a finer susceptibility, or a newer mode of thought, acts or passions that with the common would be commonplace, or with the uneducated ignoble, or with the shameful vile. Is this dangerous? Yes; it is dangerous – all ideas, as I told you, are so.

The inherent dangers of Gilbert's arguments are translated into actuality in the fate of two of Wilde's characters. Dorian Gray, in his search for newer and more bizarre experiences, becomes a criminal. So does Thomas Wainewright, who is the subject of the second of Wilde's essays in *Intentions*, 'Pen, Pencil and Poison'. Wainewright is both an artist and a poisoner, there being, as Wilde observed, 'no essential incongruity between crime and culture'. In fact his study demonstrates there is every reason why the two should happily

1 Oscar Wilde, 'The Critic as Artist'. See pp. 98–9 below.

co-exist within the same personality, for it was Wilde's case that the conflict between the artist's sensibility and that of the received moral values of the world leads inevitably to his challenging his society. In Wilde's own career this challenge became more flagrant, finally criminal and ended in his imprisonment. So the artist-critic, existing in a sphere removed from ordinary ethical choices, is of a type which only finds its full expression in criminality – in the type of the sinful man.

The fictional career, then, of most of Wilde's main characters, and indeed his own career, leads ineluctably back to the main paradox of Aestheticism. Aesthetics and ethics could not be the distinct philosophical categories that Wilde had proclaimed them to be. Finally for Wilde art is an ambiguous quantity, for by his own testimony it is implicated in criminality. That is, in Wilde's eyes it can never be moral in its effects, but it can certainly be immoral. Art is therefore dangerous, for it is radically subversive of a society.

All of this, of course, was but dimly discernible in the early 1880s, when Wilde was provoking a wide but basically amused reaction in the press. There is nothing at all sinister, for example, in the activities of Bunthorne in *Patience*, Gilbert and Sullivan's wildly popular comic opera of 1881. He was a character modelled upon the popular image of the Aesthete: the dress, the mannerisms, the regard for flowers were all precisely rendered. But Bunthorne is above all else grossly self-deceived; his Aestheticism is a fad, a passport to social, and particularly to sexual success. What was being lampooned in the opera was not the inherent immorality of Aestheticism but the extravagance and precious, mannered behaviour that it seemed not only to sanction but to encourage. There was, however, in the early 1880s another more sceptical observer – the dauntingly intelligent Violet Paget, who, under the pseudonym of Vernon Lee, published during the decade a series of books on aesthetics and one juvenile and embarrassingly transparent, if highly topical, novel, *Miss Brown* (1884).

Vernon Lee had recently arrived in England from Italy and in the early 1880s had mixed freely with the artistic and literary celebrities of London society where she won respect, if not exactly admiration, for her caustic wit and intellectual brilliance. That society was depicted with biting accuracy and frankness in her novel when Walter Hamlin, an Aesthetic poet and painter (who, perhaps unfortunately, was strikingly reminiscent of the recently dead Dante

Gabriel Rossetti), brings Anne Brown, an earnest and (by the standards of Aestheticism) startlingly beautiful servant from Italy to England in order to educate her. Anne, like her creator, soon meets London literary society and behind the most transparent of fictional disguises, Vernon Lee represented Rossetti, Swinburne, Burne-Jones, Oscar Wilde and what she elsewhere called his 'lyrico-sarcastic maudlin cultschah'. In the novel these figures were implicated in a corrupting and sinful world in which prostitution, effeminacy and the abuse of both alcohol and drugs are the specified, and so the least sordid and harmful vices. To his considerable embarrassment the novel was dedicated to Henry James: he found it 'without delicacy', formless and too overtly moral in its tone. Walter Pater, who was also mentioned by name in the novel maintained a tactful silence after receiving a complimentary copy of it. Elsewhere, though, the response was less polite. Indeed the novel aroused considerable hostility in some quarters, for William Rossetti, Wilde, Edmund Gosse and the Morrises all openly avoided Vernon Lee's company: predictably enough, perhaps, in the light of the novel's final contemptuous dismissal of them as belonging to a 'demoralised school of literature which glorified in moral indifference'.

However what artistic merit *Miss Brown* possesses – and it amounts to very little – derives from precisely those qualities which made it appear so without delicacy or taste to its contemporary readership. It contrasts the moral earnestness of Anne Brown and her cousin Richard with the moral ambivalence of the Aesthetic movement. Hamlin defends his morbid and indecorous love-poetry by asserting – as Swinburne had already done and as Wilde and Whistler were later to do – that all of life is the proper subject for art and that consequently in matters of art the charge of immorality has no meaning. Anne Brown – partly Vernon Lee's portrait of herself – refuses to free art from morality and at one point exclaims to a group of affronted and amazed Aesthetes, 'Is there nothing higher than taste in the world?' And within the novel's terms, of course, Anne's expostulation is quite justified, for the amoral art of Aestheticism is implicated in a host of nameless vices, all hinted at in the sordid depravity of Edmund Lewis, Hamlin's dark angel, who at one point tries to proposition Anne, rather unbelievably, by offering her a copy of *Mademoiselle de Maupin*. But if, as a novelist, Vernon Lee was far too deeply involved in the moral choices presented in her fiction, as a writer on aesthetics it was this very quality which lent her work authority. In a volume of essays entitled *Juvenilia* (1887) she made substantially the same case as she had intended in *Miss Brown*:[1]

> Little by little we begin to perceive that there are ugly things in the world, apathy, selfishness, vice, want, and a terrible wicked logic that binds them together in thousands of vicious meshes. And perceiving the ugly things in the world, we perceive for the first time, perhaps, the ugly things within ourselves: for of each there is somewhat in each of us. Then comes the moment of choice: we have learned, or guessed, that in continuing to live only for and with the beautiful serenities of art, we are passively abetting, leaving unfought, untouched, the dreadful, messy, irritating, loathsomeness of life; and, on the contrary, in trying to tackle even the smallest of these manifold evils, we are bringing into our existence ugliness and unrest.

It was a theme to which Vernon Lee was to return insistently during the next decade and it is one of the strangest coincidences of the history of the Aesthetic movement that the two voices that dwelt longest upon the darker implications of Aestheticism were those of the basically amoral Oscar Wilde and of the ardently moralistic young art-critic from Italy.

In spite of the fact that Aestheticism assigned such a position of pre-eminence to art in its hierarchy of human values and in spite of the revolutionary nature of much of its critical practice, it can be fairly claimed that Aesthetic writers actually produced few works of real literary significance. The lyrics that comprised *Poems and Ballads* were certainly among the most impassioned and valuable of Swinburne's prolific output. But apart from Swinburne's work and the occasionally really successful poem by Wilde or Lionel Johnson, no writer involved with Aestheticism produced verse that is more than merely proficient. However the fiction that the movement produced was undoubtedly more interesting and certainly Pater's *Marius the Epicurean* (1885) and *Imaginary Portraits* (1887) and Wilde's *The Picture of Dorian Gray* are among the most distinguished fictions produced in the last quarter of the nineteenth century. There are sound reasons why this should be the case. The lyrics of the 1880s, taking as their subject fine nuances of sensibility and mood could quite easily become merely capricious by dwelling upon moments too fine to be other than inconsequential. The fiction of Wilde and Pater, however, at its deepest levels, amply proves that ethics and

---

1 Vernon Lee, *Juvenilia* (1887) I, 10.

aesthetics are profoundly connected. In *The Picture of Dorian Gray* the dilettantism of both Lord Henry Wotton and Dorian himself compares unfavourably with the artistic (and moral) conscience of Basil Hallward, the painter: and the death of Pater's hero Marius, despite his epicureanism, is in 'the nature of a martyrdom . . . a kind of sacrament with plenary grace'. Morality, as it were, had refused to be banished.

And so, finally, what significance did the Aesthetic movement have? Its critics, then as much as now, have found it a decadent retreat into a private world of fantasy. Of course, for many of the followers of Aesthetic fashions – Max Beerbohm's 'upper ten thousand' – it was precisely that: a frivolous self-indulgence by a cultural and economic élite that because of its very extravagance could never be justified. But the real achievement of Aestheticism as a literary movement is not diminished by this qualification, for it was instrumental in bringing about a significant and permanent change in the status of criticism and in forming many of the attitudes of early Modernist writers. Indeed the movement was fundamentally a reaction to the Victorian assertion that art was concerned with moral education, and probably its greatest merit lies in its sustained attempt to re-establish art as a central part of human experience.

# A NOTE ON THE TEXTS

It is a temptation for an editor of any anthology to cast his net widely in order to make his selection as comprehensive as possible. In the present volume, however, this has been a secondary consideration, for there seems to be very little purpose in reproducing some of the very minor pieces of the Aesthetic movement. Indeed, given the very varied nature of Aestheticism, there is every reason why selections should be made from only the major works. Moreover I have tried to edit these texts as minimally as possible. At all times my object has been to respect the consistency of the author's argument and where, for reasons of space, I have been forced to omit passages from particular texts I have invariably chosen digressions and not significant parts of the writer's general case. The most abbreviated piece in this volume is James Abbott McNeill Whistler's 'Ten O'Clock' lecture, which, because of its abundant use of digression, example and illustration lent itself best to that purpose. In most of the other texts what has been selected has been reproduced intact, but where a passage has been excised its omission is noted thus: [. . .]

Two authorial footnotes – in Pater's 'Style' essay and in Swinburne's *Poems and Ballads* – have been omitted.

The copy texts chosen have usually been those of the author's last revision. There are, however, two important exceptions. First, in view of the absence of a standard edition of Wilde's poems from which to work, I have reprinted from the first edition of *Poems* (1881). Second, the essay by Walter Pater that finally became the conclusion to *Studies in the History of the Renaissance* – 'Poems by William Morris' – I have reproduced in its first periodical form because I take that to be more revealing of Pater's original convictions: every revision that the essay underwent was designed to minimise what was controversial in it.

To annotate the works of a movement so immersed in foreign literary cultures has presented a problem. The use of precedent or quotation by most Aesthetic writers seems to have been principally a rhetorical device aimed at producing an urbane, witty and authoritative effect. To itemise every allusion employed by classicists like

*xxxi*

Wilde and Pater would involve overburdening the texts intolerably and would probably destroy also those very qualities of urbanity that they were designed to achieve. So in the main I have confined myself to explaining references to proper names, principally those from classical literature.

# PART I

# AESTHETIC CRITICISM AND POLEMIC

# ALGERNON SWINBURNE

## From *William Blake* (1868), chapter II

To [Blake], as to others of his kind, all faith, all virtue, all moral duty or religious necessity, was not so much abrogated or superseded as summed up, included and involved, by the one matter of art. To him, as to other such workmen, it seemed better to do this well and let all the rest drift than to do incomparably well in all other things and dispense with this one. For this was the thing he had to do; and this once well done, he had the assurance of a certain faith that other things could not be wrong with him. As long as two such parties exist among men who think and act, it must always be some pleasure to deal with a man of either party who has no faith or hope in compromise. These middle-men, with some admirable self-sufficient theory of reconciliation between two directly opposite aims and forces, are fit for no great work on either side. If it be in the interest of facts really desirable that 'the poor Fine Arts should take themselves away,' let it be fairly avowed and preached in a distinct manner. That thesis, so delivered, is comprehensible, and deserves respect. One may add that if art can be destroyed it by all means ought to be. If for example the art of verse is not indispensable and indestructible, the sooner it is put out of the way the better. If anything can be done instead better worth doing than painting or poetry, let that preferable thing be done with all the might and haste that may be attainable. And if to live well be really better than to write or paint well, and a noble action more valuable than the greatest poem or most perfect picture, let us have done at once with the meaner things that stand in the way of the higher. For we cannot on any terms have everything; and assuredly no chief artist or poet has ever been fit to hold rank among the world's supreme benefactors in the way of doctrine, philanthropy, reform, guidance, or example: what is called the artistic faculty not being by any means the same thing as a general capacity for doing good work, diverted into this one strait or shallow in default of a better outlet. Even were this true for example of a man so imperfect as Burns, it would remain false of a man so

3

perfect as Keats. The great men, on whichever side one finds them, are never found trying to take truce or patch up terms. Savonarola burnt Boccaccio; Cromwell proscribed Shakespeare. The early Christians were not great at verse or sculpture. Men of immense capacity and energy who do seem to think or assert it possible to serve both masters – a Dante, a Shelley, a Hugo – poets whose work is mixed with and coloured by personal action or suffering for some cause moral or political – these even are no real exceptions. It is not as artists that they do or seem to do this. The work done may be, and in such high cases often must be, of supreme value to art; but not the moral implied. Strip the sentiments and re-clothe them in bad verse, what residue will be left of the slightest importance to art? Invert them, retaining the manner or form (supposing this feasible, which it might be), and art has lost nothing. Save the shape, and art will take care of the soul for you: unless that is all right, she will refuse to run or start at all; but the shape or style of workmanship each artist is bound to look to, whether or no he may choose to trouble himself about the moral or other bearings of his work. This principle, which makes the manner of doing a thing the essence of the thing done, the purpose or result of it the accident, thus reversing the principle of moral or material duty, must inevitably expose art to the condemnation of the other party – the party of those who (as aforesaid) regard what certain of their leaders call an earnest life or a great acted poem (that is, material virtue or the mere doing and saying of good or instructive deeds and words) as infinitely preferable to any possible feat of art. Opinion is free, and the choice always open; but if any man leaning on crutches of theory chooses to halt between the two camps, it shall be at his own peril – imminent peril of conviction as one unfit for service on either side. For Puritanism is in this one thing absolutely right about art; they cannot live and work together, or the one under the other. All ages which were great enough to have space for both, to hold room for a fair fighting-field between them, have always accepted and acted upon this evident fact. Take the Renaissance age for one example; you must have Knox or Ronsard, Scotch or French; not both at once; there is no place under reformers for the singing of a 'Pléiade.'[1] Take the mediæval period in its broadest sense; not to speak of the notably heretical and immoral Albigeois

---

1 i.e. John Knox (1505–72), the Scottish Church reformer; and Pierre de Ronsard (1524–85) a member of the 'Pléiade', a group of poets of the French Renaissance which included also Du Bellay.

with their exquisite school of heathenish verse, or of that other rebel-
lious gathering under the great emperor Frederick II,[1] a poet and
pagan, when eastern arts and ideas began to look up westward at one
man's bidding and open out Saracenic prospects in the very face and
teeth of the Church – look at home into familiar things, and see by
such poems as Chaucer's 'Court of Love,' absolutely one in tone and
handling as it is with the old Albigensian 'Aucassin'[2] and all its
paganism, how the poets of the time, with their eager nascent worship of beautiful form and external nature, dealt with established
opinion and the incarnate moralities of church or household. It is
easy to see why the Church on its own principle found it (as in the
Albigensian case) a matter of the gravest necessity to have such
schools of art and thought cut down or burnt out. Priest and poet, all
those times through, were proverbially on terms of reciprocal biting
and striking. That magnificent invention of making 'Art the handmaid of Religion' had not been stumbled upon in the darkness of
those days. Neither minstrel nor monk would have caught up the
idea with any rapture. As indeed they would have been unwise to do;
for the thing is impossible. Art is not like fire or water, a good
servant and bad master; rather the reverse. She will help in nothing,
of her own knowledge or freewill: upon terms of service you will get
worse than nothing out of her. Handmaid of religion, exponent of
duty, servant of fact, pioneer of morality, she cannot in any way
become; she would be none of these things though you were to bray
her in a mortar. All the battering in the world will never hammer her
into fitness for such an office as that. It is at her peril, if she tries to do
good: one might say, borrowing terms from the other party, 'she
shall not try that under penalty of death and damnation.' Her
business is not to do good on other grounds, but to be good on her
own: all is well with her while she sticks fast to that. To ask help or
furtherance from her in any extraneous good work is exactly as
rational as to expect lyrical beauty of form and flow in a logical
treatise. The contingent result of having good art about you and
living in a time of noble writing or painting may no doubt be this;
that the spirit and mind of men then living will receive on some

1 The Albigensian heretics of the south of France in the twelfth and thirteenth
centuries, whose violent suppression by Rome saw also the suppression
of Provençal culture. This period of French history also interested Pater.
Frederick II (1194–1250), Elector Palatine of the Rhine, who, accused of
heresy, united German opposition to Pope Gregory.
2 i.e. the medieval Provençal story 'Aucassin et Nicolette'.

points a certain exaltation and insight caught from the influence of such forms and colours of verse or painting; will become for one thing incapable of tolerating bad work, and capable therefore of reasonably relishing the best; which of course implies and draws with it many other advantages of a sort you may call moral or spiritual. But if the artist does his work with an eye to such results or for the sake of bringing about such improvements, he will too probably fail even of them. Art for art's sake first of all, and afterwards we may suppose all the rest shall be added to her (or if not she need hardly be overmuch concerned); but from the man who falls to artistic work with a moral purpose, shall be taken away even that which he has – whatever of capacity for doing well in either way he may have at starting. A living critic[1] of incomparably delicate insight and subtly good sense, himself 'impeccable' as an artist, calls this 'the heresy of instruction' (*l'hérésie de l'enseignement*): one might call it, for the sake of a shorter and more summary name, the great moral heresy. Nothing can be imagined more futile; nothing so ruinous. Once let art humble herself, plead excuses, try at any compromise with the Puritan principle of doing good, and she is worse than dead. Once let her turn apologetic, and promise or imply that she really will now be 'loyal to fact' and useful to men in general (say, by furthering their moral work or improving their moral nature), she is no longer of any human use or value. The one fact for her which is worth taking account of is simply mere excellence of verse or colour, which involves all manner of truth and loyalty necessary to her well-being. That is the important thing; to have her work supremely well done, and to disregard all contingent consequences. You may extract out of Titian's work or Shakespeare's any moral or immoral inference you please; it is none of their business to see after that. Good painting or writing, on any terms, is a thing quite sufficiently in accordance with fact and reality for them. Supplant art by all means if you can; root it out and try to plant in its place something useful or at least safe, which at all events will not impede the noble moral labour and trammel the noble moral life of Puritanism. But in the name of sense and fact itself let us have done with all abject and ludicrous pretence of coupling the two in harness or grafting the one on the other's stock: let us hear no more of the moral mission of earnest art; let us no longer be pestered with the frantic and flatulent assumptions of quasi-secular clericalism willing to think the best of all sides, and

1 i.e. Charles Baudelaire.

ready even, with consecrating hand, to lend meritorious art and poetry a timely pat or shove. Philistia had far better (always providing it be possible) crush art at once, hang or burn it out of the way, than think of plucking out its eyes and setting it to grind moral corn in the Philistine mills;[1] which it is certain not to do at all well. Once and again the time has been that there was no art worth speaking of afloat anywhere in the world; but there never has been or can have been a time when art, or any kind of art worth having, took active service under Puritanism, or indulged for its part in the deleterious appetite of saving souls or helping humanity in general along the way of labour and progress. Let no artist or poet listen to the bland bark of those porter dogs of the Puritan kingdom even when they fawn and flirt with tongue or tail. *Cave canem.*[2] That Cerberus[3] of the portals of Philistia will swallow your honey-cake to no purpose; if he does not turn and rend you, his slaver as he licks your hand will leave it impotent and palsied for all good work.

# ALGERNON SWINBURNE

## From *Notes on Poems and Reviews* (1866)

Why grudge them lotus-leaf and laurel,
 O toothless mouth or swinish maw,
Who never grudged you bells and coral,
 Who never grudged you troughs and straw?

Lie still in kennel, sleek in stable,
 Good creatures of the stall or sty;
Shove snouts for crumbs below the table;
 Lie still; and rise not up to lie.

To all this, however, there is a grave side. The question at issue is wider than any between a single writer and his critics, or it might well be allowed to drop. It is this: whether or not the first and last

---

1 'Philistine' was the term Matthew Arnold had recently used to characterise the uncultured English middle classes.
2 i.e. Beware of the dog.
3 The three-headed dog which in classical mythology guarded the entrance to the underworld.

requisite of art is to give no offence; whether or not all that cannot be lisped in the nursery or fingered in the schoolroom is therefore to be cast out of the library; whether or not the domestic circle is to be for all men and writers the outer limit and extreme horizon of their world of work. For to this we have come; and all students of art must face the matter as it stands. Who has not heard it asked, in a final and triumphant tone, whether this book or that can be read aloud by her mother to a young girl? whether such and such a picture can properly be exposed to the eyes of young persons? If you reply that this is nothing to the point, you fall at once into the ranks of the immoral. Never till now, and nowhere but in England, could so monstrous an absurdity rear for one moment its deformed and eyeless head. In no past century were artists ever bidden to work on these terms; nor are they now, except among us. The disease, of course, afflicts the meanest members of the body with most virulence. Nowhere is cant at once so foul-mouthed and so tight-laced as in the penny, twopenny, threepenny, or sixpenny press. Nothing is so favourable to the undergrowth of real indecency as this overshadowing foliage of fictions, this artificial network of proprieties. *L'Ariosto rit au soleil, l'Arétin ricane à l'ombre.*[1] The whiter the sepulchre without, the ranker the rottenness within. Every touch of plaster is a sign of advancing decay. The virtue of our critical journals is a dowager of somewhat dubious antecedents: every day that thins and shrivels her cheek thickens and hardens the paint on it; she consumes more chalk and ceruse than would serve a whole courtful of crones. 'It is to be presumed,' certainly, that in her case 'all is not sweet, all is not sound.' The taint on her fly-blown reputation is hard to overcome by patches and perfumery. Literature, to be worthy of men, must be large, liberal, sincere; and cannot be chaste if it be prudish. Purity and prudery cannot keep house together. Where free speech and fair play are interdicted, foul hints and evil suggestions are hatched into fetid life. And if literature indeed is not to deal with the full life of man and the whole nature of things, let it be cast aside with the rods and rattles of childhood. Whether it affect to teach or to amuse, it is equally trivial and contemptible to us; only less so than the charge of immorality. Against how few really great names has not this small and dirt-encrusted pebble been thrown! A reputation seems imperfect without this tribute also: one jewel is wanting to the crown. It is

---

1 Literally, 'Ariosto laughs in the sunshine, Aretin sniggers in the shade'. This is clearly a quotation but I have been unable to locate its origin.

good to be praised by those whom all men should praise; it is better to be reviled by those whom all men should scorn.

Various chances and causes must have combined to produce a state of faith or feeling which would turn all art and literature 'into the line of children.' One among others may be this: where the heaven of invention holds many stars at once, there is no fear that the highest and largest will either efface or draw aside into its orbit all lesser lights. Each of these takes its own way and sheds its proper lustre. But where one alone is dominant in heaven, it is encircled by a pale procession of satellite moons, filled with shallow and stolen radiance. Thus, with English versifiers now, the idyllic form is alone in fashion. The one great and prosperous poet of the time has given out the tune, and the hoarser choir takes it up. His highest lyrical work remains unimitated, being in the main inimitable. But the trick of tone which suits an idyl is easier to assume; and the note has been struck so often that the shrillest songsters can affect to catch it up. We have idyls good and bad, ugly and pretty; idyls of the farm and the mill; idyls of the dining-room and the deanery; idyls of the gutter and the gibbet. If the Muse of the minute will not feast with 'gig-men' and their wives, she must mourn with costermongers and their trulls. I fear the more ancient Muses are guests at neither house of mourning nor house of feasting.

For myself, I begrudge no man his taste or his success; I can enjoy and applaud all good work, and would always, when possible, have the workman paid in full. There is much excellent and some admirable verse among the poems of the day: to none has it given more pleasure than to me, and from none, had I been a man of letters to whom the ways were open, would it have won heartier applause. I have never been able to see what should attract men to the profession of criticism but the noble pleasure of praising. But I have no right to claim a place in the silver flock of idyllic swans. I have never worked for praise or pay, but simply by impulse, and to please myself; I must therefore, it is to be feared, remain where I am, shut out from the communion of these. At all events, I shall not be hounded into emulation of other men's work by the baying of unleashed beagles. There are those with whom I do not wish to share the praise of their praisers. I am content to abide a far different judgment:

> I write as others wrote
> On Sunium's height.

I need not be over-careful to justify my ways in other men's eyes; it is enough for me that they also work after their kind, and earn the suffrage, as they labour after the law, of their own people. The idyllic form is best for domestic and pastoral poetry. It is naturally on a lower level than that of tragic or lyric verse. Its gentle and maidenly lips are somewhat narrow for the stream and somewhat cold for the fire of song. It is very fit for the sole diet of girls; not very fit for the sole sustenance of men.

When England has again such a school of poetry, so headed and so followed, as she has had at least twice before, or as France has now; when all higher forms of the various art are included within the larger limits of a stronger race; then, if such a day should ever rise or return upon us, it will be once more remembered that the office of adult art is neither puerile nor feminine, but virile; that its purity is not that of the cloister or the harem; that all things are good in its sight, out of which good work may be produced. Then the press will be as impotent as the pulpit to dictate the laws and remove the landmarks of art; and those will be laughed at who demand from one thing the qualities of another – who seek for sermons in sonnets and morality in music. Then all accepted work will be noble and chaste in the wider masculine sense, not truncated and curtailed, but outspoken and fullgrown; art will be pure by instinct and fruitful by nature, no clipped and forced growth of unhealthy heat and unnatural air; all baseness and all triviality will fall off from it, and be forgotten; and no one will then need to assert, in defence of work done for the work's sake, the simple laws of his art which no one will then be permitted to impugn.

# WALTER PATER

## From the Preface to *The Renaissance* (1873)

Many attempts have been made by writers on art and poetry to define beauty in the abstract, to express it in the most general terms, to find some universal formula for it. The value of these attempts has most often been in the suggestive and penetrating things said by the way. Such discussions help us very little to enjoy what has been well done in art or poetry, to discriminate between what is more and what is less excellent in them, or to use words like beauty, excellence, art, poetry, with a more precise meaning than they would otherwise have. Beauty, like all other qualities presented to human experience, is relative; and the definition of it becomes unmeaning and useless in proportion to its abstractness. To define beauty, not in the most abstract but in the most concrete terms possible, to find not its universal formula, but the formula which expresses most adequately this or that special manifestation of it, is the aim of the true student of aesthetics.

'To see the object as in itself it really is,'[1] has been justly said to be the aim of all true criticism whatever; and in aesthetic criticism the first step towards seeing one's object as it really is, is to know one's own impression as it really is, to discriminate it, to realise it distinctly. The objects with which aesthetic criticism deals – music, poetry, artistic and accomplished forms of human life – are indeed receptacles of so many powers or forces: they possess, like the products of nature, so many virtues or qualities. What is this song or picture, this engaging personality presented in life or in a book, to *me*? What effect does it really produce on me? Does it give me pleasure? and if so, what sort or degree of pleasure? How is my nature modified by its presence, and under its influence? The answers to these questions are the original facts with which the aesthetic critic has to do; and, as in the study of light, of morals, of number, one must realise such primary data for one's self, or not at all. And he who experiences these impressions strongly, and drives directly at the discrimination and analysis of them, has no need to trouble himself with the abstract question what beauty is in itself, or what its exact relation to truth or experience – metaphysical questions, as unprofitable as metaphysical questions elsewhere. He may pass them all by as being, answerable or not, of no interest to him.

The aesthetic critic, then, regards all the objects with which he has to do, all works of art, and the fairer forms of nature and human life, as powers or forces producing pleasurable sensations, each of a more or less peculiar or unique kind. This influence he feels, and wishes to explain, by analysing and reducing it to its elements. To him, the picture, the landscape, the engaging personality in life or

---

1 i.e. by Matthew Arnold in his lecture 'On Translating Homer' (1861).

11

in a book, *La Gioconda*, the hills of Carrara, Pico of Mirandola, are valuable for their virtues, as we say, in speaking of a herb, a wine, a gem; for the property each has of affecting one with a special, a unique, impression of pleasure. Our education becomes complete in proportion as our susceptibility to these impressions increases in depth and variety. And the function of the aesthetic critic is to distinguish, to analyse, and separate from its adjuncts, the virtue by which a picture, a landscape, a fair personality in life or in a book, produces this special impression of beauty or pleasure, to indicate what the source of that impression is, and under what conditions it is experienced. His end is reached when he has disengaged that virtue, and noted it, as a chemist notes some natural element, for himself and others; and the rule for those who would reach this end is stated with great exactness in the words of a recent critic of Sainte-Beuve: – *De se borner à connaître de près les belles choses, et à s'en nourrir en exquis amateurs, en humanistes accomplis.*[1]

What is important, then, is not that the critic should possess a correct abstract definition of beauty for the intellect, but a certain kind of temperament, the power of being deeply moved by the presence of beautiful objects. He will remember always that beauty exists in many forms. To him all periods, types, schools of taste, are in themselves equal. In all ages there have been some excellent workmen, and some excellent work done. The question he asks is always: – In whom did the stir, the genius, the sentiment of the period find itself? where was the receptacle of its refinement, its elevation, its taste? 'The ages are all equal,' says William Blake, 'but genius is always above its age.'

# WALTER PATER

### From 'The School of Giorgione' in *The Renaissance* (1873)

It is the mistake of much popular criticism to regard poetry, music, and painting – all the various products of art – as but translations

---

1 Literally, 'to restrict oneself to knowing beautiful things intimately and to nourish oneself with them as an exquisite amateur, as an accomplished humanist'.

into different languages of one and the same fixed quantity of imaginative thought, supplemented by certain technical qualities of colour, in painting; of sound, in music; of rhythmical words, in poetry. In this way, the sensuous element in art, and with it almost everything in art that is essentially artistic, is made a matter of indifference; and a clear apprehension of the opposite principle – that the sensuous material of each art brings with it a special phase or quality of beauty, untranslatable into the forms of any other, an order of impressions distinct in kind – is the beginning of all true aesthetic criticism. For, as art addresses not pure sense, still less the pure intellect, but the 'imaginative reason' through the senses, there are differences of kind in aesthetic beauty, corresponding to the differences in kind of the gifts of sense themselves. Each art, therefore, having its own peculiar and untranslatable sensuous charm, has its own special mode of reaching the imagination, its own special responsibilities to its material. One of the functions of aesthetic criticism is to define these limitations; to estimate the degree in which a given work of art fulfils its responsibilities to its special material; to note in a picture that true pictorial charm, which is neither a mere poetical thought or sentiment, on the one hand, nor a mere result of communicable technical skill in colour or design, on the other; to define in a poem that true poetical quality, which is neither descriptive nor meditative merely, but comes of an inventive handling of rhythmical language, the element of song in the singing; to note in music the musical charm, that essential music, which presents no words, no matter of sentiment or thought, separable from the special form in which it is conveyed to us.

To such a philosophy of the variations of the beautiful, Lessing's analysis of the spheres of sculpture and poetry, in the *Laocoon*,[1] was an important contribution. But a true appreciation of these things is possible only in the light of a whole system of such art-casuistries. Now painting is the art in the criticism of which this truth most needs enforcing, for it is in popular judgments on pictures that the false generalisation of all art into forms of poetry is most prevalent. To suppose that all is mere technical acquirement in delineation or touch, working through and addressing itself to the intelligence, on the one side, or a merely poetical, or what may be called literary interest, addressed also to the pure intelligence, on the other: –

1 i.e. Gotthold Ephraim Lessing's *Laocoön* (1766), an essay on the first principles of criticism and the relative limits of particular art-forms.

this is the way of most spectators, and of many critics, who have never caught sight all the time of that true pictorial quality which lies between, unique pledge, as it is, of the possession of the pictorial gift, that inventive or creative handling of pure line and colour, which, as almost always in Dutch painting, as often also in the works of Titian or Veronese, is quite independent of anything definitely poetical in the subject it accompanies. It is the *drawing* – the design projected from that peculiar pictorial temperament or constitution, in which, while it may possibly be ignorant of true anatomical proportions, all things whatever, all poetry, all ideas however abstract or obscure, float up as visible scene or image: it is the *colouring* – that weaving of light, as of just perceptible gold threads, through the dress, the flesh, the atmosphere, in Titian's *Lace-girl*, that staining of the whole fabric of the thing with a new, delightful physical quality. This *drawing*, then – the arabesque traced in the air by Tintoret's flying figures, by Titian's forest branches; this colouring – the magic conditions of light and hue in the atmosphere of Titian's *Lace-girl*, or Rubens's *Descent from the Cross* : – these essential pictorial qualities must first of all delight the sense, delight it as directly and sensuously as a fragment of Venetian glass; and through this delight alone become the vehicle of whatever poetry or science may lie beyond them in the intention of the composer. In its primary aspect, a great picture has no more definite message for us than an accidental play of sunlight and shadow for a few moments on the wall or floor: is itself, in truth, a space of such fallen light, caught as the colours are in an Eastern carpet, but refined upon, and dealt with more subtly and exquisitely than by nature itself. And this primary and essential condition fulfilled, we may trace the coming of poetry into painting, by fine gradations upwards; from Japanese fan-painting, for instance, where we get, first, only abstract colour; then, just a little interfused sense of the poetry of flowers; then, sometimes, perfect flower-painting; and so, onwards, until in Titian we have, as his poetry in the *Ariadne*, so actually a touch of true childlike humour in the diminutive, quaint figure with its silk gown, which ascends the temple stairs, in his picture of the *Presentation of the Virgin*, at Venice.

But although each art has thus its own specific order of impressions, and an untranslatable charm, while a just apprehension of the ultimate differences of the arts is the beginning of aesthetic criticism; yet is is noticeable that, in its special mode of handling its given material, each art may be observed to pass into the condition of some other art, by what German critics term an *Anders-streben*[1] – a partial alienation from its own limitations, through which the arts are able, not indeed to supply the place of each other, but reciprocally to lend each other new forces.

Thus some of the most delightful music seems to be always approaching to figure, to pictorial definition. Architecture, again, though it has its own laws – laws esoteric enough, as the true architect knows only too well – yet sometimes aims at fulfilling the conditions of a picture, as in the *Arena* chapel; or of sculpture, as in the flawless unity of Giotto's tower at Florence; and often finds a true poetry, as in those strangely twisted staircases of the *châteaux* of the country of the Loire, as if it were intended that among their odd turnings the actors in a theatrical mode of life might pass each other unseen; there being a poetry also of memory and of the mere effect of time, by which architecture often profits greatly. Thus, again, sculpture aspires out of the hard limitation of pure form towards colour, or its equivalent; poetry also, in many ways, finding guidance from the other arts, the analogy between a Greek tragedy and a work of Greek sculpture, between a sonnet and a relief, of French poetry generally with the art of engraving, being more than mere figures of speech; and all the arts in common aspiring towards the principle of music; music being the typical, or ideally consummate art, the object of the great *Anders-streben* of all art, of all that is artistic, or partakes of artistic qualities.

*All art constantly aspires towards the condition of music.* For while in all other kinds of art it is possible to distinguish the matter from the form, and the understanding can always make this distinction, yet it is the constant effort of art to obliterate it. That the mere matter of a poem, for instance, its subject, namely, its given incidents or situation – that the mere matter of a picture, the actual circumstances of an event, the actual topography of a landscape – should be nothing without the form, the spirit, of the handling, that this form, this mode of handling, should become an end in itself, should penetrate every part of the matter: this is what all art constantly strives after, and achieves in different degrees.

This abstract language becomes clear enough, if we think of actual examples. In an actual landscape we see a long white road,

---

1 Literally, 'striving for something different'.

lost suddenly on the hill-verge. That is the matter of one of the etchings of M. Alphonse Legros:[1] only, in this etching, it is informed by an indwelling solemnity of expression, seen upon it or half-seen, within the limits of an exceptional moment, or caught from his own mood perhaps, but which he maintains as the very essence of the thing, throughout his work. Sometimes a momentary tint of stormy light may invest a homely or too familiar scene with a character which might well have been drawn from the deep places of the imagination. Then we might say that this particular effect of light, this sudden inweaving of gold thread through the texture of the haystack, and the poplars, and the grass, gives the scene artistic qualities, that it is like a picture. And such tricks of circumstance are commonest in landscape which has little salient character of its own; because, in such scenery, all the material details are so easily absorbed by that informing expression of passing light, and elevated, throughout their whole extent, to a new and delightful effect by it. And hence the superiority, for most conditions of the picturesque, of a river-side in France to a Swiss valley, because, on the French river-side, mere topography, the simple material, counts for so little, and, all being very pure, untouched, and tranquil in itself, mere light and shade have such easy work in modulating it to one dominant tone. The Venetian landscape, on the other hand, has in its material conditions much which is hard, or harshly definite; but the masters of the Venetian school have shown themselves little burdened by them. Of its Alpine background they retain certain abstracted elements only, of cool colour and tranquillising line; and they use its actual details, the brown windy turrets, the straw-coloured fields, the forest arabesques, but as the notes of a music which duly accompanies the presence of their men and women, presenting us with the spirit or essence only of a certain sort of landscape – a country of the pure reason or half-imaginative memory.

Poetry, again, works with words addressed in the first instance to the pure intelligence; and it deals, most often, with a definite subject or situation. Sometimes it may find a noble and quite legitimate function in the conveyance of moral or political aspiration,

---

[1] Alphonse Legros (1837–1911). French etcher and painter, a friend of Rossetti and Whistler, who came to England in the 1860s and was appointed Slade Professor at University College, London in 1876.

as often in the poetry of Victor Hugo. In such instances it is easy enough for the understanding to distinguish between the matter and the form, however much the matter, the subject, the element which is addressed to the mere intelligence, has been penetrated by the informing, artistic spirit. But the ideal types of poetry are those in which this distinction is reduced to its *minimum;* so that lyrical poetry, precisely because in it we are least able to detach the matter from the form, without a deduction of something from that matter itself, is, at least artistically, the highest and most complete form of poetry. And the very perfection of such poetry often appears to depend, in part, on a certain suppression or vagueness of mere subject, so that the meaning reaches us through ways not distinctly traceable by the understanding, as in some of the most imaginative compositions of William Blake, and often in Shakespeare's songs, as pre-eminently in that song of Mariana's page in *Measure for Measure*, in which the kindling force and poetry of the whole play seems to pass for a moment into an actual strain of music.

And this principle holds good of all things that partake in any degree of artistic qualities, of the furniture of our houses, and of dress, for instance, of life itself, of gesture and speech, and the details of daily intercourse; these also, for the wise, being susceptible of a suavity and charm, caught from the way in which they are done, which gives them a worth in themselves. Herein, again, lies what is valuable and justly attractive, in what is called the fashion of a time, which elevates the trivialities of speech, and manner, and dress, into 'ends in themselves,' and gives them a mysterious grace and attractiveness in the doing of them.

Art, then, is thus always striving to be independent of the mere intelligence, to become a matter of pure perception, to get rid of its responsibilities to its subject or material; the ideal examples of poetry and painting being those in which the constituent elements of the composition are so welded together, that the material or subject no longer strikes the intellect only: nor the form, the eye or the ear only; but form and matter, in their union or identity, present one single effect to the 'imaginative reason,' that complex faculty for which every thought and feeling is twin-born with its sensible analogue or symbol.

It is the art of music which most completely realises this artistic ideal, this perfect identification of matter and form. In its consummate moments, the end is not distinct from the means, the form from the matter, the subject from the expression; they inhere in and completely saturate each other; and to it, therefore, to the condition of its perfect moments, all the arts may be supposed constantly to tend and aspire. In music, then, rather than in poetry, is to be found the true type or measure of perfected art. Therefore, although each art has its incommunicable element, its untranslatable order of impressions, its unique mode of reaching the 'imaginative reason,' yet the arts may be represented as continually struggling after the law or principle of music, to a condition which music alone completely realises; and one of the chief functions of aesthetic criticism, dealing with the products of art, new or old, is to estimate the degree in which each of those products approaches, in this sense, to musical law.

# WALTER PATER

## From 'Poems by William Morris', *Westminster Review*, vol. XXXIV (1868)

[Λέγει που ʽΗράκλειτος ὅτι πάντα χωρεῖ καὶ οὐδὲν μένει][1]

To regard all things and principles of things as inconstant modes or fashions has more and more become the tendency of modern thought. Let us begin with that which is without, – our physical life. Fix upon it in one of its more exquisite intervals – the moment, for instance, of delicious recoil from the flood of water in summer heat. What is the whole physical life in that moment but a combination of natural elements to which science gives their names? But those elements, phosphorus and lime, and delicate fibres, are present not in the human body alone; we detect them in places most remote from it. Our physical life is a perpetual motion of them – the passage of the blood, the wasting and repairing of the lenses of the eye, the modification of the tissues of the brain by

---

1 When this essay became the Conclusion to *Studies in the History of the Renaissance* in 1873, Pater included this sentence as an epigraph. Literally, 'Heraclitus says that everything is in motion and nothing rests.' Plato, *Phaedrus*.

every ray of light and sound – processes which science reduces to simpler and more elementary forces. Like the elements of which we are composed, the action of these forces extends beyond us; it rusts iron and ripens corn. Far out on every side of us these elements are broadcast, driven by many forces; and birth and gesture and death and the springing of violets from the grave are but a few out of ten thousand resulting combinations. That clear, perpetual outline of face and limb is but an image of ours under which we group them – a design in a web the actual threads of which pass out beyond it. This at least of flame-like our life has, that it is but the concurrence renewed from moment to moment of forces parting sooner or later on their ways.

Or if we begin with the inward world of thought and feeling, the whirlpool is still more rapid, the flame more eager and devouring. There it is no longer the gradual darkening of the eye and fading of colour from the wall, the movement of the shore side, where the water flows down indeed, though in apparent rest, but the race of the midstream, a drift of momentary acts of sight and passion and thought. At first sight experience seems to bury us under a flood of external objects, pressing upon us with a sharp, importunate reality, calling us out of ourselves in a thousand forms of action. But when reflection begins to act upon those objects they are dissipated under its influence, the cohesive force is suspended like a trick of magic, each object is loosed into a group of impressions, colour, odour, texture, in the mind of the observer. And if we continue to dwell on this world, not of objects in the solidity with which language invests them, but of impressions unstable, flickering, inconsistent, which burn, and are extinguished with our consciousness of them, it contracts still further, the whole scope of observation is dwarfed to the narrow chamber of the individual mind. Experience, already reduced to a swarm of impressions, is ringed round for each one of us by that thick wall of personality through which no real voice has ever pierced on its way to us, or from us to that, which we can only conjecture to be without. Every one of those impressions is the impression of an individual in his isolation, each mind keeping as a solitary prisoner its own dream of a world.

Analysis goes a step further still, and tells us that those impressions of the individual to which, for each one of us, experience dwindles down, are in perpetual flight; that each of them is limited by time, and that as time is infinitely divisible, each of them is infinitely divisible also, all that is actual in it being a single moment, gone while we try to apprehend it, of which it may ever be more truly said that it has ceased to be than that it is. To such a tremulous wisp constantly reforming itself on the stream, to a single sharp impression, with a sense in it, a relic more or less fleeting, of such moments gone by, what is real in our life fines itself down. It is with the movement, the passage and dissolution of impressions, images, sensations, that analysis leaves off, that continual vanishing away, that strange perpetual weaving and unweaving of ourselves.

Such thoughts seem desolate at first; at times all the bitterness of life seems concentrated in them. They bring the image of one washed out beyond the bar in a sea at ebb, losing even his personality, as the elements of which he is composed pass into new combinations. Struggling, as he must, to save himself, it is himself that he loses at every moment.

*Philosophiren*, says Novalis, *ist dephlegmatisiren, vivificiren*.[1] The service of philosophy, and of religion and culture as well, to the human spirit, is to startle it into a sharp and eager observation. Every moment some form grows perfect in hand or face; some tone on the hills or sea is choicer than the rest; some mood of passion or insight or intellectual excitement is irresistibly real and attractive for us for that moment only. Not the fruit of experience but experience itself is the end. A counted number of pulses only is given to us of a variegated, dramatic life. How may we see in them all that is to be seen in them by the finest senses? How can we pass most swiftly from point to point, and be present always at the focus where the greatest number of vital forces unite in their purest energy?

To burn always with this hard gem-like flame, to maintain this ecstasy, is success in life. Failure is to form habits; for habit is relative to a stereotyped world; meantime it is only the roughness of the eye that makes any two things, persons, situations – seem alike. While all melts under our feet, we may well catch at any exquisite passion, or any contribution to knowledge that seems by a lifted horizon to set the spirit free for a moment, or any stirring of the senses, strange dyes, strange flowers and curious odours, or work of the artist's hands, or the face of one's friend. Not to discriminate every moment some passionate attitude in those about us and in

---

[1] Literally, 'to philosophise is to be drawn out of apathy, to be revivified'.

the brilliance of their gifts some tragic dividing of forces on their ways, is on this short day of frost and sun to sleep before evening. With this sense of the splendour of our experience and of its awful brevity, gathering all we are into one desperate effort to see and touch, we shall hardly have time to make theories about the things we see and touch. What we have to do is to be for ever curiously testing opinion and courting new impressions, never acquiescing in a facile orthodoxy of Comte or of Hegel or of our own. Theories, religious or philosophical ideas, as points of view, instruments of criticism, may help us to gather up what might otherwise pass unregarded by us. '*La philosophie*,' says Victor Hugo, '*c'est le microscope de la pensée*.'[1] The theory or idea or system which requires of us the sacrifice of any part of this experience, in consideration of some interest into which we cannot enter, or some abstract morality we have not identified with ourselves, or what is only conventional, has no real claim upon us.

One of the most beautiful places in the writings of Rousseau is that in the sixth book of the *Confessions*, where he describes the awakening in him of the literary sense. An undefinable taint of death had always clung about him, and now in early manhood he believed himself stricken by mortal disease. He asked himself how he might make as much as possible of the interval that remained; and he was not biassed by anything in his previous life when he decided that it must be by intellectual excitement, which he found in the clear, fresh writings of Voltaire. Well, we are all *condamnés*, as Victor Hugo somewhere says: we have an interval and then we cease to be. Some spend this interval in listlessness, some in high passions, the wisest in art and song. For our one chance is in expanding that interval, in getting as many pulsations as possible into the given time. High passions give one this quickened sense of life, ecstasy and sorrow of love, political or religious enthusiasm, or the 'enthusiasm of humanity.' Only, be sure it is passion, that it does yield you this fruit of a quickened, multiplied consciousness. Of this wisdom, the poetic passion, the desire of beauty, the love of art for art's sake, has most; for art comes to you professing frankly to give nothing but the highest quality to your moments as they pass, and simply for those moments' sake.

1 Literally, 'Philosophy is the microscope of thought'.

# JAMES ABBOTT McNEILL WHISTLER

## From the 'Ten O'Clock' lecture (1885) in
### *The Gentle Art of Making Enemies* (1890)

LADIES AND GENTLEMEN:

It is with great hesitation and much misgiving that I appear before you, in the character of The Preacher.

If timidity be at all allied to the virtue modesty, and can find favour in your eyes, I pray you, for the sake of that virtue, accord me your utmost indulgence.

I would plead for my want of habit, did it not seem preposterous, judging from precedent, that aught save the most efficient effrontery could be ever expected in connection with my subject – for I will not conceal from you that I mean to talk about Art. Yes, Art – that has of late become, as far as much discussion and writing can make it, a sort of common topic for the tea-table.

Art is upon the Town! – to be chucked under the chin by the passing gallant – to be enticed within the gates of the householder – to be coaxed into company, as a proof of culture and refinement.

If familiarity can breed contempt, certainly Art – or what is currently taken for it – has been brought to its lowest stage of intimacy.

The people have been harassed with Art in every guise, and vexed with many methods as to its endurance. They have been told how they shall love Art, and live with it. Their homes have been invaded, their walls covered with paper, their very dress taken to task – until, roused at last, bewildered and filled with the doubts and discomforts of senseless suggestion, they resent such intrusion, and cast forth the false prophets, who have brought the very name of the beautiful into disrepute, and derision upon themselves.

Alas! ladies and gentlemen, Art has been maligned. She has naught in common with such practices. She is a goddess of dainty thought – reticent of habit, abjuring all obtrusiveness, purposing in no way to better others.

She is, withal, selfishly occupied with her own perfection only – having no desire to teach – seeking and finding the beautiful in all conditions and in all times, as did her high priest Rembrandt, when he saw picturesque grandeur and noble dignity in the Jews' quarter of Amsterdam, and lamented not that its inhabitants were not Greeks [ . . . ].

Humanity takes the place of Art, and God's creations are excused by their usefulness. Beauty is confounded with virtue, and, before a work of Art, it is asked: 'What good shall it do?'

Hence it is that nobility of action, in this life, is hopelessly linked with the merit of the work that portrays it; and thus the people have acquired the habit of looking, as who should say, not *at* a picture, but *through* it, at some human fact, that shall, or shall not, from a social point of view, better their mental or moral state. So we have come to hear of the painting that elevates, and of the duty of the painter – of the picture that is full of thought, and of the panel that merely decorates.

A favourite faith, dear to those who teach, is that certain periods were especially artistic, and that nations, readily named, were notably lovers of Art.

So we are told that the Greeks were, as a people, worshippers of the beautiful, and that in the fifteenth century Art was engrained in the multitude.

That the great masters lived in common understanding with their patrons – that the early Italians were artists – all – and that the demand for the lovely thing produced it.

That we, of to-day, in gross contrast to this Arcadian[1] purity, call for the ungainly, and obtain the ugly.

That, could we but change our habits and climate – were we willing to wander in groves – could we be roasted out of broadcloth – were we to do without haste, and journey without speed, we should again *require* the spoon of Queen Anne, and pick at our peas with the fork of two prongs. And so, for the flock, little hamlets grow near Hammersmith, and the steam horse is scorned.

Useless! quite hopeless and false is the effort! – built upon fable, and all because 'a wise man has uttered a vain thing and filled his belly with the East wind.'

Listen! There never was an artistic period.

There never was an Art-loving nation.

In the beginning, man went forth each day – some to do battle,

1 Arcadia, in classical literature, is the region of pastoral contentment.

some to the chase; others, again, to dig and to delve in the field – all that they might gain and live, or lose and die. Until there was found among them one, differing from the rest, whose pursuits attracted him not, and so he stayed by the tents with the women, and traced strange devices with a burnt stick upon a gourd.

This man, who took no joy in the ways of his brethren – who cared not for conquest, and fretted in the field – this designer of quaint patterns – this deviser of the beautiful – who perceived in Nature about him curious curvings, as faces are seen in the fire – this dreamer apart, was the first artist [ . . . ].

And presently there came to this man another – and, in time, others – of like nature, chosen by the Gods – and so they worked together; and soon they fashioned, from the moistened earth, forms resembling the gourd. And with the power of creation, the heirloom of the artist, presently they went beyond the slovenly suggestion of Nature, and the first vase was born, in beautiful proportion [ . . . ].

And time, with more state, brought more capacity for luxury, and it became well that men should dwell in large houses, and rest upon couches, and eat at tables; whereupon the artist, with his artificers, built palaces, and filled them with furniture, beautiful in proportion and lovely to look upon.

And the people lived in marvels of art – and ate and drank out of masterpieces – for there was nothing else to eat and to drink out of, and no bad building to live in; no article of daily life, of luxury, or of necessity, that had not been handed down from the design of the master, and made by his workmen.

And the people questioned not, *and had nothing to say in the matter*.

So Greece was in its splendour, and Art reigned supreme – by force of fact, not by election – and there was no meddling from the outsider. The mighty warrior would no more have ventured to offer a design for the temple of Pallas Athene than would the sacred poet have proffered a plan for constructing the catapult.

And the Amateur was unknown – and the Dilettante undreamed of!

And history wrote on, and conquest accompanied civilisation, and Art spread, or rather its products were carried by the victors among the vanquished from one country to another. And the customs of cultivation covered the face of the earth, so that all peoples continued to use what *the artist alone produced*.

And centuries passed in this using, and the world was flooded with all that was beautiful, until there arose a new class, who discovered the cheap, and foresaw fortune in the facture of the sham.

Then sprang into existence the tawdry, the common, the gewgaw [ . . . ].

And the artist's occupation was gone, and the manufacturer and the huckster took his place [ . . . ].

And the people – this time – had much to say in the matter – and all were satisfied. And Birmingham and Manchester arose in their might – and Art was relegated to the curiosity shop.

Nature contains the elements, in colour and form, of all pictures, as the keyboard contains the notes of all music.

But the artist is born to pick, and choose, and group with science, these elements, that the result may be beautiful – as the musician gathers his notes, and forms his chords, until he bring forth from chaos glorious harmony.

To say to the painter, that Nature is to be taken as she is, is to say to the player, that he may sit on the piano.

That Nature is always right, is an assertion, artistically, as untrue, as it is one whose truth is universally taken for granted. Nature is very rarely right, to such an extent even, that it might almost be said that Nature is usually wrong: that is to say, the condition of things that shall bring about the perfection of harmony worthy a picture is rare, and not common at all.

This would seem, to even the most intelligent, a doctrine almost blasphemous. So incorporated with our education has the supposed aphorism become, that its belief is held to be part of our moral being, and the words themselves have, in our ear, the ring of religion. Still, seldom does Nature succeed in producing a picture.

The sun blares, the wind blows from the east, the sky is bereft of cloud, and without, all is of iron. The windows of the Crystal Palace are seen from all points of London. The holiday-maker rejoices in the glorious day, and the painter turns aside to shut his eyes.

How little this is understood, and how dutifully the casual in Nature is accepted as sublime, may be gathered from the unlimited admiration daily produced by a very foolish sunset.

The dignity of the snow-capped mountain is lost in distinctness, but the joy of the tourist is to recognise the traveller on the top. The desire to see, for the sake of seeing, is, with the mass, alone the one to be gratified, hence the delight in detail.

And when the evening mist clothes the riverside with poetry, as with a veil, and the poor buildings lose themselves in the dim sky, and the tall chimneys become campanili, and the warehouses are palaces in the night, and the whole city hangs in the heavens, and fairy-land is before us – then the wayfarer hastens home; the working man and the cultured one, the wise man and the one of pleasure, cease to understand, as they have ceased to see, and Nature, who, for once, has sung in tune, sings her exquisite song to the artist alone, her son and her master – her son in that he loves her, her master in that he knows her.

To him her secrets are unfolded, to him her lessons have become gradually clear. He looks at her flower, not with the enlarging lens, that he may gather facts for the botanist, but with the light of the one who sees in her choice selection of brilliant tones and delicate tints, suggestions of future harmonies.

He does not confine himself to purposeless copying, without thought, each blade of grass, as commended by the inconsequent, but, in the long curve of the narrow leaf, corrected by the straight tall stem, he learns how grace is wedded to dignity, how strength enhances sweetness, that elegance shall be the result [ . . . ].

Through his brain, as through the last alembic, is distilled the refined essence of that thought which began with the Gods, and which they left him to carry out.

Set apart by them to complete their works, he produces that wondrous thing called the masterpiece, which surpasses in perfection all that they have contrived in what is called Nature; and the Gods stand by and marvel, and perceive how far away more beautiful is the Venus of Melos than was their own Eve.

For some time past, the unattached writer has become the middleman in this matter of Art, and his influence, while it has widened the gulf between the people and the painter, has brought about the most complete misunderstanding as to the aim of the picture.

For him a picture is more or less a hieroglyph or symbol of story. Apart from a few technical terms, for the display of which he finds an occasion, the work is considered absolutely from a literary point of view; indeed, from what other can he consider it? And in his essays he deals with it as with a novel – a history – or an anecdote. He fails entirely and most naturally to see its excellences, or demerits – artistic – and so degrades Art, by supposing it a method of bringing about a literary climax [ . . . ].

Meanwhile, the *painter's* poetry is quite lost to him – the amazing invention that shall have put form and colour into such perfect harmony, that exquisiteness is the result, he is without understanding – the nobility of thought, that shall have given the artist's dignity to the whole, says to him absolutely nothing [ . . . ].

A curious matter, in its effect upon the judgment of these gentlemen, is the accepted vocabulary of poetic symbolism, that helps them, by habit, in dealing with Nature: a mountain, to them, is synonymous with height – a lake, with depth – the ocean, with vastness – the sun, with glory.

So that a picture with a mountain, a lake, and an ocean – however poor in paint – is inevitably 'lofty,' 'vast,' 'infinite,' and 'glorious' – on paper [ . . . ].

Then the Preacher 'appointed'!

He stands in high places – harangues and holds forth.

Sage of the Universities – learned in many matters, and of much experience in all, save his subject.

Exhorting – denouncing – directing.

Filled with wrath and earnestness.

Bringing powers of persuasion, and polish of language, to prove – nothing.

Torn with much teaching – having naught to impart.

Impressive – important – shallow.

Defiant – distressed – desperate.

Crying out, and cutting himself – while the gods hear not.

Gentle priest of the Philistine withal, again he ambles pleasantly from all point, and through many volumes, escaping scientific assertion – 'babbles of green fields' [ . . . ].

Art happens – no hovel is safe from it, no Prince may depend upon it, the vastest intelligence cannot bring it about, and puny efforts to make it universal end in quaint comedy, and coarse farce.

This is as it should be – and all attempts to make it otherwise are due to the eloquence of the ignorant, the zeal of the conceited.

The boundary line is clear. Far from me to propose to bridge it over – that the pestered people be pushed across. No! I would save them from further fatigue. I would come to their relief, and would lift from their shoulders this incubus of Art.

Why, after centuries of freedom from it, and indifference to it, should it now be thrust upon them by the blind – until wearied and puzzled, they know no longer how they shall eat or drink – how they shall sit or stand – or wherewithal they shall clothe themselves – without afflicting Art.

But, lo! there is much talk without!

Triumphantly they cry, 'Beware! This matter does indeed concern us. We also have our part in all true Art! – for, remember the "one touch of Nature" that "makes the whole world kin"' [ . . . ].

Vulgarity – under whose fascinating influence 'the many' have elbowed 'the few,' and the gentle circle of Art swarms with the intoxicated mob of mediocrity, whose leaders prate and counsel, and call aloud, where the Gods once spoke in whisper!

And now from their midst the Dilettante stalks abroad. The amateur is loosed. The voice of the aesthete is heard in the land, and catastrophe is upon us.

The meddler beckons the vengeance of the Gods, and ridicule threatens the fair daughters of the land.

And there are curious converts to a weird *culte*, in which all instinct for attractiveness – all freshness and sparkle – all woman's winsomeness – is to give way to a strange vocation for the unlovely – and this desecration in the name of the Graces!

Shall this gaunt, ill-at-ease, distressed, abashed mixture of *mauvaise honte*[1] and desperate assertion call itself artistic, and claim cousinship with the artist — who delights in the dainty, the sharp, bright gaiety of beauty?

No! – a thousand times no! Here are no connections of ours.

We will have nothing to do with them.

Forced to seriousness, that emptiness may be hidden, they dare not smile –

While the artist, in fulness of heart and head, is glad, and laughs aloud, and is happy in his strength, and is merry at the pompous pretension – the solemn silliness that surrounds him.

For Art and Joy go together, with bold openness, and high head, and ready hand – fearing naught, and dreading no exposure.

Know, then, all beautiful women, that we are with you. Pay no heed, we pray you, to this outcry of the unbecoming – this last plea for the plain.

It concerns you not.

Your own instinct is near the truth – your own wit far surer guide than the untaught ventures of thick heeled Apollos.

---

1 Literally, 'self-consciousness' or 'bashfulness'.

What! will you up and follow the first piper that leads you down Petticoat Lane, there, on a Sabbath, to gather, for the week, from the dull rags of ages wherewith to bedeck yourselves? that, beneath your travestied awkwardness, we have trouble to find your own dainty selves? Oh, fie! Is the world, then, exhausted? and must we go back because the thumb of the mountebank jerks the other way?

Costume is not dress.

And the wearers of wardrobes may not be doctors of taste!

For by what authority shall these be pretty masters? Look well, and nothing have they invented – nothing put together for comeliness' sake.

Haphazard from their shoulders hang the garments of the hawker – combining in their person the motley of many manners with the medley of the mummers' closet.

Set up as a warning, and a finger-post of danger, they point to the disastrous effect of Art upon the middle classes [ . . . ].

False again, the fabled link between the grandeur of Art and the glories and virtues of the State, for Art feeds not upon nations, and peoples may be wiped from the face of the earth, but Art *is*.

It is indeed high time that we cast aside the weary weight of responsibility and co-partnership, and know that, in no way, do our virtues minister to its worth, in no way do our vices impede its triumph!

How irksome! how hopeless! how superhuman the self-imposed task of the nation! How sublimely vain the belief that it shall live nobly or art perish [ . . . ].

[Art] is proud of her comrade, and promises that in after-years, others shall pass that way, and understand.

So in all time does this superb one cast about for the man worthy her love – and Art seeks the Artist alone.

Where he is, there she appears, and remains with him – loving and fruitful – turning never aside in moments of hope deferred – of insult – and of ribald misunderstanding; and when he dies she sadly takes her flight, though loitering yet in the land, from fond association, but refusing to be consoled.

With the man, then, and not with the multitude, are her intimacies; and in the book of her life the names inscribed are few – scant, indeed, the list of those who have helped to write her story of love and beauty [ . . . ].

Therefore have we cause to be merry! – and to cast away all care –

resolved that all is well – as it ever was – and that it is not meet that we should be cried at, and urged to take measures!

Enough have we endured of dulness! Surely are we weary of weeping, and our tears have been cozened from us falsely, for they have called out woe! when there was no grief – and, alas! where all is fair!

We have then but to wait – until, with the mark of the Gods upon him – there come among us again the chosen – who shall continue what has gone before. Satisfied that, even were he never to appear, the story of the beautiful is already complete – hewn in the marbles of the Parthenon – and broidered, with the birds, upon the fan of Hokusai[1] – at the foot of Fusiyama.

# WALTER PATER

## From 'Style' in *Appreciations* (1889)

I propose here to point out certain qualities of all literature as a fine art, which, if they apply to the literature of fact, apply still more to the literature of the imaginative sense of fact, while they apply indifferently to verse and prose, so far as either is really imaginative – certain conditions of true art in both alike, which conditions may also contain in them the secret of the proper discrimination and guardianship of the peculiar excellences of either.

The line between fact and something quite different from external fact is, indeed, hard to draw. In Pascal, for instance, in the persuasive writers generally, how difficult to define the point where, from time to time, argument which, if it is to be worth anything at all, must consist of facts or groups of facts, becomes a pleading – a theorem no longer, but essentially an appeal to the reader to catch the writer's spirit, to think with him, if one can or will – an expression no longer of fact but of his sense of it, his peculiar intuition of a world, prospective, or discerned below the faulty

---

1 i.e. the nineteenth-century Japanese artist: Japanese art was discovered in the last decades of the century.

conditions of the present, in either case changed somewhat from the actual world. In science, on the other hand, in history so far as it conforms to scientific rule, we have a literary domain where the imagination may be thought to be always an intruder. And as, in all science, the functions of literature reduce themselves eventually to the transcribing of fact, so all the excellences of literary form in regard to science are reducible to various kinds of painstaking; this good quality being involved in all 'skilled work' whatever, in the drafting of an act of parliament, as in sewing. Yet here again, the writer's sense of fact, in history especially, and in all those complex subjects which do but lie on the borders of science, will still take the place of fact, in various degrees. Your historian, for instance, with absolutely truthful intention, amid the multitude of facts presented to him must needs select, and in selecting assert something of his own humour, something that comes not of the world without but of a vision within. So Gibbon moulds his unwieldly material to a preconceived view. Livy, Tacitus, Michelet,[1] moving full of poignant sensibility amid the records of the past, each, after his own sense, modifies – who can tell where and to what degree? – and becomes something else than a transcriber; each, as he thus modifies, passing into the domain of art proper. For just in proportion as the writer's aim, consciously or unconsciously, comes to be the transcribing, not of the world, not of mere fact, but of his sense of it, he becomes an artist, his work *fine* art; and good art (as I hope ultimately to show) in proportion to the truth of his presentment of that sense; as in those humbler or plainer functions of literature also, truth – truth to bare fact, there – is the essence of such artistic quality as they may have. Truth! there can be no merit, no craft at all, without that. And further, all beauty is in the long run only *fineness* of truth, or what we call expression, the finer accommodation of speech to that vision within.

– The transcript of his sense of fact rather than the fact, as being preferable, pleasanter, more beautiful to the writer himself. In literature, as in every other product of human skill, in the moulding of a bell or a platter for instance, wherever this sense asserts itself, wherever the producer so modifies his work as, over and above its

---

1 i.e. Edward Gibbon, the eighteenth-century historian; Titus Livius (59 BC–AD 17) and Cornelius Tacitus (55–120), Roman historians. Jules Michelet (1789–1874), the French historian who in the nineteenth century had a reputation as a stimulating but unreliable author.

primary use or intention, to make it pleasing (to himself, of course, in the first instance) there, 'fine' as opposed to merely serviceable art, exists. Literary art, that is, like all art which is in any way imitative or reproductive of fact – form, or colour, or incident – is the representation of such fact as connected with soul, of a specific personality, in its preferences, its volition and power.

Such is the matter of imaginative or artistic literature – this transcript, not of mere fact, but of fact in its infinite variety, as modified by human preference in all its infinitely varied forms. It will be good literary art not because it is brilliant or sober, or rich, or impulsive, or severe, but just in proportion as its representation of that sense, that soul-fact, is true, verse being only one department of such literature, and imaginative prose, it may be thought, being the special art of the modern world. That imaginative prose should be the special and opportune art of the modern world results from two important facts about the latter: first, the chaotic variety and complexity of its interests, making the intellectual issue, the really master currents of the present time incalculable – a condition of mind little susceptible of the restraint proper to verse form, so that the most characteristic verse of the nineteenth century has been lawless verse; and secondly, an all-pervading naturalism, a curiosity about everything whatever as it really is, involving a certain humility of attitude, cognate to what must, after all, be the less ambitious form of literature. And prose thus asserting itself as the special and privileged artistic faculty of the present day, will be, however critics may try to narrow its scope, as varied in its excellence as humanity itself reflecting on the facts of its latest experience – an instrument of many stops, meditative, observant, descriptive, eloquent, analytic, plaintive, fervid. Its beauties will be not exclusively 'pedestrian': it will exert, in due measure, all the varied charms of poetry, down to the rhythm which, as in Cicero, or Michelet, or Newman,[1] at their best, gives its musical value to every syllable.

The literary artist is of necessity a scholar, and in what he proposes to do will have in mind, first of all, the scholar and the scholarly conscience – the male conscience in this matter, as we

---

1 i.e. Marcus Tullius Cicero (106–43 BC), the Roman orator, statesman and stoic; John Henry Newman (1801–90) a central figure in the Oxford Movement, whose *The Idea of a University* was published in 1852.

must think it, under a system of education which still to so large an extent limits real scholarship to men. In his self-criticism, he supposes always that sort of reader who will go (full of eyes) warily, considerately, though without consideration for him, over the ground which the female conscience traverses so lightly, so amiably. For the material in which he works is no more a creation of his own than the sculptor's marble. Product of a myriad various minds and contending tongues, compact of obscure and minute association, a language has its own abundant and often recondite laws, in the habitual and summary recognition of which scholarship consists. A writer, full of a matter he is before all things anxious to express, may think of those laws, the limitations of vocabulary, structure, and the like, as a restriction, but if a real artist will find in them an opportunity. His punctilious observance of the proprieties of his medium will diffuse through all he writes a general air of sensibility, of refined usage. *Exclusiones debitae naturae* – the exclusions, or rejections, which nature demands – we know how large a part these play, according to Bacon, in the science of nature. In a somewhat changed sense, we might say that the art of the scholar is summed up in the observance of those rejections demanded by the nature of his medium, the material he must use. Alive to the value of an atmosphere in which every term finds its utmost degree of expression, and with all the jealousy of a lover of words, he will resist a constant tendency on the part of the majority of those who use them to efface the distinctions of language, the facility of writers often reinforcing in this respect the work of the vulgar. He will feel the obligation not of the laws only, but of those affinities, avoidances, those mere preferences, of his language, which through the associations of literary history have become a part of its nature, prescribing the rejection of many a neology, many a license, many a gipsy phrase which might present itself as actually expressive. His appeal, again, is to the scholar, who has great experience in literature, and will show no favour to short-cuts, or hackneyed illustration, or an affectation of learning designed for the unlearned. Hence a contention, a sense of self-restraint and renunciation, having for the susceptible reader the effect of a challenge for minute consideration; the attention of the writer, in every minutest detail, being a pledge that it is worth the reader's while to be attentive too, that the writer is dealing scrupulously with his instrument, and therefore, indirectly, with the reader himself also, that he has the science of the instrument he plays on, perhaps, after all, with a freedom which in such case will be the freedom of a master.

For meanwhile, braced only by those restraints, he is really vindicating his liberty in the making of a vocabulary, an entire system of composition, for himself, his own true manner; and when we speak of the manner of a true master we mean what is essential in his art. Pedantry being only the scholarship of *le cuistre*[1] (we have no English equivalent) he is no pedant, and does but show his intelligence of the rules of language in his freedoms with it, addition or expansion, which like the spontaneities of manner in a well-bred person will still further illustrate good taste. – The right vocabulary! Translators have not invariably seen how all-important that is in the work of translation, driving for the most part at idiom or construction; whereas, if the original be first-rate, one's first care should be with its elementary particles, Plato, for instance, being often reproducible by an exact following, with no variation in structure, of word after word, as the pencil follows a drawing under tracing-paper, so only each word or syllable be not of false colour, to change my illustration a little.

Well! that is because any writer worth translating at all has winnowed and searched through his vocabulary, is conscious of the words he would select in systematic reading of a dictionary, and still more of the words he would reject were the dictionary other than Johnson's; and doing this with his peculiar sense of the world ever in view, in search of an instrument for the adequate expression of that, he begets a vocabulary faithful to the colouring of his own spirit, and in the strictest sense original. That living authority which language needs lies, in truth, in its scholars, who recognising always that every language possesses a genius, a very fastidious genius, of its own, expand at once and purify its very elements, which must needs change along with the changing thoughts of living people. Ninety years ago, for instance, great mental force, certainly, was needed by Wordsworth, to break through the consecrated poetic associations of a century, and speak the language that was his, that was to become in a measure the language of the next generation. But he did it with the tact of a scholar also. English, for a quarter of a century past, has been assimilating the phraseology of pictorial art; for half a century, the phraseology of the great German meta-

1 There is no equivalent word, for *le cuistre* means a pedant but carries the overtones of caddishness or posing.

physical movement of eighty years ago; in part also the language of mystical theology: and none but pedants will regret a great consequent increase of its resources. For many years to come its enterprise may well lie in the naturalisation of the vocabulary of science, so only it be under the eye of a sensitive scholarship – in a liberal naturalisation of the ideas of science too, for after all the chief stimulus of good style is to possess a full, rich, complex matter to grapple with. The literary artist, therefore, will be well aware of physical science; science also attaining, in its turn, its true literary ideal. And then, as the scholar is nothing without the historic sense, he will be apt to restore not really obsolete or really worn-out words, but the finer edge of words still in use: *ascertain*, *communicate*, *discover* – words like these it has been part of our 'business' to misuse. And still, as language was made for man, he will be no authority for correctnesses which, limiting freedom of utterance, were yet but accidents in their origin; as if one vowed not to say '*its*,' which ought to have been in Shakespeare; '*his*' and '*hers*,' for inanimate objects, being but a barbarous and really inexpressive survival. Yet we have known many things like this. Racy Saxon monosyllables, close to us as touch and sight, he will intermix readily with those long, savoursome, Latin words, rich in 'second intention.' In this late day certainly, no critical process can be conducted reasonably without eclecticism. Of such eclecticism we have a justifying example in one of the first poets of our time. How illustrative of monosyllabic effect, of sonorous Latin, of the phraseology of science, of metaphysic, of colloquialism even, are the writings of Tennyson; yet with what a fine, fastidious scholarship throughout!

A scholar writing for the scholarly, he will of course leave something to the willing intelligence of his reader. 'To go preach to the first passer-by,' says Montaigne, 'to become tutor to the ignorance of the first I meet, is a thing I abhor;' a thing, in fact, naturally distressing to the scholar, who will therefore ever be shy of offering uncomplimentary assistance to the reader's wit. To really strenuous minds there is a pleasurable stimulus in the challenge for a continuous effort on their part, to be rewarded by securer and more intimate grasp of the author's sense. Self-restraint, a skilful economy of means, *ascêsis*, that too has a beauty of its own; and for the reader supposed there will be an aesthetic satisfaction in that frugal closeness of style which makes the most of a word, in the exaction from every sentence of a precise relief, in the just spacing out of word to thought, in the logically filled space connected always with the delightful sense of difficulty overcome.

Different classes of persons, at different times, make, of course, very various demands upon literature. Still, scholars, I suppose, and not only scholars, but all disinterested lovers of books, will always look to it, as to all other fine art, for a refuge, a sort of cloistral refuge, from a certain vulgarity in the actual world. A perfect poem like *Lycidas*, a perfect fiction like *Esmond*,[1] the perfect handling of a theory like Newman's *Idea of a University*, has for them something of the uses of a religious 'retreat.' Here, then, with a view to the central need of a select few, those 'men of a finer thread' who have formed and maintain the literary ideal, everything, every component element, will have undergone exact trial, and, above all, there will be no uncharacteristic or tarnished or vulgar decoration, permissible ornament being for the most part structural, or necessary. As the painter in his picture, so the artist in his book, aims at the production by honourable artifice of a peculiar atmosphere. 'The artist,' says Schiller, 'may be known rather by what he *omits*'; and in literature, too, the true artist may be best recognised by his tact of omission. For to the grave reader words too are grave; and the ornamental word, the figure, the accessory form or colour or reference, is rarely content to die to thought precisely at the right moment, but will inevitably linger awhile, stirring a long 'brainwave' behind it of perhaps quite alien associations.

Just there, it may be, is the detrimental tendency of the sort of scholarly attentiveness of mind I am recommending. But the true artist allows for it. He will remember that, as the very word ornament indicates what is in itself non-essential, so the 'one beauty' of all literary style is of its very essence, and independent, in prose and verse alike, of all removable decoration; that it may exist in its fullest lustre, as in Flaubert's *Madame Bovary*, for instance, or in Stendhal's *Le Rouge et Le Noir*, in a composition utterly unadorned, with hardly a single suggestion of visibly beautiful things. Parallel, allusion, the allusive way generally, the flowers in the garden: – he knows the narcotic force of these upon the negligent intelligence to which any *diversion*, literally, is welcome, any vagrant intruder, because one can go wandering away with it from the immediate

1 i.e. Milton's 'Lycidas' and W. M. Thackeray's novel, *The History of Henry Esmond* (1852).

subject. Jealous, if he have a really quickening motive within, of all that does not hold directly to that, of the facile, the otiose, he will never depart from the strictly pedestrian process, unless he gains a ponderable something thereby. Even assured of its congruity, he will still question its serviceableness. Is it worth while, can we afford, to attend to just that, to just that figure or literary reference, just then? – Surplusage! he will dread that, as the runner on his muscles. For in truth all art does but consist in the removal of surplusage, from the last finish of the gem-engraver blowing away the last particle of invisible dust, back to the earliest divination of the finished work to be, lying somewhere, according to Michelangelo's fancy, in the rough-hewn block of stone.

And what applies to figure or flower must be understood of all other accidental or removable ornaments of writing whatever; and not of specific ornament only, but of all that latent colour and imagery which language as such carries in it. A lover of words for their own sake, to whom nothing about them is unimportant, a minute and constant observer of their physiognomy, he will be on the alert not only for obviously mixed metaphors of course, but for the metaphor that is mixed in all our speech, though a rapid use may involve no cognition of it. Currently recognising the incident, the colour, the physical elements or particles in words like *absorb, consider, extract*, to take the first that occur, he will avail himself of them, as further adding to the resources of expression. The elementary particles of language will be realised as colour and light and shade through his scholarly living in the full sense of them. Still opposing the constant degradation of language by those who use it carelessly, he will not treat coloured glass as if it were clear; and while half the world is using figure unconsciously, will be fully aware not only of all that latent figurative texture in speech, but of the vague, lazy, half-formed personification – a rhetoric, depressing, and worse than nothing, because it has no really rhetorical motive – which plays so large a part there, and, as in the case of more ostentatious ornament, scrupulously exact of it, from syllable to syllable, its precise value.

So far I have been speaking of certain conditions of the literary art arising out of the medium or material in or upon which it works, the essential qualities of language and its aptitudes for contingent ornamentation, matters which define scholarship as science and good taste respectively. They are both subservient to a more intimate quality of good style: more intimate, as coming nearer to the artist himself. The otiose, the facile, surplusage: why are these abhorrent to the true literary artist, except because, in literary as in all other art, structure is all-important, felt, or painfully missed, everywhere? – that architectural conception of work, which foresees the end in the beginning and never loses sight of it, and in every part is conscious of all the rest, till the last sentence does but, with un-diminished vigour, unfold and justify the first – a condition of literary art, which, in contradistinction to another quality of the artist himself, to be spoken of later, I shall call the necessity of *mind* in style.

An acute philosophical writer, the late Dean Mansel[1] (a writer whose works illustrate the literary beauty there may be in closeness, and with obvious repression or economy of a fine rhetorical gift) wrote a book, of fascinating precision in a very obscure subject, to show that all the technical laws of logic are but means of securing, in each and all of its apprehensions, the unity, the strict identity with itself, of the apprehending mind. All the laws of good writing aim at a similar unity or identity of the mind in all the processes by which the word is associated to its import. The term is right, and has its essential beauty, when it becomes, in a manner, what it signifies, as with the names of simple sensations. To give the phrase, the sentence, the structural member, the entire composition, song, or essay, a similar unity with its subject and with itself: – style is in the right way when it tends towards that. All depends upon the original unity, the vital wholeness and identity, of the initiatory apprehension or view. So much is true of all art, which therefore requires always its logic, its comprehensive reason – insight, fore-sight, retrospect, in simultaneous action – true, most of all, of the literary art, as being of all the arts most closely cognate to the abstract intelligence. Such logical coherency may be evidenced not merely in the lines of composition as a whole, but in the choice of a single word, while it by no means interferes with, but may even prescribe, much variety, in the building of the sentence for instance, or in the manner, argumentative, descriptive, discursive, of this or that part or member of the entire design. The blithe, crisp sentence, decisive as a child's expression of its needs, may alternate with the long-contending, victoriously intricate sentence; the sentence, born

---

1 i.e. Henry Mansel (1820–71), the Oxford philosopher and cleric.

with the integrity of a single word, relieving the sort of sentence in which, if you look closely, you can see much contrivance, much adjustment, to bring a highly qualified matter into compass at one view. For the literary architecture, if it is to be rich and expressive, involves not only foresight of the end in the beginning, but also development or growth of design, in the process of execution, with many irregularities, surprises, and afterthoughts; the contingent as well as the necessary being subsumed under the unity of the whole. As truly, to the lack of such architectural design, of a single, almost visual, image, vigorously informing an entire, perhaps very intricate, composition, which shall be austere, ornate, argumentative, fanciful, yet true from first to last to that vision within, may be attributed those weaknesses of conscious or unconscious repetition of word, phrase, motive, or member of the whole matter, indicating, as Flaubert was aware, an original structure in thought not organically complete. With such foresight, the actual conclusion will most often get itself written out of hand, before, in the more obvious sense, the work is finished. With some strong and leading sense of the world, the tight hold of which secures true *composition* and not mere loose accretion, the literary artist, I suppose, goes on considerately, setting joint to joint, sustained by yet restraining the productive ardour, retracing the negligences of his first sketch, repeating his steps only that he may give the reader a sense of secure and restful progress, readjusting mere assonances even, that they may soothe the reader, or at least not interrupt him on his way; and then, somewhere before the end comes, is burdened, inspired, with his conclusion, and betimes delivered of it, leaving off, not in weariness and because he finds *himself* at an end, but in all the freshness of volition. His work now structurally complete, with all the accumulating effect of secondary shades of meaning, he finishes the whole up to the just proportion of that ante-penultimate conclusion, and all becomes expressive. The house he has built is rather a body he has informed. And so it happens, to its greater credit, that the better interest even of a narrative to be recounted, a story to be told, will often be in its second reading. And though there are instances of great writers who have been no artists, an unconscious tact sometimes directing work in which we may detect, very pleasurably, many of the effects of conscious art, yet one of the greatest pleasures of really good prose literature is in the critical tracing out of that conscious artistic structure, and the pervading sense of it as we read. Yet of poetic literature too; for, in truth, the kind of constructive intelligence here supposed is one of the forms of the imagination.

That is the special function of mind, in style. Mind and soul: – hard to ascertain philosophically, the distinction is real enough practically, for they often interfere, are sometimes in conflict, with each other. Blake, in the last century, is an instance of preponderating soul, embarrassed, at a loss, in an era of preponderating mind. As a quality of style, at all events, soul is a fact, in certain writers – the way they have of absorbing language, of attracting it into the peculiar spirit they are of, with a subtlety which makes the actual result seem like some inexplicable inspiration. By mind, the literary artist reaches us, through static and objective indications of design in his work, legible to all. By soul, he reaches us, somewhat capriciously perhaps, one and not another, through vagrant sympathy and a kind of immediate contact. Mind we cannot choose but approve where we recognise it; soul may repel us, not because we misunderstand it. The way in which theological interests sometimes avail themselves of language is perhaps the best illustration of the force I mean to indicate generally in literature, by the word *soul*. Ardent religious persuasion may exist, may make its way, without finding any equivalent heat in language: or, again, it may enkindle words to various degrees, and when it really takes hold of them doubles its force. Religious history presents many remarkable instances in which, through no mere phrase-worship, an unconscious literary tact has, for the sensitive, laid open a privileged pathway from one to another. 'The altar-fire,' people say, 'has touched those lips!' The Vulgate, the English Bible, the English Prayer-Book, the writings of Swedenborg,[1] the Tracts for the Times:[2] – there, we have instances of widely different and largely diffused phases of religious feeling in operation as soul in style. But something of the same kind acts with similar power in certain writers of quite other than theological literature, on behalf of some wholly personal and peculiar sense of theirs. Most easily illustrated by theological literature, this quality lends to profane writers a kind of religious influence. At their best, these writers become, as we say sometimes, 'prophets'; such character depending on the

[1] Immanuel Swedenborg (1688–1772), the Swedish philosopher and mystic.
[2] *Tracts for the Times* were religious texts published by members of the Oxford Movement (some were by Newman) in the 1830s.

effect not merely of their matter, but of their matter as allied to, in 'electric affinity' with, peculiar form, and working in all cases by an immediate sympathetic contact, on which account it is that it may be called soul, as opposed to mind, in style. And this too is a faculty of choosing and rejecting what is congruous or otherwise with a drift towards unity – unity of atmosphere here, as there of design – soul securing colour (or perfume, might we say?) as mind secures form, the latter being essentially finite, the former vague or infinite, as the influence of a living person is practically infinite. There are some to whom nothing has any real interest, or real meaning, except as operative in a given person; and it is they who best appreciate the quality of soul in literary art. They seem to know a *person*, in a book, and make way by intuition: yet, although they thus enjoy the completeness of a personal information, it is still a characteristic of soul, in this sense of the word, that it does but suggest what can never be uttered, not as being different from, or more obscure than, what actually gets said, but as containing that plenary substance of which there is only one phase or facet in what is there expressed.

If all high things have their martyrs, Gustave Flaubert might perhaps rank as the martyr of literary style. In his printed cor- respondence, a curious series of letters, written in his twenty-fifth year, records what seems to have been his one other passion – a series of letters which, with its fine casuistries, its firmly repressed anguish, its tone of harmonious grey, and the sense of disillusion in which the whole matter ends, might have been, a few slight changes supposed, one of his own fictions. Writing to Madame X. certainly he does display, by 'taking thought' mainly, by constant and delicate pondering, as in his love for literature, a heart really moved, but still more, and as the pledge of that emotion, a loyalty to his work. Madame X., too, is a literary artist, and the best gifts he can send her are precepts of perfection in art, counsels for the effectual pursuit of that better love. In his love-letters it is the pains and pleasures of art he insists on, its solaces: he communicates secrets, reproves, encourages, with a view to that [ . . . ].

The one word for the one thing, the one thought, amid the multitude of words, terms, that might just do: the problem of style was there! – the unique word, phrase, sentence, paragraph, essay, or song, absolutely proper to the single mental presentation or vision within. In that perfect justice, over and above the many contingent and removable beauties with which beautiful style may charm us, but which it can exist without, independent of them yet dexterously availing itself of them, omnipresent in good work, in function at every point, from single epithets to the rhythm of a whole book, lay the specific, indispensable, very intellectual, beauty of literature, the possibility of which constitutes it a fine art.

One seems to detect the influence of a philosophic idea there, the idea of a natural economy, of some pre-existent adaptation, between a relative, somewhere in the world of thought, and its correlative, somewhere in the world of language – both alike, rather, somewhere in the mind of the artist, desiderative, expectant, inventive – meeting each other with the readiness of 'soul and body reunited,' in Blake's rapturous design; and, in fact, Flaubert was fond of giving his theory philosophical expression. –

> There are no beautiful thoughts (he would say) without beautiful forms, and conversely. As it is impossible to extract from a physical body the qualities which really constitute it – colour, extension, and the like – without reducing it to a hollow abstraction, in a word, without destroying it; just so it is impossible to detach the form from the idea, for the idea only exists by virtue of the form.

All the recognised flowers, the removable ornaments of literature (including harmony and ease in reading aloud, very carefully considered by him) counted, certainly; for these too are part of the actual value of what one says. But still, after all, with Flaubert, the search, the unwearied research, was not for the smooth, or winsome, or forcible word, as such, as with false Ciceronians, but quite simply and honestly, for the word's adjustment to its meaning. The first condition of this must be, of course, to know yourself, to have ascertained your own sense exactly. Then, if we suppose an artist, he says to the reader, – I want you to see precisely what I see. Into the mind sensitive to 'form,' a flood of random sounds, colours, incidents, is ever penetrating from the world without, to become, by sympathetic selection, a part of its very structure, and, in turn, the visible vesture and expression of that other world it sees so steadily within, nay, already with a partial conformity thereto, to be refined, enlarged, corrected, at a hundred points; and it is just there, just at those doubtful points that the function of style, as tact or taste, intervenes. The unique term will come more quickly to one than another, at one time than another, according also to the kind of matter in question. Quickness and slowness, ease and closeness alike, have nothing to do with the artistic character of the true word found at last. As there is a charm of ease, so there is also a special charm in the signs of discovery, of effort and contention towards a due end, as so often with Flaubert himself – in the style which has been pliant, as only obstinate, durable metal can be, to the inherent perplexities and recusancy of a certain difficult thought [ . . . ].

Coming slowly or quickly, when it comes, as it came with so much labour of mind, but also with so much lustre, to Gustave Flaubert, this discovery of the word will be, like all artistic success and felicity, incapable of strict analysis: effect of an intuitive condition of mind, it must be recognised by like intuition on the part of the reader, and a sort of immediate sense. In every one of those masterly sentences of Flaubert there was, below all mere contrivance, shaping and afterthought, by some happy instantaneous concourse of the various faculties of the mind with each other, the exact apprehension of what was *needed* to carry the meaning. And that it fits with absolute justice will be a judgment of immediate sense in the appreciative reader. We all feel this in what may be called inspired translation. Well! all language involves translation from inward to outward. In literature, as in all forms of art, there are the absolute and merely relative or accessory beauties; and precisely in that exact proportion of the term to its purpose is the absolute beauty of style, prose or verse. All the good qualities, the beauties, of verse also, are such, only as precise expression.

In the highest as in the lowliest literature, then, the one indispensable beauty is, after all, truth: – truth to bare fact in the latter, as to some personal sense of fact, diverted somewhat from men's ordinary sense of it, in the former; truth there as accuracy, truth here as expression, that finest and most intimate form of truth, the *vraie vérité*.[1] And what an eclectic principle this really is! employing for its one sole purpose – that absolute accordance of expression to idea – all other literary beauties and excellences whatever: how many kinds of style it covers, explains, justifies, and at the same time safeguards! Scott's facility, Flaubert's deeply pondered evocation of 'the phrase,' are equally good art. Say what you have to say, what you have a will to say, in the simplest, the most direct and exact manner possible, with no surplusage: – there, is the justification of the sentence so fortunately born, 'entire, smooth,

1 Literally, 'the honest truth'.

and round,' that it needs no punctuation, and also (that is the point!) of the most elaborate period, if it be right in its elaboration. Here is the office of ornament: here also the purpose of restraint in ornament. As the exponent of truth, that austerity (the beauty, the function, of which in literature Flaubert understood so well) becomes not the correctness or purism of the mere scholar, but a security against the otiose, a jealous exclusion of what does not really tell towards the pursuit of relief, of life and vigour in the portraiture of one's sense. License again, the making free with rule, if it be indeed, as people fancy, a habit of genius, flinging aside or transforming all that opposes the liberty of beautiful production, will be but faith to one's own meaning. The seeming baldness of *Le Rouge et Le Noir* is nothing in itself; the wild ornament of *Les Misérables* is nothing in itself; and the restraint of Flaubert, amid a real natural opulence, only redoubled beauty – the phrase so large and so precise at the same time, hard as bronze, in service to the more perfect adaptation of words to their matter. Afterthoughts, retouchings, finish, will be of profit only so far as they too really serve to bring out the original, initiative, generative, sense in them.

In this way, according to the well-known saying, 'The style is the man,'[1] complex or simple, in his individuality, his plenary sense of what he really has to say, his sense of the world; all cautions regarding style arising out of so many natural scruples as to the medium through which alone he can expose that inward sense of things, the purity of this medium, its laws or tricks of refraction: nothing is to be left there which might give conveyance to any matter save that. Style in all its varieties, reserved or opulent, terse, abundant, musical, stimulant, academic, so long as each is really characteristic or expressive, finds thus its justification, the sumptuous good taste of Cicero being as truly the man himself, and not another, justified, yet insured inalienably to him, thereby, as would have been his portrait by Raffaelle, in full consular splendour, on his ivory chair.

A relegation, you may say perhaps – a relegation of style to the subjectivity, the mere caprice, of the individual, which must soon transform it into mannerism. Not so! since there is, under the conditions supposed, for those elements of the man, for every lineament of the vision within, the one word, the one acceptable

1 Originating with Buffon.

44

word, recognisable by the sensitive, by others 'who have intelligence' in the matter, as absolutely as ever anything can be in the evanescent and delicate region of human language. The style, the manner, would be the man, not in his unreasoned and really uncharacteristic caprices, involuntary or affected, but in absolutely sincere apprehension of what is most real to him. But let us hear our French guide again. –

> Styles (says Flaubert's commentator), *Styles*, as so many peculiar moulds, each of which bears the mark of a particular writer, who is to pour into it the whole content of his ideas, were no part of his theory. What he believed in was *Style*: that is to say, a certain absolute and unique manner of expressing a thing, in all its intensity and colour. For him the *form* was the work itself. As in living creatures, the blood, nourishing the body, determines its very contour and external aspect, just so, to his mind, the *matter*, the basis, in a work of art, imposed, necessarily, the unique, the just expression, the measure, the rhythm – the *form* in all its characteristics.

If the style be the man, in all the colour and intensity of a veritable apprehension, it will be in a real sense 'impersonal.'

I said, thinking of books like Victor Hugo's *Les Misérables*, that prose literature was the characteristic art of the nineteenth century, as others, thinking of its triumphs since the youth of Bach, have assigned that place to music. Music and prose literature are, in one sense, the opposite terms of art; the art of literature presenting to the imagination, through the intelligence, a range of interests, as free and various as those which music presents to it through sense. And certainly the tendency of what has been here said is to bring literature too under those conditions, by conformity to which music takes rank as the typically perfect art. If music be the ideal of all art whatever, precisely because in music it is impossible to distinguish the form from the substance or matter, the subject from the expression, then, literature, by finding its specific excellence in the absolute correspondence of the term to its import, will be but fulfilling the condition of all artistic quality in things everywhere, of all good art.

Good art, but not necessarily great art; the distinction between great art and good art depending immediately, as regards literature at all events, not on its form, but on the matter. Thackeray's *Esmond*, surely, is greater art than *Vanity Fair*, by the greater dignity of its interests. It is on the quality of the matter it informs or controls, its compass, its variety, its alliance to great ends, or the depth of the note of revolt, or the largeness of hope in it, that the greatness of literary art depends, as *The Divine Comedy, Paradise Lost, Les Misérables, The English Bible*, are great art. Given the conditions I have tried to explain as constituting good art; – then, if it be devoted further to the increase of men's happiness, to the redemption of the oppressed, or the enlargement of our sympathies with each other, or to such presentment of new or old truth about ourselves and our relation to the world as may ennoble and fortify us in our sojourn here, or immediately, as with Dante, to the glory of God, it will be also great art; if, over and above those qualities I summed up as mind and soul – that colour and mystic perfume, and that reasonable structure, it has something of the soul of humanity in it, and finds its logical, its architectural place, in the great structure of human life.

# OSCAR WILDE

## From 'The Critic as Artist' in *Intentions* (1891)

*With some remarks upon the importance of doing nothing.*
*A Dialogue. Part I.*
*Persons: Gilbert and Ernest.*
*Scene: the library of a house in Piccadilly, overlooking the Green Park.*

*Ernest.* [ . . . ] But, seriously speaking, what is the use of art-criticism? Why cannot the artist be left alone, to create a new world if he wishes it, or, if not, to shadow forth the world which we already know, and of which, I fancy, we would each one of us be wearied if Art, with her fine spirit of choice and delicate instinct of selection, did not, as it were, purify it for us, and give to it a momentary perfection. It seems to me that the imagination spreads, or should spread, a solitude around it, and works best in silence and in isolation. Why should the artist be troubled by the shrill clamour of criticism? Why should those who cannot create take upon themselves to estimate the value of creative work? What can they know about it? If a man's work is easy to understand, an explanation is unnecessary. . . .

*Gilbert.* And if his work is incomprehensible, an explanation is wicked.

*Ernest.* I did not say that.

*Gilbert.* Ah! but you should have. Nowadays, we have so few mysteries left to us that we cannot afford to part with one of them. The members of the Browning Society, like the theologians of the Broad Church Party, or the authors of Mr. Walter Scott's Great Writers' Series,[1] seem to me to spend their time in trying to explain their divinity away. Where one had hoped that Browning was a mystic, they have sought to show that he was simply inarticulate. Where one had fancied that he had something to conceal, they have proved that he had but little to reveal. But I speak merely of his incoherent work. Taken as a whole, the man was great. He did not belong to the Olympians, and had all the incompleteness of the Titan. He did not survey, and it was but rarely that he could sing. His work is marred by struggle, violence and effort, and he passed not from emotion to form, but from thought to chaos. Still, he was great. He has been called a thinker, and was certainly a man who was always thinking, and always thinking aloud; but it was not thought that fascinated him, but rather the processes by which thought moves. It was the machine he loved, not what the machine makes. The method by which the fool arrives at his folly was as dear to him as the ultimate wisdom of the wise. So much, indeed, did the subtle mechanism of mind fascinate him that he despised language, or looked upon it as an incomplete instrument of expression. Rhyme, that exquisite echo which in the Muse's hollow hill creates and answers its own voice; rhyme, which in the hands of the real artist becomes not merely a material element of metrical beauty, but a spiritual element of thought and passion also, waking a new mood, it may be, or stirring a fresh train of ideas, or opening by mere sweetness and suggestion of sound some golden door at which the Imagination itself had knocked in vain; rhyme, which can turn man's utterance to the speech of gods; rhyme, the one chord we have added to the Greek lyre, became in Robert Browning's

---

1 Browning Societies, dedicated to explication of his poems, were common in the last years of the nineteenth century; as were popular editions of great literary works.

hands a grotesque, misshapen thing, which at times made him masquerade in poetry as a low comedian, and ride Pegasus too often with his tongue in his cheek. There are moments when he wounds us by monstrous music. Nay, if he can only get his music by breaking the strings of his lute, he breaks them, and they snap in discord, and no Athenian tettix,[1] making melody from tremulous wings, lights on the ivory horn to make the movement perfect, or the interval less harsh. Yet, he was great: and though he turned language into ignoble clay, he made from it men and women that live. He is the most Shakespearian creature since Shakespeare. If Shakespeare could sing with myriad lips, Browning could stammer through a thousand mouths. Even now, as I am speaking, and speaking not against him but for him, there glides through the room the pageant of his persons. There, creeps Fra Lippo Lippi with his cheeks still burning from some girl's hot kiss. There, stands dread Saul with the lordly male-sapphires gleaming in his turban. Mildred Tresham is there, and the Spanish monk, yellow with hatred, and Blougram, and Ben Ezra, and the Bishop of St. Praxed's. The spawn of Setebos gibbers in the corner, and Sebald, hearing Pippa pass by, looks on Ottima's haggard face, and loathes her and his own sin, and himself. Pale as the white satin of his doublet, the melancholy king watches with dreamy treacherous eyes too loyal Strafford pass forth to his doom, and Andrea shudders as he hears the cousins whistle in the garden, and bids his perfect wife go down.[2] Yes, Browning was great. And as what will he be remembered? As a poet? Ah, not as a poet! He will be remembered as a writer of fiction, as the most supreme writer of fiction, it may be, that we have ever had. His sense of dramatic situation was unrivalled, and, if he could not answer his own problems, he could at least put problems forth, and what more should an artist do? Considered from the point of view of a creator of character he ranks next to him who made Hamlet. Had he been articulate, he might have sat beside him. The only man who can touch the hem of his garment is George Meredith. Meredith is a prose Browning, and so is Browning. He used poetry as a medium for writing in prose.

*Ernest.* There is something in what you say, but there is not

---

1 A cicada or tree-cricket.
2 The references are to Browning's poems or characters, speakers or situations in his poems.

everything in what you say. In many points you are unjust.

*Gilbert.* It is difficult not to be unjust to what one loves. But let us return to the particular point at issue. What was it that you said?

*Ernest.* Simply this: that in the best days of art there were no art-critics.

*Gilbert.* I seem to have heard that observation before, Ernest. It has all the vitality of error and all the tediousness of an old friend.

*Ernest.* It is true. Yes: there is no use your tossing your head in that petulant manner. It is quite true. In the best days of art there were no art-critics. The sculptor hewed from the marble block the great white-limbed Hermes that slept within it. The waxers and gilders of images gave tone and texture to the statue, and the world, when it saw it, worshipped and was dumb. He poured the glowing bronze into the mould of sand, and the river of red metal cooled into noble curves and took the impress of the body of a god. With enamel or polished jewels he gave sight to the sightless eyes. The hyacinth-like curls grew crisp beneath his graver. And when, in some dim frescoed fane, or pillared sunlit portico, the child of Leto[1] stood upon his pedestal, those who passed by, ἁβρῶς βαίνοντες διὰ λαμπροτάτου αἰθέρος,[2] became conscious of a new influence that had come across their lives, and dreamily, or with a sense of strange and quickening joy, went to their homes or daily labour, or wandered, it may be, through the city gates to that nymph-haunted meadow where young Phaedrus[3] bathed his feet, and, lying there on the soft grass, beneath the tall wind-whispering planes and flowering *agnus castus*, began to think of the wonder of beauty, and grew silent with unaccustomed awe. In those days the artist was free. From the river valley he took the fine clay in his fingers, and with a little tool of wood or bone, fashioned it into forms so exquisite that the people gave them to the dead as their playthings, and we find them still in the dusty tombs on the yellow hillside by Tanagra,[4] with the faint gold and the fading crimson still lingering about hair and lips and raiment. On a wall of fresh plaster, stained with bright sandyx or mixed with milk and saffron, he pictured one who trod with tired feet the purple white-starred fields of asphodel,

1 i.e. Apollo, the Greek god who presided over the arts.
2 Literally, 'treading lightly through the shining air'.
3 Wilde is almost certainly thinking of Phaedrus, the friend of Plato.
4 In ancient Greece, a town in Boeotia.

one 'in whose eyelids lay the whole of the Trojan War,' Polyxena,[1] the daughter of Priam; or figured Odysseus, the wise and cunning, bound by tight cords to the mast-step, that he might listen without hurt to the singing of the Sirens,[2] or wandering by the clear river of Acheron,[3] where the ghosts of fishes flitted over the pebbly bed; or showed the Persian in trews and mitre flying before the Greek at Marathon, or the galleys clashing their beaks of brass in the little Salaminian bay. He drew with silver-point and charcoal upon parchment and prepared cedar. Upon ivory and rose-coloured terracotta he painted with wax, making the wax fluid with juice of olives, and with heated irons making it firm. Panel and marble and linen canvas became wonderful as his brush swept across them; and life seeing her own image, was still, and dared not speak. All life, indeed, was his, from the merchants seated in the market-place to the cloaked shepherd lying on the hill; from the nymph hidden in the laurels and the faun that pipes at noon, to the king whom, in long green-curtained litter, slaves bore upon oil-bright shoulders and fanned with peacock fans. Men and women, with pleasure or sorrow in their faces, passed before him. He watched them, and their secret became his. Through form and colour he recreated a world.

All subtle arts belonged to him also. He held the gem against the revolving disk, and the amethyst became the purple couch for Adonis,[4] and across the veined sardonyx sped Artemis[5] with her hounds. He beat out the gold into roses, and strung them together for necklace or armlet. He beat out the gold into wreaths for the conqueror's helmet, or into palmates for the Tyrian robe, or into masks for the royal dead. On the back of the silver mirror he graved Thetis[6] borne by her Nereids, or love-sick Phædra[7] with her nurse, or Persephone,[8] weary of memory, putting poppies in her hair. The potter sat in his shed, and, flower-like from the silent wheel, the

1 Polyxena, in the *Iliad*, is the betrothed of Achilles.
2 Nymphs whose songs irresistibly lured sailors to destruction.
3 One of the rivers of Hell, receiving the souls of the dead.
4 A lover of Venus, and the type of classical lover.
5 The Greek goddess of hunting (the Roman Diana).
6 In Greek mythology the goddess of the sea.
7 Daughter of Minos and Pasiphaë, wife of Theseus but enamoured of Theseus' son Hippolytus, Phaedra was the subject of plays by Euripides and Seneca.
8 Daughter of Zeus and Demeter (the Roman Ceres), abducted to the underworld, where she was obliged to spend one third of each year.

vase rose up beneath his hands. He decorated the base and stem and ears with pattern of dainty olive-leaf, or foliated acanthus, or curved and crested wave. Then in black or red he painted lads wrestling, or in the race: knights in full armour, with strange heraldic shields and curious visors, leaning from shell-shaped chariot over rearing steeds: the gods seated at the feast or working their miracles: the heroes in their victory or in their pain. Sometimes he would etch in thin vermilion lines upon a ground of white the languid bridegroom and his bride, with Eros hovering round them – an Eros like one of Donatello's angels, a little laughing thing with gilded or with azure wings. On the curved side he would write the name of his friend *ΚΑΛΟΣ ΑΛΚΙΒΙΑΔΗΣ* or *ΚΑΛΟΣ ΧΑΡΜΙΔΗΣ*[1] tells us the story of his days. Again, on the rim of the wide flat cup he would draw the stag browsing, or the lion at rest, as his fancy willed it. From the tiny perfume-bottle laughed Aphrodite at her toilet, and, with bare-limbed Mænads in his train, Dionysus danced round the wine-jar on naked must-stained feet, while, satyr-like, the old Silenus[2] sprawled upon the bloated skins, or shook that magic spear which was tipped with a fretted fir-cone, and wreathed with dark ivy. And no one came to trouble the artist at his work. No irresponsible chatter disturbed him. He was not worried by opinions. By the Ilyssus,[3] says Arnold somewhere, there was no Higginbotham. By the Ilyssus, my dear Gilbert, there were no silly art-congresses, bringing provincialism to the provinces and teaching the mediocrity how to mouth. By the Ilyssus there were no tedious magazines about art, in which the industrious prattle of what they do not understand. On the reed-grown banks of that little stream strutted no ridiculous journalism monopolizing the seat of judgment when it should be apologizing in the dock. The Greeks had no art-critics.

*Gilbert.* Ernest, you are quite delightful, but your views are terribly unsound. I am afraid that you have been listening to the conversation of someone older than yourself. That is always a dangerous thing to do, and if you allow it to degenerate into a habit, you will find it absolutely fatal to any intellectual development. As for modern journalism, it is not my business to defend it.

---

1 Noble Alcibiades or noble Charmides.
2 A Greek demi-god, attendant of Bacchus.
3 A small river in Attica.

It justifies its own existence by the great Darwinian principle of the survival of the vulgarest. I have merely to do with literature.

*Ernest.* But what is the difference between literature and journalism?

*Gilbert.* Oh! journalism is unreadable, and literature is not read. That is all. But with regard to your statement that the Greeks had no art-critics, I assure you that is quite absurd. It would be more just to say that the Greeks were a nation of art-critics.

*Ernest.* Really?

*Gilbert.* Yes, a nation of art-critics. But I don't wish to destroy the delightfully unreal picture that you have drawn of the relation of the Hellenic artist to the intellectual spirit of his age. To give an accurate description of what has never occurred is not merely the proper occupation of the historian, but the inalienable privilege of any man of parts and culture. Still less do I desire to talk learnedly. Learned conversation is either the affectation of the ignorant or the profession of the mentally unemployed. And, as for what is called improving conversation, that is merely the foolish method by which the still more foolish philanthropist feebly tries to disarm the just rancour of the criminal classes. No: let me play to you some mad scarlet thing by Dvořák. The pallid figures on the tapestry are smiling at us, and the heavy eyelids of my bronze Narcissus are folded in sleep. Don't let us discuss anything solemnly. I am but too conscious of the fact that we are born in an age when only the dull are treated seriously, and I live in terror of not being mis-understood. Don't degrade me into the position of giving you useful information. Education is an admirable thing, but it is well to remember from time to time that nothing that is worth knowing can be taught. Through the parted curtains of the window I see the moon like a clipped piece of silver. Like gilded bees the stars cluster round her. The sky is a hard hollow sapphire. Let us go out into the night. Thought is wonderful, but adventure is more wonderful still. Who knows but we may meet Prince Florizel of Bohemia, and hear the fair Cuban tell us that she is not what she seems?[1]

*Ernest.* You are horribly wilful. I insist on your discussing this matter with me. You have said that the Greeks were a nation of art-critics. What art-criticism have they left us?

1 See *The Winter's Tale.*

52

*Gilbert.* My dear Ernest, even if not a single fragment of art-criticism had come down to us from Hellenic or Hellenistic days, it would be none the less true that the Greeks were a nation of art-critics, and that they invented the criticism of art just as they invented the criticism of everything else. For, after all, what is our primary debt to the Greeks? Simply the critical spirit. And, this spirit, which they exercised on questions of religion and science, of ethics and metaphysics, of politics and education, they exercised on questions of art also, and, indeed, of the two supreme and highest arts, they have left us the most flawless system of criticism that the world has ever seen.

*Ernest.* But what are the two supreme and highest arts?

*Gilbert.* Life and Literature, life and the perfect expression of life. The principles of the former, as laid down by the Greeks, we may not realize in an age so marred by false ideals of our own. The principles of the latter, as they laid them down, are, in many cases, so subtle that we can hardly understand them. Recognizing that the most perfect art is that which most fully mirrors man in all his infinite variety, they elaborated the criticism of language, considered in the light of the mere material of that art, to a point to which we, with our accentual system of reasonable or emotional emphasis, can barely if at all attain; studying, for instance, the metrical movements of a prose as scientifically as a modern musician studies harmony and counter point, and, I need hardly say, with much keener aesthetic instinct. In this they were right, as they were right in all things. Since the introduction of printing, and the fatal development of the habit of reading amongst the middle and lower classes of this country, there has been a tendency in literature to appeal more and more to the eye, and less and less to the ear which is really the sense which, from the standpoint of pure art, it should seek to please, and by whose canons of pleasure it should abide always. Even the work of Mr. Pater, who is, on the whole, the most perfect master of English prose now creating amongst us, is often far more like a piece of mosaic than a passage in music, and seems, here and there, to lack the true rhythmical life of words and the fine freedom and richness of effect that such rhythmical life produces. We, in fact, have made writing a definite mode of composition, and have treated it as a form of elaborate design. The Greeks, upon the other hand, regarded writing simply as a method of chronicling. Their test was always the spoken word in its musical and metrical relations. The voice was the medium, and the ear the critic. I have sometimes thought that the story of Homer's blindness might be really an artistic myth, created in critical days, and serving to remind us, not merely that the great poet is always a seer, seeing less with the eyes of the body than he does with the eyes of the soul, but that he is a true singer also, building his song out of music, repeating each line over and over again to himself till he has caught the secret of its melody, chaunting in darkness the words that are winged with light. Certainly, whether this be so or not, it was to his blindness, as an occasion if not as a cause, that England's great poet owed much of the majestic movement and sonorous splendour of his later verse. When Milton could no longer write, he began to sing. Who would match the measures of *Comus* with the measures of *Samson Agonistes*, or of *Paradise Lost* or *Regained?* When Milton became blind he composed, as everyone should compose, with the voice purely, and so the pipe or reed of earlier days became that mighty many-stopped organ whose rich reverberant music has all the stateliness of Homeric verse, if it seeks not to have its swiftness, and is the one imperishable inheritance of English literature, sweeping through all the ages, because above them, and abiding with us ever, being immortal in its form. Yes: writing has done much harm to writers. We must return to the voice. That must be our test, and perhaps then we shall be able to appreciate some of the subtleties of Greek art-criticism.

As it now is, we cannot do so. Sometimes, when I have written a piece of prose that I have been modest enough to consider absolutely free from fault, a dreadful thought comes over me that I may have been guilty of the immoral effeminacy of using trochaic and tribrachic movements, a crime for which a learned critic of the Augustan age censures with most just severity the brilliant if somewhat para-doxical Hegesias.[1] I grow cold when I think of it, and wonder to myself if the admirable ethical effect of the prose of that charming writer, who once in a spirit of reckless generosity towards the uncultivated portion of our community proclaimed the monstrous doctrine that conduct is three-fourths of life, will not some day be entirely annihilated by the discovery that the pæons have been wrongly placed.

---

1 I am not sure of the 'learned critic', but Wilde was thinking of Hegesias of Magnesia, a writer of florid prose.

*Ernest.* Ah! now you are flippant.

*Gilbert.* Who would not be flippant when he is gravely told that the Greeks had no art-critics? I can understand it being said that the constructive genius of the Greeks lost itself in criticism, but not that the race to whom we owe the critical spirit did not criticise. You will not ask me to give you a survey of Greek art-criticism from Plato to Plotinus. The night is too lovely for that, and the moon, if she heard us, would put more ashes on her face than are there already. But think merely of one perfect little work of aesthetic criticism, Aristotle's *Treatise on Poetry*. It is not perfect in form, for it is badly written, consisting perhaps of notes jotted down for an art lecture, or of isolated fragments destined for some larger book, but in temper and treatment it is perfect absolutely. The ethical effect of art, its importance to culture, and its place in the formation of character, had been done once for all by Plato;[1] but here we have art treated, not from the moral, but from the purely aesthetic point of view. Plato had, of course, dealt with many definitely artistic subjects, such as the importance of unity in a work of art, the necessity for tone and harmony, the aesthetic value of appearances, the relation of the visible arts to the external world, and the relation of fiction to fact. He first perhaps stirred in the soul of man that desire which we have not yet satisfied, the desire to know the connection between Beauty and Truth, and the place of Beauty in the moral and intellectual order of the Kosmos. The problems of idealism and realism, as he sets them forth, may seem to many to be somewhat barren of results in the metaphysical sphere of abstract being in which he places them, but transfer them to the sphere of art, and you will find that they are still vital and full of meaning. It may be that it is as a critic of Beauty that Plato is destined to live, and by altering the name of the sphere of his speculation we shall find a new philosophy. But Aristotle, like Goethe, deals with art primarily in its concrete manifestations, taking Tragedy, for instance, and investigating the material it uses, which is language, its subject-matter, which is life, the method by which it works, which is action, the conditions under which it reveals itself, which are those of theatric presentation, its logical structure, which is plot, and its final aesthetic appeal, which is to the sense of beauty realized through the passions of pity and awe. That purification and

---

1 A topic upon which Wilde had heard Pater lecture at Oxford.

spiritualizing of the nature which he calls κάθαρσις[1] is, as Goethe saw, essentially aesthetic, and is not moral, as Lessing fancied. Concerning himself primarily with the impression that the work of art produces, Aristotle sets himself to analyse that impression, to investigate its source, to see how it is engendered. As a physiologist and psychologist, he knows that the health of a function resides in energy. To have a capacity for a passion and not to realize it, is to make oneself incomplete and limited. The mimic spectacle of life that Tragedy affords cleanses the bosom of much 'perilous stuff,' and by presenting high and worthy objects for the exercise of the emotions purifies and spiritualizes the man; nay, not merely does it spiritualize him, but it initiates him also into noble feelings of which he might else have known nothing, the word κάθαρσις having, it has sometimes seemed to me, a definite allusion to the rite of initiation, if indeed that be not, as I am occasionally tempted to fancy, its true and only meaning here. This is of course a mere outline of the book. But you see what a perfect piece of aesthetic criticism it is. Who indeed but a Greek could have analysed art so well? After reading it, one does not wonder any longer that Alexandria devoted itself so largely to art-criticism, and that we find the artistic temperaments of the day investigating every question of style and manner, discussing the great Academic schools of painting, for instance, such as the school of Sicyon,[2] that sought to preserve the dignified traditions of the antique mode, or the realistic and impressionist schools, that aimed at reproducing actual life, or the elements of ideality in portraiture, or the artistic value of the epic form in an age so modern as theirs, or the proper subject-matter for the artist. Indeed, I fear that the inartistic temperaments of the day busied themselves also in matters of literature and art, for the accusations of plagiarism were endless, and such accusations proceed either from the thin colourless lips of impotence, or from the grotesque mouths of those who, possessing nothing of their own, fancy that they can gain a reputation for wealth by crying out that they have been robbed. And I assure you, my dear Ernest, that the Greeks chattered about painters quite as much as people do nowadays, and had their private views, and shilling exhibitions, and Arts and Crafts guilds, and Pre-Raphaelite movements, and move-

[1] Catharsis or cleansing.
[2] The most famous school of painting in ancient Greece where, according to legend, the art was invented.

ments towards realism, and lectured about art, and wrote essays on art, and produced their art-historians, and their archaeologists, and all the rest of it. Why, even the theatrical managers of travelling companies brought their dramatic critics with them when they went on tour, and paid them very handsome salaries for writing laudatory notices. Whatever, in fact, is modern in our life we owe to the Greeks. Whatever is an anachronism is due to mediaevalism. It is the Greeks who have given us the whole system of art-criticism, and how fine their critical instinct was, may be seen from the fact that the material they criticised with most care was, as I have already said, language. For the material that painter or sculptor uses is meagre in comparison with that of words. Words have not merely music as sweet as that of viol and lute, colour as rich and vivid as any that makes lovely for us the canvas of the Venetian or the Spaniard, and plastic form no less sure and certain than that which reveals itself in marble or in bronze, but thought and passion and spirituality are theirs also, are theirs indeed alone. If the Greeks had criticised nothing but language, they would still have been the great art-critics of the world. To know the principles of the highest art, is to know the principles of the arts.

But I see that the moon is hiding behind a sulphur-coloured cloud. Out of a tawny mane of drift she gleams like a lion's eye. She is afraid that I will talk to you of Lucian and Longinus, of Quinctilian and Dionysius, of Pliny and Fronto and Pausanias, of all those who in the antique world wrote or lectured upon art-matters.[1] She need not be afraid. I am tired of my expedition into the dim, dull abyss of facts. There is nothing left for me now but the divine μονόχρονος ἡδονή[2] of another cigarette. Cigarettes have at least the charm of leaving one unsatisfied.

*Ernest.* Try one of mine. They are rather good. I get them direct from Cairo. The only use of our *attachés* is that they supply their friends with excellent tobacco. And as the moon has hidden herself, let us talk a little longer. I am quite ready to admit that I was wrong in what I said about the Greeks. They were, as you have pointed out, a nation of art-critics. I acknowledge it, and feel a little sorry

---

1 Lucian: a Greek philosophical writer; Longinus: the name given to the unknown author of *On the Sublime*; Quintilian: a Roman grammarian; Dionysius: either a Greek grammarian or a Greek poet; Pliny: a Roman historian; Fronto: a Roman rhetorician; Pausanias: a Greek geographer.
2 Undivided pleasure.

for them. For the creative faculty is higher than the critical. There is really no comparison between them.

*Gilbert.* The antithesis between them is entirely arbitrary. Without the critical faculty, there is no artistic creation at all, worthy of the name. You spoke a little while ago of that fine spirit of choice and delicate instinct of selection by which the artist realizes life for us, and gives to it a momentary perfection. Well, that spirit of choice, that subtle tact of omission, is really the critical faculty in one of its most characteristic moods, and no one who does not possess this critical faculty can create anything at all in art. Arnold's definition of literature as a criticism of life, was not very felicitous in form, but it showed how keenly he recognized the importance of the critical element in all creative work.[1]

*Ernest.* I should have said that great artists worked unconsciously, that they were 'wiser than they knew,' as, I think, Emerson remarks somewhere.

*Gilbert.* It is really not so, Ernest. All fine imaginative work is self-conscious and deliberate. No poet sings because he must sing. At least, no great poet does. A great poet sings because he chooses to sing. It is so now, and it has always been so. We are sometimes apt to think that the voices that sounded at the dawn of poetry were simpler, fresher, and more natural than ours, and that the world which the early poets looked at, and through which they walked, had a kind of poetical quality of its own, and almost without changing could pass into song. The snow lies thick now upon Olympus, and its steep scarped sides are bleak and barren, but once, we fancy, the white feet of the Muses brushed the dew from the anemones in the morning, and at evening came Apollo to sing to the shepherds in the vale. But in this we are merely lending to other ages what we desire, or think we desire, for our own. Our historical sense is at fault. Every century that produces poetry is, so far, an artificial century, and the work that seems to us to be the most natural and simple product of its time is always the result of the most self-conscious effort. Believe me, Ernest, there is no fine art without self-consciousness, and self-consciousness and the critical spirit are one.

*Ernest.* I see what you mean, and there is much in it. But surely you would admit that the great poems of the early world, the

1 See 'The Function of Criticism at the Present Time', *Essays in Criticism* (first series 1865).

primitive, anonymous collective poems, were the result of the imagination of races, rather than of the imagination of individuals?

*Gilbert.* Not when they became poetry. Not when they received a beautiful form. For there is no art where there is no style, and no style where there is no unity, and unity is of the individual. No doubt Homer had old ballads and stories to deal with, as Shakespeare had chronicles and plays and novels from which to work, but they were merely his rough material. He took them, and shaped them into song. They become his, because he made them lovely. They were built out of music,

> And so not built at all,
> And therefore built for ever.

The longer one studies life and literature, the more strongly one feels that behind everything that is wonderful stands the individual, and that it is not the moment that makes the man, but the man who creates the age. Indeed, I am inclined to think that each myth and legend that seems to us to spring out of the wonder, or terror, or fancy of tribe and nation, was in its origin the invention of one single mind. The curiously limited number of the myths seems to me to point to this conclusion. But we must not go off into questions of comparative mythology. We must keep to criticism. And what I want to point out is this. An age that has no criticism is either an age in which art is immobile, hieratic, and confined to the repro-duction of formal types, or an age that possesses no art at all. There have been critical ages that have not been creative, in the ordinary sense of the word, ages in which the spirit of man has sought to set in order the treasures of his treasure-house, to separate the gold from the silver, and the silver from the lead, to count over the jewels, and to give names to the pearls. But there has never been a creative age that has not been critical also. For it is the critical faculty that invents fresh forms. The tendency of creation is to repeat itself. It is to the critical instinct that we owe each new school that springs up, each new mould that art finds ready to its hand. There is really not a single form that art now uses that does not come to us from the critical spirit of Alexandria, where these forms were either stereotyped, or invented, or made perfect. I say Alexandria, not merely because it was there that the Greek spirit became most self-conscious, and indeed ultimately expired in scepticism and theology, but because it was to that city, and not to Athens, that Rome turned for her models, and it was through the survival, such as it was, of the Latin language that culture lived at all. When, at the Renaissance, Greek literature dawned upon Europe, the soil had been in some measure prepared for it. But, to get rid of the details of history, which are always wearisome and usually inaccurate, let us say generally, that the forms of art have been due to the Greek critical spirit. To it we owe the epic, the lyric, the entire drama in every one of its developments, including burlesque, the idyll, the romantic novel, the novel of adventure, the essay, the dialogue, the oration, the lecture, for which perhaps we should not forgive them, and the epigram, in all the wide meaning of that word. In fact, we owe it everything, except the sonnet, to which, however, some curious parallels of thought-movement may be traced in the Anthology, American journalism, to which no parallel can be found anywhere and the ballad in sham Scotch dialect, which one of our most industrious writers has recently proposed should be made the basis for a final and unanimous effort on the part of our second-rate poets to make themselves really romantic. Each new school, as it appears, cries out against criticism, but it is to the critical faculty in man that it owes its origin. The mere creative instinct does not innovate, but reproduces.

*Ernest.* You have been talking of criticism as an essential part of the creative spirit, and I now fully accept your theory. But what of criticism outside creation? I have a foolish habit of reading periodicals, and it seems to me that most modern criticism is perfectly valueless.

*Gilbert.* So is most modern creative work also. Mediocrity weighing mediocrity in the balance, and incompetence applauding its brother – that is the spectacle which the artistic activity of England affords us from time to time. And yet, I feel I am a little unfair in this matter. As a rule, the critics – I speak, of course, of the higher class, of those in fact who write for the sixpenny papers – are far more cultured than the people whose work they are called upon to review. This is, indeed, only what one would expect, for criticism demands infinitely more cultivation than creation does.

*Ernest.* Really?

*Gilbert.* Certainly. Anybody can write a three-volumed novel.[1] It

---

[1] The general form in which novels were published in the last half of the century, to the increasing dissatisfaction of some authors and publishers.

merely requires a complete ignorance of both life and literature. The
difficulty that I should fancy the reviewer feels is the difficulty of
sustaining any standard. Where there is no style a standard must be
impossible. The poor reviewers are apparently reduced to be the
reporters of the police-court of literature, the chroniclers of the
doings of the habitual criminals of art. It is sometimes said of them
that they do not read all through the works they are called upon to
criticise. They do not. Or at least they should not. If they did so,
they would become confirmed misanthropes, or if I may borrow a
phrase from the one of the pretty Newnham graduates, confirmed
womanthropes for the rest of their lives. Nor is it necessary. To
know the vintage and quality of a wine one need not drink the whole
cask. It must be perfectly easy in half an hour to say whether a book
is worth anything or worth nothing. Ten minutes are really sufficient,
if one has the instinct for form. Who wants to wade through a dull
volume? One tastes it, and that is quite enough – more than enough,
I should imagine. I am aware that there are many honest workers
in painting as well as in literature who object to criticism entirely.
They are quite right. Their work stands in no intellectual relation
to their age. It brings us no new element of pleasure. It suggests
no fresh departure of thought, or passion, or beauty. It should not
be spoken of. It should be left to the oblivion that it deserves.

*Ernest.* But, my dear fellow – excuse me for interrupting you – you
seem to me to be allowing your passion for criticism to lead you a
great deal too far. For, after all, even you must admit that it is much
more difficult to do a thing than to talk about it.

*Gilbert.* More difficult to do a thing than to talk about it? Not at
all. That is a gross popular error. It is very much more difficult to
talk about a thing than to do it. In the sphere of actual life that is
of course obvious. Anybody can make history. Only a great man
can write it. There is no mode of action, no form of emotion, that
we do not share with the lower animals. It is only by language that
we rise above them, or above each other – by language, which is
the parent, and not the child, of thought. Action, indeed, is always
easy, and when presented to us in its most aggravated, because
most continuous form, which I take to be that of real industry,
becomes simply the refuge of people who have nothing whatsoever
to do. No, Ernest, don't talk about action. It is a blind thing
dependent on external influences, and moved by an impulse of
whose nature it is unconscious. It is a thing incomplete in its essence,

because limited by accident, and ignorant of its direction, being always at variance with its aim. Its basis is the lack of imagination. It is the last resource of those who know not how to dream.

*Ernest.* Gilbert, you treat the world as if it were a crystal ball. You hold it in your hand, and reverse it to please a wilful fancy. You do nothing but rewrite history.

*Gilbert.* The one duty we owe to history is to rewrite it. That is not the least of the tasks in store for the critical spirit. When we have fully discovered the scientific laws that govern life, we shall realize that the one person who has more illusions than the dreamer is the man of action. He, indeed, knows neither the origin of his deeds nor their results. From the field in which he thought that he had sown thorns, we have gathered our vintage, and the fig-tree that he planted for our pleasure is as barren as the thistle, and more bitter. It is because humanity has never known where it was going that it has been able to find its way.

*Ernest.* You think, then, that in the sphere of action a conscious aim is a delusion?

*Gilbert.* It is worse than a delusion. If we lived long enough to see the results of our actions it may be that those who call themselves good would be sickened with a dull remorse, and those whom the world calls evil stirred by a noble joy. Each little thing that we do passes into the great machine of life which may grind our virtues to powder and make them worthless, or transform our sins into elements of a new civilization, more marvellous and more splendid than any that has gone before. But men are the slaves of words. They rage against Materialism, as they call it, forgetting that there has been no material improvement that has not spiritualized the world, and that there have been few, if any, spiritual awakenings that have not wasted the world's faculties in barren hopes, and fruitless aspirations, and empty or trammelling creeds. What is termed Sin is an essential element of progress. Without it the world would stagnate, or grow old, or become colourless. By its curiosity, Sin increases the experience of the race. Through its intensified assertion of individualism, it saves us from monotony of type. In its rejection of the current notions about morality, it is one with the higher ethics. And as for the virtues! What are the virtues? Nature, M. Renan[1] tells us, cares little about chastity, and it may be that

---

1 i.e. Ernest Renan (1823–92), the French historian and scholar.

it is to the shame of the Magdalen, and not to their own purity, that the Lucretias of modern life owe their freedom from stain. Charity, as even those of whose religion it makes a formal part have been compelled to acknowledge, creates a multitude of evils. The mere existence of conscience, that faculty of which people prate so much nowadays, and are so ignorantly proud, is a sign of our imperfect development. It must be merged in instinct before we become fine. Self-denial is simply a method by which man arrests his progress, and self-sacrifice a survival of the mutilation of the savage, part of that old worship of pain which is so terrible a factor in the history of the world, and which even now makes its victims day by day, and has its altars in the land. Virtues! Who knows what the virtues are? Not you. Not I. Not anyone. It is well for our vanity that we slay the criminal, for if we suffered him to live he might show us what we had gained by his crime. It is well for his peace that the saint goes to his martyrdom. He is spared the sight of the horror of his harvest.

*Ernest.* Gilbert, you sound too harsh a note. Let us go back to the more gracious fields of literature. What was it you said? That it was more difficult to talk about a thing than to do it?

*Gilbert (after a pause).* Yes: I believe I ventured upon that simple truth. Surely you see now that I am right? When man acts he is a puppet. When he describes he is a poet. The whole secret lies in that. It was easy enough on the sandy plains by windy Ilion[1] to send the notched arrow from the painted bow, or to hurl against the shield of hide and flame-like brass the long ash-handled spear. It was easy for the adulterous queen to spread the Tyrian carpets for her lord, and then, as he lay couched in the marble bath, to throw over his head the purple net, and call to her smooth-faced lover to stab through the meshes at the heart that should have broken at Aulis.[2] For Antigone[3] even, with Death waiting for her as her bridegroom, it was easy to pass through the tainted air at noon, and climb the hill, and strew with kindly earth the wretched naked corse that had no tomb. But what of those who wrote about these things? What of those who gave them reality, and made them

---

1 Troy.

2 By tradition the starting point of the Greek fleet for the Trojan war. The references are chiefly to Aeschylus' *Agamemnon*.

3 Who, in Sophocles' *Antigone*, is entombed alive by Creon for burying her brother Polyneices.

live forever? Are they not greater than the men and women they sing of? 'Hector that sweet knight is dead,' and Lucian tells us how in the dim underworld Menippus saw the bleaching skull of Helen, and marvelled that it was for so grim a favour that all those horned ships were launched, those beautiful mailed men laid low, those towered cities brought to dust. Yet, every day the swan-like daughter of Leda comes out on the battlements, and looks down at the tide of war. The greybeards wonder at her loveliness, and she stands by the side of the king. In his chamber of stained ivory lies her leman. He is polishing his dainty armour, and combing the scarlet plume. With squire and page, her husband passes from tent to tent. She can see his bright hair, and hears, or fancies that she hears, that clear cold voice. In the courtyard below, the son of Priam is buckling on his brazen cuirass. The white arms of Andromache are around his neck. He sets his helmet on the ground, lest their babe should be frightened. Behind the embroidered curtains of his pavilion sits Achilles, in perfumed raiment, while in harness of gilt and silver the friend of his soul arrays himself to go forth to the fight. From a curiously carven chest that his mother Thetis has brought to his ship-side, the Lord of the Myrmidons takes out that mystic chalice that the lip of man had never touched, and cleanses it with brimstone, and with fresh water cools it, and, having washed his hands, fills with black wine its burnished hollow, and spills the thick grape-blood upon the ground in honour of Him whom at Dodona barefooted prophets worshipped,[1] and prays to Him, and knows not that he prays in vain, and that by the hands of two knights from Troy, Panthous' son, Euphorbus, whose love-locks were looped with gold, and the Priamid, the lion-hearted, Patroklus, the comrade of comrades, must meet his doom.[2] Phantoms, are they? Heroes of mist and mountain? Shadows in a song? No: they are real. Action! What is action? It dies at the moment of its energy. It is a base concession to fact. The world is made by the singer for the dreamer.

*Ernest.* While you talk it seems to me to be so.

*Gilbert.* It is so in truth. On the mouldering citadel of Troy lies the lizard like a thing of green bronze. The owl has built her nest in the palace of Priam. Over the empty plain wander shepherd and goatherd with their flocks, and where, on the wine-surfaced, oily sea, οἶνοψ πόντος,[3] as Homer calls it, copper-prowed and streaked

---

1 i.e. Zeus.    3 References to the action of the *Iliad*.    3 Wine-coloured sea.

with vermilion, the great galleys of the Danaoi came in their gleaming crescent; the lonely tunny-fisher sits in his little boat and watches the bobbing corks of his net. Yet, every morning the doors of the city are thrown open, and on foot, or in horse-drawn chariot, the warriors go forth to battle, and mock their enemies from behind their iron masks. All day long the fight rages, and when night comes the torches gleam by the tents, and the cresset burns in the hall. Those who live in marble or on painted panel, know of life but a single exquisite instant, eternal indeed in its beauty, but limited to one note of passion or one mood of calm. Those whom the poet makes live have their myriad emotions of joy and terror, of courage and despair, of pleasure and of suffering. The seasons come and go in glad or saddening pageant, and with winged or leaden feet the years pass by before them. They have their youth and their manhood, they are children, and they grow old. It is always dawn for St. Helena, as Veronese saw her at the window. Through the still morning air the angels bring her the symbol of God's pain. The cool breezes of the morning lift the gilt threads from her brow. On that little hill by the city of Florence, where the lovers of Giorgione are lying, it is always the solstice of noon, of noon made so languorous by summer suns that hardly can the slim naked girl dip into the marble tank the round bubble of clear glass, and the long fingers of the lute-player rest idly upon the chords. It is twilight always for the dancing nymphs whom Corot[1] set free among the silver poplars of France. In eternal twilight they move, those frail diaphanous figures, whose tremulous white feet seem not to touch the dew-drenched grass they tread on. But those who walk in epos, drama, or romance, see through the labouring months the young moons wax and wane, and watch the night from evening unto morning star, and from sunrise unto sunsetting can note the shifting day with all its gold and shadow. For them, as for us, the flowers bloom and wither, and the Earth, that Green-tressed Goddess as Coleridge calls her, alters her raiment for their pleasure. The statue is concentrated to one moment of perfection. The image stained upon the canvas possesses no spiritual element of growth or change. If they know nothing of death, it is because they know little of life, for the secrets of life and death belong to those, and those only, whom the sequence of time affects, and who

---

1 Jean-Baptiste-Camille Corot (1796–1875), the French landscape painter.

possess not merely the present but the future, and can rise or fall from a past of glory or of shame. Movement, that problem of the visible arts, can be truly realized by Literature alone. It is Literature that shows us the body in its swiftness and the soul in its unrest.

*Ernest.* Yes; I see now what you mean. But, surely, the higher you place the creative artist, the lower must the critic rank.

*Gilbert.* Why so?

*Ernest.* Because the best that he can give us will be but an echo of rich music, a dim shadow of clear-outlined form. It may, indeed, be that life is chaos, as you tell me that it is; that its martyrdoms are mean and its heroisms ignoble; and that it is the function of Literature to create, from the rough material of actual existence, a new world that will be more marvellous, more enduring, and more true than the world that common eyes look upon, and through which common natures seek to realize their perfection. But surely, if this new world has been made by the spirit and touch of a great artist, it will be a thing so complete and perfect that there will be nothing left for the critic [to do. I quite understand now, and indeed admit most readily, that it is far more difficult to talk about a thing than to do it. But it seems to me that this sound and sensible maxim, which is really extremely soothing to one's feelings, and should be adopted as its motto by every Academy of Literature all over the world, applies only to the relations that exist between Art and Life, and not to any relations that there may be between Art and Criticism.

*Gilbert.* But, surely, Criticism is itself an art. And just as artistic creation implies the working of the critical faculty, and, indeed, without it cannot be said to exist at all, so Criticism is really creative in the highest sense of the word. Criticism is, in fact, both creative and independent.

*Ernest.* Independent?

*Gilbert.* Yes; independent. Criticism is no more to be judged by any low standard of imitation or resemblance than is the work of poet or sculptor. The critic occupies the same relation to the work of art that he criticises as the artist does to the visible world of form and colour, or the unseen world of passion and of thought. He does not even require for the perfection of his art the finest materials. Anything will serve his purpose. And just as out of the sordid and sentimental amours of the silly wife of a small country doctor in the squalid village of Yonville-l'Abbaye, near Rouen,[1] Gustave Flaubert was able to create a classic, and make a masterpiece of style, so, from subjects of little or of no importance, such as the pictures in this year's Royal Academy, or in any year's Royal Academy for that matter, Mr. Lewis Morris's[2] poems, M. Ohnet's novels,[3] or the plays of Mr. Henry Arthur Jones,[4] the true critic can, if it be his pleasure so to direct or waste his faculty of contemplation, produce work that will be flawless in beauty and instinct with intellectual subtlety. Why not? Dulness is always an irresistible temptation for brilliancy, and stupidity is the permanent *Bestia Trionfans*[5] that calls wisdom from its cave. To an artist so creative as the critic, what does subject-matter signify? No more and no less than it does to the novelist and the painter. Like them, he can find his motives everywhere. Treatment is the test. There is nothing that has not in it suggestion or challenge.

*Ernest.* But is Criticism really a creative art?

*Gilbert.* Why should it not be? It works with materials, and puts them into a form that is at once new and delightful. What more can one say of poetry? Indeed, I would call criticism a creation within a creation. For just as the great artists, from Homer and Æschylus, down to Shakespeare and Keats, did not go directly to life for their subject-matter, but sought for it in myth, and legend and ancient tale, so the critic deals with materials that others have, as it were, purified for him, and to which imaginative form and colour have been already added. Nay, more, I would say that the highest Criticism, being the purest form of personal impression, is in its way more creative than creation, as it has least reference to any standard external to itself, and is, in fact, its own reason for existing, and, as the Greeks would put it, in itself, and to itself, an end. Certainly, it is never trammelled by any shackles of verisimilitude. No ignoble considerations of probability, that cowardly concession to the tedious repetitions of domestic or public life, affect it ever. One may appeal from fiction unto fact. But from the soul there is no appeal.

*Ernest.* From the soul?

---

1 The action of Flaubert's novel, *Madame Bovary*.
2 A popular, but poor, late nineteenth-century poet.
3 Georges Ohnet (1848–1918), French novelist and man of letters, bitterly opposed to realism.
4 A popular late nineteenth-century dramatist.     5 Triumphant beast.

*Gilbert.* Yes, from the soul. That is what the highest criticism really is, the record of one's own soul. It is more fascinating than history, as it is concerned simply with oneself. It is more delightful than philosophy, as its subject is concrete and not abstract, real and not vague. It is the only civilized form of autobiography, as it deals not with the events, but with the thoughts of one's life; not with life's physical accidents of deed or circumstance, but with the spiritual moods and imaginative passions of the mind. I am always amused by the silly vanity of those writers and artists of our day who seem to imagine that the primary function of the critic is to chatter about their second-rate work. The best that one can say of most modern creative art is that it is just a little less vulgar than reality, and so the critic, with his fine sense of distinction and sure instinct of delicate refinements, will prefer to look into the silver mirror or through the woven veil, and will turn his eyes away from the chaos and clamour of actual existence, though the mirror be tarnished and the veil be torn. His sole aim is to chronicle his own impressions. It is for him that pictures are painted, books written, and marble hewn into form.

*Ernest.* I seem to have heard another theory of Criticism.

*Gilbert.* Yes: it has been said by one whose gracious memory we all revere, and the music of whose pipe once lured Proserpina from her Sicilian fields, and made those white feet stir, and not in vain, the Cumnor cowslips, that the proper aim of Criticism is to see the object as in itself it really is.[1] But this is a very serious error, and takes no cognizance of Criticism's most perfect form, which is in its essence purely subjective, and seeks to reveal its own secret and not the secret of another. For the highest Criticism deals with art not as expressive but as impressive purely.

*Ernest.* But is that really so?

*Gilbert.* Of course it is. Who cares whether Mr. Ruskin's views on Turner[2] are sound or not? What does it matter? That mighty and majestic prose of his, so fervid and so fiery-coloured in its noble eloquence, so rich in its elaborate symphonic music, so sure and certain, at its best, in subtle choice of word and epithet, is at least as great a work of art as any of those wonderful sunsets that bleach or rot on their corrupted canvases in England's Gallery; greater

---

1 i.e. Matthew Arnold.
2 Ruskin's reputation had been made as a populariser of Turner's work.

indeed, one is apt to think at times, not merely because its equal beauty is more enduring, but on account of the fuller variety of its appeal, soul speaking to soul in those long-cadenced lines, not through form and colour alone, though through these, indeed, completely and without loss, but with intellectual and emotional utterance, with lofty passion and with loftier thought, with imaginative insight, and with poetic aim; greater, I always think, even as Literature is the greater art. Who, again, cares whether Mr. Pater has put into the portrait of Monna Lisa something that Lionardo never dreamed of?[1] The painter may have been merely the slave of an archaic smile, as some have fancied, but whenever I pass into the cool galleries of the Palace of the Louvre, and stand before that strange figure 'set in its marble chair in that cirque of fantastic rocks, as in some faint light under sea,' I murmur to myself, 'She is older than the rocks among which she sits; like the vampire, she has been dead many times, and learned the secrets of the grave; and has been a diver in deep seas, and keeps their fallen day about her; and trafficked for strange webs with Eastern merchants; and, as Leda, was the mother of Helen of Troy, and, as St. Anne, the mother of Mary; and all this has been to her but as the sound of lyres and flutes, and lives only in the delicacy with which it has moulded the changing lineaments, and tinged the eyelids and the hands.' And I say to my friend, 'The presence that thus so strangely rose beside the waters is expressive of what in the ways of a thousand years man had come to desire;' and he answers me, 'Hers is the head upon which all "the ends of the world are come," and the eyelids are a little weary.'

And so the picture becomes more wonderful to us than it really is, and reveals to us a secret of which, in truth, it knows nothing, and the music of the mystical prose is as sweet in our ears as was that flute-player's music that lent to the lips of La Gioconda those subtle and poisonous curves. Do you ask me what Lionardo would have said had anyone told him of this picture that 'all the thoughts and experience of the world had etched and moulded there in that which they had of power to refine and make expressive the outward form, the animalism of Greece, the lust of Rome, the reverie of the Middle Age with its spiritual ambition and imaginative loves, the return of the Pagan world, the sins of the Borgias?' He would

1 See Pater's essay on Leonardo da Vinci in *The Renaissance*.

probably have answered that he had contemplated none of these things, but had concerned himself simply with certain arrangements of lines and masses, and with new and curious colour-harmonies of blue and green. And it is for this very reason that the criticism which I have quoted is criticism of the highest kind. It treats the work of art simply as a starting-point for a new creation. It does not confine itself – let us at least suppose so for the moment – to discovering the real intention of the artist and accepting that as final. And in this it is right, for the meaning of any beautiful created thing is, at least, as much in the soul of him who looks at it, as it was in his soul who wrought it. Nay, it is rather the beholder who lends to the beautiful thing its myriad meanings, and makes it marvellous for us, and sets it in some new relation to the age, so that it becomes a vital portion of our lives, and a symbol of what we pray for, or perhaps of what, having prayed for, we fear that we may receive. The longer I study, Ernest, the more clearly I see that the beauty of the visible arts is, as the beauty of music, impressive primarily, and that it may be marred, and indeed often is so, by any excess of intellectual intention on the part of the artist. For when the work is finished it has, as it were, an independent life of its own, and may deliver a message far other than that which was put into its lips to say. Sometimes, when I listen to the overture to *Tannhäuser*,[1] I seem indeed to see that comely knight treading delicately on the flower-strewn grass, and to hear the voice of Venus calling to him from the caverned hill. But at other times it speaks to me of a thousand different things, of myself, it may be, and my own life, or of the lives of others whom one has loved and grown weary of loving, or of the passions that man has known, or of the passions that man has not known, and so has sought for. To-night it may fill one with that *ΕΡΩΣ ΤΩΝ ΑΔΥΝΑΤΩΝ*, that *Amour de l'Impossible*,[2] which falls like a madness on many who think they live securely and out of reach of harm, so that they sicken suddenly with the poison of unlimited desire, and, in the infinite pursuit of what they may not obtain, grow faint and swoon or stumble. To-morrow, like the music of which Aristotle and Plato tell us, the noble Dorian music of the Greek, it may perform the office of a physician, and give us an anodyne against pain, and heal the spirit that is wounded, and 'bring the soul into harmony with all right things.' And what

---

1 i.e. Wagner's opera, *Tannhäuser*.    2 Love of the impossible.

is true about music is true about all the arts. Beauty has as many meanings as man has moods. Beauty is the symbol of symbols. Beauty reveals everything, because it expresses nothing. When it shows us itself, it shows us the whole fiery-coloured world.

*Ernest.* But is such work as you have talked about really criticism?

*Gilbert.* It is the highest Criticism, for it criticises not merely the individual work of art, but Beauty itself, and fills with wonder a form which the artist may have left void, or not understood, or understood incompletely.

*Ernest.* The highest Criticism, then, is more creative than creation, and the primary aim of the critic is to see the object as in itself it really is not; that is your theory, I believe?

*Gilbert.* Yes, that is my theory. To the critic the work of art is simply a suggestion for a new work of his own, that need not necessarily bear any obvious resemblance to the thing it criticises. The one characteristic of a beautiful form is that one can put into it whatever one wishes, and see in it whatever one chooses to see; and the Beauty, that gives to creation its universal and aesthetic element, makes the critic a creator in his turn, and whispers of a thousand different things which were not present in the mind of him who carved the statue or painted the panel or graved the gem.

It is sometimes said by those who understand neither the nature of the highest Criticism nor the charm of the highest Art, that the pictures that the critic loves most to write about are those that belong to the anecdotage of painting, and that deal with scenes taken out of literature or history. But this is not so. Indeed, pictures of this kind are far too intelligible. As a class, they rank with illustrations, and even considered from this point of view are failures, as they do not stir the imagination, but set definite bounds to it. For the domain of the painter is, as I suggested before, widely different from that of the poet. To the latter belongs life in its full and absolute entirety; not merely the beauty that men look at, but the beauty that men listen to also; not merely the momentary grace of form or the transient gladness of colour, but the whole sphere of feeling, the perfect cycle of thought. The painter is so far limited that it is only through the mask of the body that he can show us the mystery of the soul; only through conventional images that he can handle ideas; only through its physical equivalents that he can deal with psychology. And how inadequately does he do it then, asking us to accept the torn turban of the Moor for the noble rage of Othello, or a dotard in a storm for the wild madness of Lear! Yet it seems as if nothing could stop him. Most of our elderly English painters spend their wicked and wasted lives in poaching upon the domain of the poets, marring their motives by clumsy treatment, and striving to render, by visible form or colour, the marvel of what is invisible, the splendour of what is not seen. Their pictures are, as a natural consequence, insufferably tedious. They have degraded the visible arts into the obvious arts, and the one thing not worth looking at is the obvious. I do not say that poet and painter may not treat of the same subject. They have always done so, and will always do so. But while the poet can be pictorial or not, as he chooses, the painter must be pictorial always. For a painter is limited, not to what he sees in nature, but to what upon canvas may be seen.

And so, my dear Ernest, pictures of this kind will not really fascinate the critic. He will turn from them to such works as make him brood and dream and fancy, to works that possess the subtle quality of suggestion, and seem to tell one that even from them there is an escape into a wider world. It is sometimes said that the tragedy of an artist's life is that he cannot realize his ideal. But the true tragedy that dogs the steps of most artists is that they realize their ideal too absolutely. For, when the ideal is realized, it is robbed of its wonder and its mystery, and becomes simply a new starting-point for an ideal that is other than itself. This is the reason why music is the perfect type of art. Music can never reveal its ultimate secret. This, also, is the explanation of the value of limitations in art. The sculptor gladly surrenders imitative colour, and the painter the actual dimensions of form, because by such renunciations they are able to avoid too definite a presentation of the Real, which would be mere imitation, and too definite a realization of the Ideal, which would be too purely intellectual. It is through its very incompleteness that Art becomes complete in beauty, and so addresses itself, not to the faculty of recognition nor to the faculty of reason, but to the aesthetic sense alone, which, while accepting both reason and recognition as stages of apprehension, subordinates them both to a pure synthetic impression of the work of art as a whole, and, taking whatever alien emotional elements the work may possess, uses their very complexity as a means by which a richer unity may be added to the ultimate impression itself. You see, then, how it is that the aesthetic critic rejects those obvious modes of art that have but one message to deliver, and having delivered it become dumb and sterile, and seeks rather for such modes as suggest reverie and mood, and by their imaginative beauty make all interpretations true and no interpretation final. Some resemblance, no doubt, the creative work of the critic will have to the work that has stirred him to creation, but it will be such resemblance as exists, not between Nature and the mirror that the painter of landscape or figure may be supposed to hold up to her, but between Nature and the work of the decorative artist. Just as on the flowerless carpets of Persia, tulip and rose blossom indeed and are lovely to look on, though they are not reproduced in visible shape or line; just as the pearl and purple of the sea-shell is echoed in the church of St. Mark at Venice; just as the vaulted ceiling of the wondrous chapel of Ravenna is made gorgeous by the gold and green and sapphire of the peacock's tail, though the birds of Juno[1] fly not across it; so the critic reproduces the work that he criticises in a mode that is never imitative, and part of whose charm may really consist in the rejection of resemblance, and shows us in this way not merely the meaning but also the mystery of Beauty, and, by transforming each art into literature, solves once for all the problem of Art's unity.

But I see it is time for supper. After we have discussed some Chambertin and a few ortolans,[2] we will pass on to the question of the critic considered in the light of the interpreter.

*Ernest.* Ah! you admit, then, that the critic may occasionally be allowed to see the object as in itself it really is.

*Gilbert.* I am not quite sure. Perhaps I may admit it after supper. There is a subtle influence in supper.


## 'The Critic as Artist'

*With some remarks upon the importance of discussing everything.*
*A Dialogue. Part II.*
*Persons: the same.*
*Scene: the same.*

*Ernest.* The ortolans were delightful, and the Chambertin perfect. And now let us return to the point at issue.

1 i.e. peacocks.
2 Chambertin is a superior Burgundy, and ortolans are delicately flavoured buntings.

*Gilbert.* Ah! don't let us do that. Conversation should touch everything, but should concentrate itself on nothing. Let us talk about *Moral Indignation, its Cause and Cure*, a subject on which I think of writing: or about *The Survival of Thersites*, as shown by the English comic papers; or about any topic that may turn up.

*Ernest.* No: I want to discuss the critic and criticism. You have told me that the highest criticism deals with art, not as expressive, but as impressive purely, and is consequently both creative and independent, is in fact an art by itself, occupying the same relation to creative work that creative work does to the visible world of form and colour, or the unseen world of passion and of thought. Well, now tell me, will not the critic be sometimes a real interpreter?

*Gilbert.* Yes; the critic will be an interpreter, if he chooses. He can pass from his synthetic impression of the work of art as a whole, to an analysis or exposition of the work itself, and in this lower sphere, as I hold it to be, there are many delightful things to be said and done. Yet his object will not always be to explain the work of art. He may seek rather to deepen its mystery, to raise round it, and round its maker, that mist of wonder which is dear to both gods and worshippers alike. Ordinary people are 'terribly at ease in Zion.'[1] They propose to walk arm in arm with the poets, and have a glib ignorant way of saying 'Why should we read what is written about Shakespeare and Milton? We can read the plays and the poems. That is enough.' But an appreciation of Milton is, as the late Rector of Lincoln[2] remarked once, the reward of consummate scholarship. And he who desires to understand Shakespeare truly must understand the relations in which Shakespeare stood to the Renaissance and the Reformation, to the age of Elizabeth and the age of James; he must be familiar with the history of the struggle for supremacy between the old classical forms and the new spirit of romance, between the school of Sidney, and Daniel,[3] and Jonson, and the school of Marlowe and Marlowe's greater son; he must know the materials that were at Shakespeare's disposal, and the method in which he used them, and the conditions of theatric presentation in the sixteenth and seventeenth century, their limita-

---

1 'Socrates is *terribly at ease in Zion*'; a saying attributed by Matthew Arnold to Carlyle. See *Culture and Anarchy*, chapter IV.
2 Mark Pattison (1813–84), an advocate of greater scholarship in English universities.
3 i.e. Samuel Daniel (1562–1619), the English poet.

tions and their opportunities for freedom, and the literary criticism of Shakespeare's day, its aims and modes and canons; he must study the English language in its progress, and blank or rhymed verse in its various developments; he must study the Greek drama, and the connection between the art of the creator of the Agamemnon and the art of the creator of Macbeth; in a word, he must be able to bind Elizabethan London to the Athens of Pericles, and to learn Shakespeare's true position in the history of European drama and the drama of the world. The critic will certainly be an interpreter, but he will not treat Art as a riddling Sphinx, whose shallow secret may be guessed and revealed by one whose feet are wounded and who knows not his name.[1] Rather, he will look upon Art as a goddess whose mystery it is his province to intensify, and whose majesty his privilege to make more marvellous in the eyes of men.

And here, Ernest, this strange thing happens. The critic will indeed be an interpreter, but he will not be an interpreter in the sense of one who simply repeats in another form a message that has been put into his lips to say. For, just as it is only by contact with the art of foreign nations that the art of a country gains that individual and separate life that we call nationality, so, by curious inversion, it is only by intensifying his own personality that the critic can interpret the personality and work of others, and the more strongly this personality enters into the interpretation the more real the interpretation becomes, the more satisfying, the more convincing, and the more true.

*Ernest.* I would have said that personality would have been a disturbing element.

*Gilbert.* No; it is an element of revelation. If you wish to understand others you must intensify your own individualism.

*Ernest.* What, then, is the result?

*Gilbert.* I will tell you, and perhaps I can tell you best by definite example. It seems to me that, while the literary critic stands of course first, as having the wider range, and larger vision, and nobler material, each of the arts has a critic, as it were, assigned to it. The actor is a critic of the drama. He shows the poet's work under new conditions, and by a method special to himself. He takes the written word, and action, gesture, and voice become the media of

---

1 i.e. Oedipus.

revelation. The singer, or the player on lute and viol, is the critic of music. The etcher of a picture robs the painting of its fair colours, but shows us by the use of a new material its true colour-quality, its tones and values, and the relations of its masses, and so is, in his way, a critic of it, for the critic is he who exhibits to us a work of art in a form different from that of the work itself, and the employment of a new material is a critical as well as a creative element. Sculpture, too, has its critic, who may be either the carver of a gem, as he was in Greek days, or some painter like Mantegna, who sought to reproduce on canvas the beauty of plastic line and the symphonic dignity of processional bas-relief. And in the case of all these creative critics of art it is evident that personality is an absolute essential for any real interpretation. When Rubinstein plays to us the *Sonata Appassionata* of Beethoven, he gives us not merely Beethoven, but also himself, and so gives us Beethoven absolutely – Beethoven reinterpreted through a rich artistic nature, and made vivid and wonderful to us by a new and intense personality. When a great actor plays Shakespeare we have the same experience. His own individuality becomes a vital part of the interpretation. People sometimes say that actors give us their own Hamlets, and not Shakespeare's; and this fallacy – for it is a fallacy – is, I regret to say, repeated by that charming and graceful writer who has lately deserted the turmoil of literature for the peace of the House of Commons, I mean the author of *Obiter Dicta*.[1] In point of fact, there is no such thing as Shakespeare's Hamlet. If Hamlet has something of the definiteness of a work of art, he has also all the obscurity that belongs to life. There are as many Hamlets as there are melancholies.

*Ernest.* As many Hamlets as there are melancholies?

*Gilbert.* Yes; and as art springs from personality, so it is only to personality that it can be revealed, and from the meeting of the two comes right interpretative criticism.

*Ernest.* The critic, then, considered as the interpreter, will give no less than he receives, and lend as much as he borrows?

*Gilbert.* He will be always showing us the work of art in some new relation to our age. He will always be reminding us that great works of art are living things – are, in fact, the only things that live. So much, indeed, will he feel this, that I am certain that, as civilization progresses and we become more highly organized, the elect spirits

---

1 Augustine Birrell. The very popular *Obiter Dicta* was published in 1884.

of each age, the critical and cultured spirits, will grow less and less interested in actual life, and *will seek to gain their impressions almost entirely from what Art has touched.* For Life is terribly deficient in form. Its catastrophes happen in the wrong way and to the wrong people. There is a grotesque horror about its comedies, and its tragedies seem to culminate in farce. One is always wounded when one approaches it. Things last either too long, or not long enough.

*Ernest.* Poor life! Poor human life! Are you not even touched by the tears that the Roman poet tells us are part of its essence?[1]

*Gilbert.* Too quickly touched by them, I fear. For when one looks back upon the life that was so vivid in its emotional intensity, and filled with such fervent moments of ecstasy or of joy, it all seems to be a dream and an illusion. What are the unreal things, but the passions that once burned one like fire? What are the incredible things, but the things that one has faithfully believed? What are the improbable things? The things that one has done oneself. No, Ernest; life cheats us with shadows, like a puppet-master. We ask it for pleasure. It gives it to us, with bitterness and disappointment in its train. We come across some noble grief that we think will lend the purple dignity of tragedy to our days, but it passes away from us, and things less noble take its place, and on some grey windy dawn, or odorous eve of silence and of silver, we find ourselves looking with callous wonder, or dull heart of stone, at the trees of gold-flecked hair that we had once so wildly worshipped and so madly kissed.

*Ernest.* Life then is a failure?

*Gilbert.* From the artistic point of view, certainly. And the chief thing that makes life a failure from this artistic point of view is the thing that lends to life its sordid security, the fact that one can never repeat exactly the same emotion. How different it is in the world of Art! On a shelf of the bookcase behind you stands the *Divine Comedy,* and I know that, if I open it at a certain place, I shall be filled with a fierce hatred of some one who has never wronged me, or stirred by a great love for some one whom I shall never see. There is no mood or passion that Art cannot give us, and those of us who have discovered her secret can settle beforehand what our experiences are going to be [ ... ].

---

1 Wilde is referring to *Aeneid* I, 462: 'sunt lacrimae rerum et mentem mortalia tangunt', and wrongly construing the line to be indicative of the pathos of the *Aeneid.*

Life! Life! Don't let us go to life for our fulfilment or our experience. It is a thing narrowed by circumstances, incoherent in its utterance, and without that fine correspondence of form and spirit which is the only thing that can satisfy the artistic and critical temperament. It makes us pay too high a price for its wares, and we purchase the meanest of its secrets at a cost that is monstrous and infinite.

*Ernest.* Must we go, then, to Art for everything?

*Gilbert.* For everything. Because Art does not hurt us. The tears that we shed at a play are a type of the exquisite sterile emotions that it is the function of Art to awaken. We weep, but we are not wounded. We grieve, but our grief is not bitter. In the actual life of man, sorrow, as Spinoza[1] says somewhere, is a passage to a lesser perfection. But the sorrow with which Art fills us both purifies and initiates, if I may quote once more from the great art-critic of the Greeks. It is through Art, and through Art only, that we can realize our perfection; through Art, and through Art only, that we can shield ourselves from the sordid perils of actual existence. This results not merely from the fact that nothing that one can imagine is worth doing, and that one can imagine everything, but from the subtle law that emotional forces, like the forces of the physical sphere, are limited in extent and energy. One can feel so much, and no more. And how can it matter with what pleasure life tries to tempt one, or with what pain it seeks to maim and mar one's soul, if in the spectacle of the lives of those who have never existed one has found the true secret of joy, and wept away one's tears over their deaths who, like Cordelia and the daughter of Brabantio,[2] can never die?

*Ernest.* Stop a moment. It seems to me that in everything that you have said there is something radically immoral.

*Gilbert.* All art is immoral.

*Ernest.* All art?

*Gilbert.* Yes. For emotion for the sake of emotion is the aim of art, and emotion for the sake of action is the aim of life, and of that practical organization of life that we call society. Society, which is the beginning and basis of morals, exists simply for the concentration of human energy, and in order to ensure its own continuance and

---

1 Benedict Spinoza in the *Ethics*.
2 i.e. Cordelia in *King Lear* and Desdemona in *Othello*.

healthy stability it demands, and no doubt rightly demands, of each of its citizens that he should contribute some form of productive labour to the common weal, and toil and travail that the day's work may be done. Society often forgives the criminal; it never forgives the dreamer. The beautiful sterile emotions that art excites in us, are hateful in its eyes, and so completely are people dominated by the tyranny of this dreadful social ideal that they are always coming shamelessly up to one at Private Views and other places that are open to the general public, and saying in a loud stentorian voice, 'What are you doing?' whereas 'What are you thinking?' is the only question that any single civilized being should ever be allowed to whisper to another. They mean well, no doubt, these honest beaming folk. Perhaps that is the reason why they are so excessively tedious. But some one should teach them that while, in the opinion of society, Contemplation is the gravest sin of which any citizen can be guilty, in the opinion of the highest culture it is the proper occupation of man.

*Ernest.* Contemplation?

*Gilbert.* Contemplation. I said to you some time ago that it was far more difficult to talk about a thing than to do it. Let me say to you now that to do nothing at all is the most difficult thing in the world, the most difficult and the most intellectual. To Plato, with his passion for wisdom, this was the noblest form of energy. To Aristotle, with his passion for knowledge, this was the noblest form of energy also. It was to this that the passion for holiness led the saint and the mystic of medieval days.

*Ernest.* We exist, then, to do nothing?

*Gilbert.* It is to do nothing that the elect exist. Action is limited and relative. Unlimited and absolute is the vision of him who sits at ease and watches, who walks in loneliness and dreams. But we who are born at the close of this wonderful age, are at once too cultured and too critical, too intellectually subtle and too curious of exquisite pleasures, to accept any speculations about life in exchange for life itself. To us the *citta divina*[1] is colourless, and the *fruitio Dei*[2] without meaning. Metaphysics do not satisfy our temperaments, and religious ecstasy is out of date. The world through which the Academic philosopher[3] becomes 'the spectator of all time and of all existence' is not really an ideal world, but

---

1 Divine City.    2 Enjoyment of God.    3 i.e. Plato.

simply a world of abstract ideas. When we enter it, we starve amidst the chill mathematics of thought. The courts of the city of God are not open to us now. Its gates are guarded by Ignorance, and to pass them we have to surrender all that in our nature is most divine. It is enough that our fathers believed. They have exhausted the faith-faculty of the species. Their legacy to us is the scepticism of which they were afraid. Had they put it into words, it might not live within us as thought. No, Ernest, no. We cannot go back to the saint. There is far more to be learned from the sinner. We cannot go back to the philosopher, and the mystic leads us astray. Who, as Mr. Pater suggests somewhere, would exchange the curve of a single rose-leaf for that formless intangible Being which Plato rates so high? What to us is the Illumination of Philo, the Abyss of Eckhart, the Vision of Böhme, the monstrous Heaven itself that was revealed to Swedenborg's blinded eyes?[1] Such things are less than the yellow trumpet of one daffodil of the field, far less than the meanest of the visible arts; for, just as Nature is matter struggling into mind, so Art is mind expressing itself under the conditions of matter, and thus, even in the lowliest of her manifestations, she speaks to both sense and soul alike. To the aesthetic temperament the vague is always repellent. The Greeks were a nation of artists, because they were spared the sense of the infinite. Like Aristotle, like Goethe after he had read Kant, we desire the concrete, and nothing but the concrete can satisfy us.

*Ernest.* What then do you propose?

*Gilbert.* It seems to me that with the development of the critical spirit we shall be able to realize, not merely our own lives, but the collective life of the race, and so to make ourselves absolutely modern, in the true meaning of the word modernity. For he to whom the present is the only thing that is present, knows nothing of the age in which he lives. To realize the nineteenth century, one must realize every century that has preceded it and that has contributed to its making. To know anything about oneself, one must know all about others. There must be no mood with which one cannot sympathize, no dead mode of life that one cannot make alive. Is this impossible? I think not. By revealing to us the absolute

---

1 Philo (b. *c.* 10–20 BC), the Jewish philosopher; Johannes Eckhart (1260–1327), the German speculative philosopher and mystic; Jakob Böhme (1575–1624), the German philosopher; Immanuel Swedenborg (1688–1772), the Swedish philosopher and mystic.

mechanism of all action, and so freeing us from the self-imposed and trammelling burden of moral responsibility, the scientific principle of Heredity has become, as it were, the warrant for the contemplative life. It has shown us that we are never less free than when we try to act. It has hemmed us round with the nets of the hunter, and written upon the wall the prophecy of our doom. We may not watch it, for it is within us. We may not see it, save in a mirror that mirrors the soul. It is Nemesis without her mask. It is the last of the Fates, and the most terrible. It is the only one of the Gods whose real name we know.

And yet, while in the sphere of practical and external life it has robbed energy of its freedom and activity of its choice, in the subjective sphere, where the soul is at work, it comes to us, this terrible shadow, with many gifts in its hands, gifts of strange temperaments and subtle susceptibilities, gifts of wild ardours and chill moods of indifference, complex multiform gifts of thoughts that are at variance with each other, and passions that war against themselves. And so, it is not our own life that we live, but the lives of the dead, and the soul that dwells within us is no single spiritual entity, making us personal and individual, created for our service, and entering into us for our joy. It is something that has dwelt in fearful places, and in ancient sepulchres has made its abode. It is sick with many maladies, and has memories of curious sins. It is wiser than we are, and its wisdom is bitter. It fills us with impossible desires, and makes us follow what we know we cannot gain. One thing, however, Ernest, it can do for us. It can lead us away from surroundings whose beauty is dimmed to us by the mist of familiarity, or whose ignoble ugliness and sordid claims are marring the perfection of our development. It can help us to leave the age in which we were born, and to pass into other ages, and find ourselves not exiled from their air. It can teach us how to escape from our experience, and to realize the experiences of those who are greater than we are. The pain of Leopardi[1] crying out against life becomes our pain. Theocritus blows on his pipe, and we laugh with the lips of nymph and shepherd. In the wolfskin of Pierre Vidal[2] we flee before the hounds, and in the armour of Lancelot we ride from the

---

1 Giacomo Leopardi (1798–1837), the Italian poet whose physical suffering was life-long.
2 Pierre Vidal, the twelfth-century Provençal poet, dressed in a wolf-skin because his lover's name was Loba or wolf.

bower of the Queen. We have whispered the secret of our love beneath the cowl of Abelard,[1] and in the stained raiment of Villon[2] have put our shame into song. We can see the dawn through Shelley's eyes, and when we wander with Endymion the Moon grows amorous of our youth. Ours is the anguish of Atys,[3] and ours the weak rage and noble sorrows of the Dane. Do you think that it is the imagination that enables us to live these countless lives? Yes: it is the imagination; and the imagination is the result of heredity. It is simply concentrated race-experience.

*Ernest.* But where in this is the function of the critical spirit?

*Gilbert.* The culture that this transmission of racial experiences makes possible can be made perfect by the critical spirit alone, and indeed may be said to be one with it. For who is the true critic but he who bears within himself the dreams, and ideas, and feelings of myriad generations, and to whom no form of thought is alien, no emotional impulse obscure? And who the true man of culture, if not he who by fine scholarship and fastidious rejection has made instinct self-conscious and intelligent, and can separate the work that has distinction from the work that has it not, and so by contact and comparison makes himself master of the secrets of style and school, and understands their meanings, and listens to their voices, and develops that spirit of disinterested curiosity which is the real root, as it is the real flower, of the intellectual life, and thus attains to intellectual clarity, and, having learned 'the best that is known and thought in the world,'[4] lives – it is not fanciful to say so – with those who are the Immortals.

Yes, Ernest: the contemplative life, the life that has for its aim not *doing* but *being*, and not *being* merely, but *becoming* – that is what the critical spirit can give us. The gods live thus: either brooding over their own perfection, as Aristotle tells us, or, as Epicurus fancied, watching with the calm eyes of the spectator the tragi-comedy of the world that they have made. We, too, might live like them, and set ourselves to witness with appropriate emotions the varied scenes that man and nature afford. We might make ourselves

1 Pierre Abelard (1079–1142), medieval French theologian, mainly remembered (from their famous correspondence) as the secret lover of Héloïse.
2 François Villon (1431–63), the French poet who was noted for his riotous life.
3 Atys (Attis), a Phrygian deity who, driven mad by the jealousy of his lover Agdistis, castrated himself.
4 Arnold's advice to the critic in 'The Function of Criticism at the Present Time'.

spiritual by detaching ourselves from action, and become perfect by the rejection of energy. It has often seemed to me that Browning felt something of this. Shakespeare hurls Hamlet into active life, and makes him realize his mission by effort. Browning might have given us a Hamlet who would have realized his mission by thought. Incident and event were to him unreal or unmeaning. He made the soul the protagonist of life's tragedy, and looked on action as the one undramatic element of a play. To us, at any rate, the *ΒΙΟΣ ΘΕΩΡΗΤΙΚΟΣ*[1] is the true ideal. From the high tower of Thought we can look out at the world. Calm, and self-centred, and complete, the aesthetic critic contemplates life, and no arrow drawn at a venture can pierce between the joints of his harness. He at least is safe. He has discovered how to live.

Is such a mode of life immoral? Yes: all the arts are immoral, except those baser forms of sensual or didactic art that seek to excite to action of evil or of good. For action of every kind belongs to the sphere of ethics. The aim of art is simply to create a mood. Is such a mode of life unpractical? Ah! it is not so easy to be unpractical as the ignorant Philistine[2] imagines. It were well for England if it were so. There is no country in the world so much in need of unpractical people as this country of ours. With us, Thought is degraded by its constant association with practice [ . . . ].

No, Ernest, self-culture is the true ideal of man. Goethe saw it, and the immediate debt that we owe to Goethe is greater than the debt we owe to any man since Greek days. The Greeks saw it, and have left us, as their legacy to modern thought, the conception of the contemplative life as well as the critical method by which alone can that life be truly realized. It was the one thing that made the Renaissance great, and gave us Humanism. It is the one thing that could make our own age great also; for the real weakness of England lies, not in incomplete armaments or unfortified coasts, not in the poverty that creeps through sunless lanes, or the drunkenness that brawls in loathsome courts, but simply in the fact that her ideals are emotional and not intellectual.

I do not deny that the intellectual ideal is difficult of attainment, still less that it is, and perhaps will be for years to come, unpopular with the crowd. It is so easy for people to have sympathy with suffering. It is so difficult for them to have sympathy with thought.

---

1 The contemplative life.     2 See note to p. 7.

Indeed, so little do ordinary people understand what thought really is, that they seem to imagine that, when they have said that a theory is dangerous, they have pronounced its condemnation, whereas it is only such theories that have any true intellectual value. An idea that is not dangerous is unworthy of being called an idea at all.

*Ernest.* Gilbert, you bewilder me. You have told me that all art is, in its essence, immoral. Are you going to tell me now that all thought is, in its essence, dangerous?

*Gilbert.* Yes, in the practical sphere it is so. The security of society lies in custom and unconscious instinct, and the basis of the stability of society, as a healthy organism, is the complete absence of any intelligence amongst its members. The great majority of people being fully aware of this, rank themselves naturally on the side of that splendid system that elevates them to the dignity of machines, and rage so wildly against the intrusion of the intellectual faculty into any question that concerns life, that one is tempted to define man as a rational animal who always loses his temper when he is called upon to act in accordance with the dictates of reason. But let us turn from the practical sphere, and say no more about the wicked philanthropists, who, indeed, may well be left to the mercy of the almond-eyed sage of the Yellow River, Chuang Tsŭ the wise, who has proved that such well-meaning and offensive busy-bodies have destroyed the simple and spontaneous virtue that there is in man. They are a wearisome topic, and I am anxious to get back to the sphere in which criticism is free.

*Ernest.* The sphere of the intellect?

*Gilbert.* Yes. You remember that I spoke of the critic as being in his own way as creative as the artist, whose work, indeed, may be merely of value in so far as it gives to the critic a suggestion for some new mood of thought and feeling which he can realize with equal, or perhaps greater, distinction of form, and, through the use of a fresh medium of expression, make differently beautiful and more perfect. Well, you seemed to me to be a little sceptical about the theory. But perhaps I wronged you?

*Ernest.* I am not really sceptical about it, but I must admit that I feel very strongly that such work as you describe the critic producing – and creative such work must undoubtedly be admitted to be – is, of necessity, purely subjective, whereas the greatest work is objective always, objective and impersonal.

*Gilbert.* The difference between objective and subjective work is one of external form merely. It is accidental, not essential. All artistic creation is absolutely subjective. The very landscape that Corot looked at was, as he said himself, but a mood of his own mind; and those great figures of Greek or English drama that seem to us to possess an actual existence of their own, apart from the poets who shaped and fashioned them, are, in their ultimate analysis, simply the poets themselves, not as they thought they were, but as they thought they were not; and by such thinking came in strange manner, though but for a moment, really so to be. For out of ourselves we can never pass, nor can there be in creation what in the creator was not. Nay, I would say that the more objective a creation appears to be, the more subjective it really is. Shakespeare might have met Rosencrantz and Guildenstern in the white streets of London, or seen the serving-men of rival houses bite their thumbs at each other in the open square; but Hamlet came out of his soul, and Romeo out of his passion. They were elements of his nature to which he gave visible form, impulses that stirred so strongly within him that he had, as it were perforce, to suffer them to realize their energy, not on the lower plane of actual life, where they would have been trammelled and constrained and so made imperfect, but on that imaginative plane of art where Love can indeed find in Death its rich fulfilment, where one can stab the eavesdropper behind the arras, and wrestle in a new-made grave, and make a guilty king drink his own hurt, and see one's father's spirit, beneath the glimpses of the moon, stalking in complete steel from misty wall to wall. Action being limited would have left Shakespeare unsatisfied and unexpressed; and, just as it is because he did nothing that he has been able to achieve everything, so it is because he never speaks to us of himself in his plays that his plays reveal him to us absolutely, and show us his true nature and temperament far more completely than do those strange and exquisite sonnets, even, in which he bares to crystal eyes the secret closet of his heart. Yes, the objective form is the most subjective in matter. Man is least himself when he talks in his own person. Give him a mask, and he will tell you the truth.

*Ernest.* The critic, then, being limited to the subjective form, will necessarily be less able to fully express himself than the artist, who has always at his disposal the forms that are impersonal and objective.

*Gilbert.* Not necessarily, and certainly not at all if he recognizes that each mode of criticism is, in its highest development, simply a mood, and that we are never more true to ourselves than when we are inconsistent. The aesthetic critic, constant only to the principle of beauty in all things, will ever be looking for fresh impressions, winning from the various schools the secret of their charm, bowing, it may be, before foreign altars, or smiling, if it be his fancy, at strange new gods. What other people call one's past has, no doubt, everything to do with them, but has absolutely nothing to do with oneself. The man who regards his past is a man who deserves to have no future to look forward to. When one has found expression for a mood, one has done with it. You laugh; but believe me it is so. Yesterday it was Realism that charmed one. One gained from it that *nouveau frisson*[1] which it was its aim to produce. One analysed it, explained it, and wearied of it. At sunset came the *Luministe*[2] in painting, and the *Symboliste* in poetry, and the spirit of mediaevalism, that spirit which belongs not to time but to temperament, woke suddenly in wounded Russia, and stirred us for a moment by the terrible fascination of pain. To-day the cry is for Romance, and already the leaves are tremulous in the valley, and on the purple hill-tops walks Beauty with slim gilded feet. The old modes of creation linger, of course. The artists reproduce either themselves or each other, with wearisome iteration. But Criticism is always moving on, and the critic is always developing.

Nor, again, is the critic really limited to the subjective form of expression. The method of the drama is his, as well as the method of the epos. He may use dialogue, as he did who set Milton talking to Marvel on the nature of comedy and tragedy, and made Sidney and Lord Brooke discourse on letters beneath the Penshurst oaks;[3] or adopt narration, as Mr. Pater is fond of doing, each of whose Imaginary Portraits – is not that the title of the book? – presents to us, under the fanciful guise of fiction, some fine and exquisite piece of criticism, one on the painter Watteau, another on the philosophy of Spinoza, a third on the Pagan elements of the early Renaissance, and the last, and in some respects the most suggestive, on the source of that Aufklärung, that enlightening which dawned on Germany in the last century, and to which our own culture owes so great a

1 New thrill.
2 Painting concerned with rendering the effects of light.
3 The reference is to Walter Savage Landor's two Imaginary Conversations, 'Lord Brooke and Sir Philip Sidney' and 'Milton and Andrew Marvell'.

debt. Dialogue, certainly, that wonderful literary form which, from Plato to Lucian,[1] and from Lucian to Giordano Bruno,[2] and from Bruno to that grand old Pagan[3] in whom Carlyle took such delight, the creative critics of the world have always employed, can never lose for the thinker its attraction as a mode of expression. By its means he can both reveal and conceal himself, and give form to every fancy, and reality to every mood. By its means he can exhibit the object from each point of view, and show it to us in the round, as a sculptor shows us things, gaining in this manner all the richness and reality of effect that comes from those side issues that are suddenly suggested by the central idea in its progress, and really illumine the idea more completely, or from those felicitous after-thoughts that give a fuller completeness to the central scheme, and yet convey something of the delicate charm of chance.

*Ernest.* By its means, too, he can invent an imaginary antagonist, and convert him when he chooses by some absurdly sophistical argument.

*Gilbert.* Ah! it is so easy to convert others. It is so difficult to convert oneself. To arrive at what one really believes, one must speak through lips different from one's own. To know the truth one must imagine myriads of falsehoods. For what is Truth? In matters of religion, it is simply the opinion that has survived. In matters of science, it is the ultimate sensation. In matters of art, it is one's last mood. And you see now, Ernest, that the critic has at his disposal as many objective forms of expression as the artist has. Ruskin put his criticism into imaginative prose, and is superb in his changes and contradictions; and Browning put his into blank verse, and made painter and poet yield us their secret; and M. Renan uses dialogue, and Mr. Pater fiction, and Rossetti translated into sonnet-music the colour of Giorgione and the design of Ingres, and his own design and colour also, feeling, with the instinct of one who had many modes of utterance, that the ultimate art is literature, and the finest and fullest medium that of words.

*Ernest.* Well, now that you have settled that the critic has at his disposal all objective forms, I wish you would tell me what are the qualities that should characterize the true critic.

*Gilbert.* What would you say they were?

1 Lucian, see note to p. 57.
2 Giordano Bruno (1548–1600), the Italian Renaissance philosopher.
3 This is perhaps a reference to Goethe.

*Ernest.* Well, I should say that a critic should above all things be fair.

*Gilbert.* Ah! not fair. A critic cannot be fair in the ordinary sense of the word. It is only about things that do not interest one that one can give a really unbiassed opinion, which is no doubt the reason why an unbiassed opinion is always absolutely valueless. The man who sees both sides of a question, is a man who sees absolutely nothing at all. Art is a passion, and, in matters of art, Thought is inevitably coloured by emotion, and so is fluid rather than fixed, and, depending upon fine moods and exquisite moments, cannot be narrowed into the rigidity of a scientific formula or a theological dogma. It is to the soul that Art speaks, and the soul may be made the prisoner of the mind as well as of the body. One should, of course, have no prejudices; but, as a great Frenchman remarked a hundred years ago, it is one's business in such matters to have preferences, and when one has preferences one ceases to be fair. It is only an auctioneer who can equally and impartially admire all schools of Art. No: fairness is not one of the qualities of the true critic. It is not even a condition of criticism. Each form of Art with which we come in contact dominates us for the moment to the exclusion of every other form. We must surrender ourselves absolutely to the work in question, whatever it may be, if we wish to gain its secret. For the time, we must think of nothing else, can think of nothing else, indeed.

*Ernest.* The true critic will be rational, at any rate, will he not?

*Gilbert.* Rational? There are two ways of disliking art, Ernest. One is to dislike it. The other, to like it rationally. For Art, as Plato saw, and not without regret, creates in listener and spectator a form of divine madness. It does not spring from inspiration, but it makes others inspired. Reason is not the faculty to which it appeals. If one loves Art at all, one must love it beyond all other things in the world, and against such love, the reason, if one listened to it, would cry out. There is nothing sane about the worship of beauty. It is too splendid to be sane. Those of whose lives it forms the dominant note will always seem to the world to be pure visionaries.

*Ernest.* Well, at least, the critic will be sincere.

*Gilbert.* A little sincerity is a dangerous thing, and a great deal of it is absolutely fatal. The true critic will, indeed, always be sincere in his devotion to the principle of beauty, but he will seek for beauty in every age and in each school, and will never suffer himself to be limited to any settled custom of thought, or stereotyped mode of looking at things. He will realize himself in many forms, and by a thousand different ways, and will ever be curious of new sensations and fresh points of view. Through constant change, and through constant change alone, he will find his true unity. He will not consent to be the slave of his own opinions. For what is mind but motion in the intellectual sphere? The essence of thought, as the essence of life, is growth. You must not be frightened by words, Ernest. What people call insincerity is simply a method by which we can multiply our personalities.

*Ernest.* I am afraid I have not been fortunate in my suggestions.

*Gilbert.* Of the three qualifications you mentioned, two, sincerity and fairness, were, if not actually moral, at least on the border-land of morals, and the first condition of criticism is that the critic should be able to recognize that the sphere of Art and the sphere of Ethics are absolutely distinct and separate. When they are confused, Chaos has come again. They are too often confused in England now, and though our modern Puritans cannot destroy a beautiful thing, yet, by means of their extraordinary prurience, they can almost taint beauty for a moment. It is chiefly, I regret to say, through journalism that such people find expression. I regret it because there is much to be said in favour of modern journalism. By giving us the opinions of the uneducated, it keeps us in touch with the ignorance of the community. By carefully chronicling the current events of contemporary life, it shows us of what very little importance such events really are. By invariably discussing the unnecessary, it makes us understand what things are requisite for culture, and what are not. But it should not allow poor Tartuffe to write articles upon modern art. When it does this it stultifies itself. And yet Tartuffe's articles, and Chadband's[1] notes do this good, at least. They serve to show how extremely limited is the area over which ethics, and ethical considerations, can claim to exercise influence. Science is out of the reach of morals, for her eyes are fixed upon eternal truths. Art is out of the reach of morals, for her eyes are fixed upon things beautiful and immortal and ever-changing. To morals belong the lower and less intellectual spheres. However, let these mouthing Puritans pass; they have their comic side. Who can help laughing

---

1 From Molière's *Tartuffe*; Chadband is a character in Dickens's *Bleak House.*
Both are types of the hypocrite.

when an ordinary journalist seriously proposes to limit the subject-matter at the disposal of the artist? Some limitation might well, and will soon, I hope, be placed upon some of our newspapers and newspaper writers. For they give us the bald, sordid, disgusting facts of life. They chronicle, with degrading avidity, the sins of the second-rate, and with the conscientiousness of the illiterate give us accurate and prosaic details of the doings of people of absolutely no interest whatsoever. But the artist, who accepts the facts of life, and yet transforms them into shapes of beauty, and makes them vehicles of pity or of awe, and shows their colour-element, and their wonder, and their true ethical import also, and builds out of them a world more real than reality itself, and of loftier and more noble import – who shall set limits to him? Not the apostles of that new Journalism which is but the old vulgarity 'writ large.' Not the apostles of that new Puritanism, which is but the whine of the hypocrite, and is both writ and spoken badly. The mere suggestion is ridiculous. Let us leave these wicked people, and proceed to the discussion of the artistic qualifications necessary for the true critic.

*Ernest.* And what are they? Tell me yourself.

*Gilbert.* Temperament is the primary requisite for the critic – a temperament exquisitely susceptible to beauty, and to the various impressions that beauty gives us. Under what conditions, and by what means, this temperament is engendered in race or individual, we will not discuss at present. It is sufficient to note that it exists, and that there is in us a beauty-sense, separate from the other senses and above them, separate from the reason and of nobler import, separate from the soul and of equal value – a sense that leads some to create, and others, the finer spirits as I think, to contemplate merely. But to be purified and made perfect, this sense requires some form of exquisite environment [ . . . ].

We have got rid of what was bad. We have now to make what is beautiful. And though the mission of the aesthetic movement is to lure people to contemplate, not to lead them to create, yet, as the creative instinct is strong in the Celt, and it is the Celt who leads in art, there is no reason why in future years this strange Renaissance should not become almost as mighty in its way as was that new birth of Art that woke many centuries ago in the cities of Italy.

Certainly, for the cultivation of temperament, we must turn to the decorative arts: to the arts that touch us, not to the arts that teach us. Modern pictures are, no doubt, delightful to look at. At least, some of them are. But they are quite impossible to live with; they are too clever, too assertive, too intellectual. Their meaning is too obvious, and their method too clearly defined [ . . . ].

But even the Impressionists, earnest and industrious as they are, will not do. I like them. Their white keynote, with its variations in lilac, was an era in colour. Though the moment does not make the man, the moment certainly makes the Impressionist, and for the moment in art, and the 'moment's monument' as Rossetti phrased it, what may not be said? They are suggestive also. If they have not opened the eyes of the blind, they have at least given great encouragement to the short-sighted, and while their leaders may have all the inexperience of old age, their young men are far too wise to be ever sensible. Yet they will insist on treating painting as if it were a mode of autobiography invented for the use of the illiterate, and are always prating to us on their coarse gritty canvases of their unnecessary selves and their unnecessary opinions, and spoiling by a vulgar over-emphasis that fine contempt of nature which is the best and only modest thing about them. One tires, at the end, of the work of individuals whose individuality is always noisy, and generally uninteresting. There is far more to be said in favour of that newer school at Paris, the *Archaicistes*, as they call themselves, who, refusing to leave the artist entirely at the mercy of the weather, do not find the ideal of art in mere atmospheric effect, but seek rather for the imaginative beauty of design and the loveliness of fair colour, and rejecting the tedious realism of those who merely paint what they see, try to see something worth seeing, and to see it not merely with actual and physical vision, but with that nobler vision of the soul which is as far wider in spiritual scope as it is far more splendid in artistic purpose. They, at any rate, work under those decorative conditions that each art requires for its perfection, and have sufficient aesthetic instinct to regret those sordid and stupid limitations of absolute modernity of form which have proved the ruin of so many of the Impressionists. Still, the art that is frankly decorative is the art to live with. It is, of all visible arts, the one art that creates in us both mood and temperament. Mere colour, unspoiled by meaning, and unallied with definite form, can speak to the soul in a thousand different ways. The harmony that resides in the delicate proportions of lines and masses becomes mirrored in the mind. The repetitions of pattern give us rest. The marvels of design stir the imagination. In the mere loveliness of the materials employed there are latent elements of culture. Nor is this all. By its deliberate rejection of Nature as the ideal of beauty, as well as of the imitative method of the ordinary painter, decorative art not merely prepares the soul for the reception of true imaginative work, but develops in it that sense of form which is the basis of creative no less than of critical achievement. For the real artist is he who proceeds, not from feeling to form, but from form to thought and passion. He does not first conceive an idea, and then say to himself, 'I will put my idea into a complex metre of fourteen lines,' but, realizing the beauty of the sonnet-scheme, he conceives certain modes of music and methods of rhyme, and the mere form suggests what is to fill it and make it intellectually and emotionally complete. From time to time the world cries out against some charming artistic poet, because, to use its hackneyed and silly phrase, he has 'nothing to say.' But if he had something to say, he would probably say it, and the result would be tedious. It is just because he has no new message, that he can do beautiful work. He gains his inspiration from form, and from form purely, as an artist should. A real passion would ruin him. Whatever actually occurs is spoiled for art. All bad poetry springs from genuine feeling. To be natural is to be obvious, and to be obvious is to be inartistic.

*Ernest.* I wonder do you really believe what you say.

*Gilbert.* Why should you wonder? It is not merely in art that the body is the soul. In every sphere of life Form is the beginning of things. The rhythmic harmonious gestures of dancing convey, Plato tells us, both rhythm and harmony into the mind. Forms are the food of faith, cried Newman in one of those great moments of sincerity that made us admire and know the man. He was right, though he may not have known how terribly right he was. The Creeds are believed, not because they are rational, but because they are repeated. Yes: Form is everything. It is the secret of life. Find expression for a sorrow, and it will become dear to you. Find expression for a joy, and you intensify its ecstasy. Do you wish to love? Use Love's Litany, and the words will create the yearning from which the world fancies that they spring. Have you a grief that corrodes your heart? Steep yourself in the language of grief, learn its utterance from Prince Hamlet and Queen Constance,[1] and you will find that mere expression is a mode of consolation, and

---

1 A reference to Constance's laments in *King John*, III.i.

that Form, which is the birth of passion, is also the death of pain. And so, to return to the sphere of Art, it is Form that creates not merely the critical temperament, but also the aesthetic instinct, that unerring instinct that reveals to one all things under their conditions of beauty. Start with the worship of form, and there is no secret in art that will not be revealed to you, and remember that in criticism, as in creation, temperament is everything, and that it is, not by the time of their production, but by the temperaments to which they appeal, that the schools of art should be historically grouped.

*Ernest.* Your theory of education is delightful. But what influence will your critic, brought up in these exquisite surroundings, possess? Do you really think that any artist is ever affected by criticism?

*Gilbert.* The influence of the critic will be the mere fact of his own existence. He will represent the flawless type. In him the culture of the century will see itself realized. You must not ask of him to have any aim other than the perfecting of himself. The demand of the intellect, as has been well said, is simply to feel itself alive. The critic may, indeed, desire to exercise influence; but, if so, he will concern himself not with the individual, but with the age, which he will seek to wake into consciousness, and to make responsive, creating in it new desires and appetites, and lending it his larger vision and his nobler moods. The actual art of to-day will occupy him less than the art of to-morrow, far less than the art of yesterday, and as for this or that person at present toiling away, what do the industrious matter? They do their best, no doubt, and consequently we get the worst from them. It is always with the best intentions that the worst work is done. And besides, my dear Ernest, when a man reaches the age of forty, or becomes a Royal Academician, or is elected a member of the Athenaeum Club, or is recognized as a popular novelist, whose books are in great demand at suburban railway stations, one may have the amusement of exposing him, but one cannot have the pleasure of reforming him. And this is, I dare say, very fortunate for him; for I have no doubt that reformation is a much more painful process than punishment, is indeed punishment in its most aggravated and moral form – a fact which accounts for our entire failure as a community to reclaim that interesting phenomenon who is called the confirmed criminal.

*Ernest.* But may it not be that the poet is the best judge of poetry, and the painter of painting? Each art must appeal primarily to the artist who works in it. His judgment will surely be the most valuable?

*Gilbert.* The appeal of all art is simply to the artistic temperament. Art does not address herself to the specialist. Her claim is that she is universal, and that in all her manifestations she is one. Indeed, so far from its being true that the artist is the best judge of art, a really great artist can never judge of other people's work at all, and can hardly, in fact, judge of his own. That very concentration of vision that makes a man an artist, limits by its sheer intensity his faculty of fine appreciation. The energy of creation hurries him blindly on to his own goal. The wheels of his chariot raise the dust as a cloud around him. The gods are hidden from each other. They can recognize their worshippers. That is all.

*Ernest.* You say that a great artist cannot recognize the beauty of work different from his own.

*Gilbert.* It is impossible for him to do so [ . . . ].

Bad artists always admire each other's work. They call it being large-minded and free from prejudice. But a truly great artist cannot conceive of life being shown, or beauty fashioned, under any conditions other than those that he has selected. Creation employs all its critical faculty within its own sphere. It may not use it in the sphere that belongs to others. It is exactly because a man cannot do a thing that he is the proper judge of it.

*Ernest.* Do you really mean that?

*Gilbert.* Yes, for creation limits, while contemplation widens, the vision.

*Ernest.* But what about technique? Surely each art has its separate technique?

*Gilbert.* Certainly: each art has its grammar and its materials. There is no mystery about either, and the incompetent can always be correct. But, while the laws upon which Art rests may be fixed and certain, to find their true realization they must be touched by the imagination into such beauty that they will seem an exception, each one of them. Technique is really personality. That is the reason why the artist cannot teach it, why the pupil cannot learn it, and why the aesthetic critic can understand it. To the great poet, there is only one method of music – his own. To the great painter, there is only one manner of painting – that which he himself employs. The aesthetic critic, and the aesthetic critic alone, can appreciate all forms and modes. It is to him that Art makes her appeal.

*Ernest.* Well, I think I have put all my questions to you. And now I must admit –

*Gilbert.* Ah! don't say that you agree with me. When people agree with me I always feel that I must be wrong.

*Ernest.* In that case I certainly won't tell you whether I agree with you or not. But I will put another question. You have explained to me that criticism is a creative art. What future has it?

*Gilbert.* It is to criticism that the future belongs. The subject-matter at the disposal of creation becomes every day more limited in extent and variety. Providence and Mr. Walter Besant[1] have exhausted the obvious. If creation is to last at all, it can only do so on the condition of becoming far more critical than it is at present. The old roads and dusty highways have been traversed too often. Their charm has been worn away by plodding feet, and they have lost that element of novelty or surprise which is so essential for romance. He who would stir us now by fiction must either give us an entirely new background, or reveal to us the soul of man in its innermost workings [ . . . ].

I myself am inclined to think that creation is doomed. It springs from too primitive, too natural an impulse. However this may be, it is certain that the subject-matter at the disposal of creation is always diminishing, while the subject-matter of criticism increases daily. There are always new attitudes for the mind, and new points of view. The duty of imposing form upon chaos does not grow less as the world advances. There was never a time when Criticism was more needed than it is now. It is only by its means that Humanity can become conscious of the point at which it has arrived.

Hours ago, Ernest, you asked me the use of Criticism. You might just as well have asked me the use of thought. It is Criticism, as Arnold points out,[2] that creates the intellectual atmosphere of the age. It is Criticism, as I hope to point out myself some day, that makes the mind a fine instrument. We, in our educational system, have burdened the memory with a load of unconnected facts, and laboriously striven to impart our laboriously-acquired knowledge. We teach people how to remember, we never teach them how to grow. It has never occurred to us to try and develop in the mind a more subtle quality of apprehension and discernment. The Greeks

1 A minor late nineteenth-century English novelist and critic, whose 'The Art of Fiction' provoked Henry James's much more famous reply.
2 In 'The Function of Criticism at the Present Time'.

did this, and when we come in contact with the Greek critical intellect, we cannot but be conscious that, while our subject-matter is in every respect larger and more varied than theirs, theirs is the only method by which this subject-matter can be interpreted. England has done one thing; it has invented and established Public Opinion, which is an attempt to organize the ignorance of the community, and to elevate it to the dignity of physical force. But Wisdom has always been hidden from it. Considered as an instrument of thought, the English mind is coarse and undeveloped. The only thing that can purify it is the growth of the critical instinct.

It is Criticism, again, that, by concentration, makes culture possible. It takes the cumbersome mass of creative work, and distils it into a finer essence. Who that desires to retain any sense of form could struggle through the monstrous multitudinous books that the world has produced, books in which thought stammers or ignorance brawls? The thread that is to guide us across the wearisome labyrinth is in the hands of Criticism. Nay more, where there is no record, and history is either lost or was never written, Criticism can recreate the past for us from the very smallest fragment of language or art, just as surely as the man of science can from some tiny bone, or the mere impress of a foot upon a rock, recreate for us the winged dragon or Titan lizard that once made the earth shake beneath its tread, can call Behemoth out of his cave, and make Leviathan swim once more across the startled sea. Prehistoric history belongs to the philological and archaeological critic. It is to him that the origins of things are revealed. The self-conscious deposits of an age are nearly always misleading. Through philological criticism alone we know more of the centuries of which no actual record has been preserved, than we do of the centuries that have left us their scrolls. It can do for us what can be done neither by physics nor metaphysics. It can give us the exact science of mind in the process of becoming. It can do for us what History cannot do. It can tell us what man thought before he learned how to write. You have asked me about the influence of Criticism. I think I have answered that question already; but there is this also to be said. It is Criticism that makes us cosmopolitan. The Manchester school[1] tried to make men realize the brotherhood of humanity, by pointing

---

1 The 'Manchester' school of political economy was responsible for the most influential theory of economics in the nineteenth century.

## ÆSTHETIC PRIDE.

*Fond Mother.* "YOU LIVE TOO MUCH ALONE, ALGERNON!"

*Young Genius (Poet, Painter, Sculptor, &c.).* "'TIS BETTER SO, MOTHER! BESIDES I ONLY CARE FOR THE SOCIETY OF MY *EQUALS*, AND—A—SUCH BEING THE CASE—A—MY CIRCLE IS NECESSARILY RATHER LIMITED."

*Fond Mother.* "BUT SURELY THE SOCIETY OF YOUR SUPERIORS——"

*Young Genius.* "MY *WHAT*, MOTHER? MY *SUPERIORS!* WHERE ARE THEY !!!"

PLATE 1

NINCOMPOOPIANA.—THE MUTUAL ADMIRATION SOCIETY.

*Our Gallant Colonel* (who is not a Member thereof, to Mrs. Cimabue Broom, who is). "AND WHO 's THIS YOUNG HERO THEY 'RE ALL SWARMING OVER NOW?"

*Mrs. Cimabue Broom.* "JELLABY POSTLETHWAITE, THE GREAT POET, YOU KNOW, WHO SAT FOR MAUDLE'S 'DEAD NARCISSUS'! HE HAS JUST DEDICATED HIS *LATTER-DAY SAPPHICS* TO ME. *Is NOT HE BEAUTIFUL?*"

*Our Gallant Colonel.* "WHY, WHAT 's THERE *BEAUTIFUL* ABOUT HIM?"

*Mrs. Cimabue Broom.* "OH, LOOK AT HIS GRAND HEAD AND POETIC FACE, WITH THOSE FLOWERLIKE EYES, AND THAT EXQUISITE SAD SMILE! LOOK AT HIS SLENDER WILLOWY FRAME, AS YIELDING AND FRAGILE AS A WOMAN'S! THAT 's YOUNG MAUDLE, STANDING JUST BEHIND HIM—THE GREAT PAINTER, YOU KNOW. HE HAS JUST PAINTED ME AS 'HÉLOÏSE,' AND MY HUSBAND AS 'ABÉLARD.' *Is NOT HE DIVINE?*"

*N.B.—Postlethwaite and Maudle are quite unknown to fame.*

[*The Colonel looks it.*]

PLATE 2

## AN ÆSTHETIC MIDDAY MEAL.

*At the Luncheon hour, Jellaby Postlethwaite enters a Pastrycook's and calls for a glass of Water,
into which he puts a freshly-cut Lily, and loses himself in contemplation thereof.*

*Waiter.* "SHALL I BRING YOU ANYTHING ELSE, SIR ?"

*Jellaby Postlethwaite.* "THANKS, NO ! I HAVE ALL I REQUIRE, AND SHALL SOON HAVE DONE !"

PLATE 3

## A REACTION IN ÆSTHETICS.

*Pilcox (the rising Æsthete, gazing at his last work, which represents Mrs. Cimabue Brown sick of Lilies, and trying to smell a Sunflower).* "I 'M AFRAID IT 'S ONE OF MY FAILURES !"

*Mrs. Cimabue Brown.* "OH, BUT YOUR FAILURES REMIND ONE OF MICHAEL ANGELO AT HIS BEST !"

*Pilcox.* "NOT QUITE SO BAD AS THAT, I HOPE !"

PLATE 4

## THE SIX-MARK TEA-POT.

*Æsthetic Bridegroom.* "It is quite consummate, is it not?"
*Intense Bride.* "It is, indeed! Oh, Algernon, let us live up to it!"

PLATE 5

## MAUDLE ON THE CHOICE OF A PROFESSION.

*Maudle.* "How CONSUMMATELY LOVELY YOUR SON IS, MRS. BROWN!"

*Mrs. Brown (a Philistine from the country).* "WHAT! HE'S A NICE, MANLY BOY, IF YOU MEAN THAT, MR. MAUDLE. HE HAS JUST LEFT SCHOOL, YOU KNOW, AND WISHES TO BE AN ARTIST."

*Maudle.* "WHY SHOULD HE BE AN ARTIST?"

*Mrs. Brown.* "WELL, HE MUST BE SOMETHING!"

*Maudle.* "WHY SHOULD HE BE ANYTHING? WHY NOT LET HIM REMAIN FOR EVER CONTENT TO EXIST BEAUTIFULLY?"

[*Mrs. Brown determines that at all events her Son shall not study Art under Maudle.*

PLATE 6

## THE APPALLING DIFFUSION OF TASTE.

*Much as he hates a joke, Sir Pompey Bedell has a still greater loathing for Nature, Poetry and Art,*
*which he chooses to identify with Postlethwaite, Maudle, & Co. ; and Grigsby's lifelike imita-*
*tions of those gentlemen—whom, by the bye, Sir Pompey has never seen—have so gratified him,*
*that he honours our funny friend with a call.*

*Sir Pompey (aghast).* "WHAT, MR. GRIGSBY, CAN THIS ROOM REALLY BE YOURS !—WITH
A DADO !—AND ARTISTIC WALL-PAPER ! !—AND A BRASS FENDER ! ! !—AND, GRACIOUS
HEAVENS, A BUNCH OF LILIES IN A BLUE POT ! ! ! !"

*Grigsby.* "THEY'RE NOT FOR LUNCHEON, SIR POMPEY ; THEY'RE ONLY TO SMELL, AND
TO LOOK AT, I ASSURE YOU ! LET ME OFFER YOU ONE !"

*Sir Pompey.* "NOT FOR THE WORLD, MR. GRIGSBY !"                    [*Beats a solemn retreat.*

PLATE 7

## FRUSTRATED SOCIAL AMBITION.

Collapse of Postlethwaite, Maudle, and Mrs. Cimabue Brown, on reading in a widely-circulated Contemporary Journal that they only exist in Mr. Punch's vivid Imagination. They had fondly flattered themselves that Universal Fame was theirs at last.

PLATE 8

out the commercial advantages of peace. It sought to degrade the wonderful world into a common market-place for the buyer and the seller. It addressed itself to the lowest instincts, and it failed. War followed upon war, and the tradesman's creed did not prevent France and Germany from clashing together in blood-stained battle. There are others of our own day who seek to appeal to mere emotional sympathies, or to the shallow dogmas of some vague system of abstract ethics. They have their Peace Societies, so dear to the sentimentalists, and their proposals for unarmed International Arbitration, so popular among those who have never read history. But mere emotional sympathy will not do. It is too variable, and too closely connected with the passions; and a board of arbitrators who, for the general welfare of the race, are to be deprived of the power of putting their decisions into execution, will not be of much avail. There is only one thing worse than Injustice, and that is Justice without her sword in her hand. When Right is not Might, it is Evil.

No: the emotions will not make us cosmopolitan, any more than the greed for gain could do so. It is only by the cultivation of the habit of intellectual criticism that we shall be able to rise superior to race prejudices. Goethe – you will not misunderstand what I say – was a German of the Germans. He loved his country – no man more so. Its people were dear to him; and he led them. Yet, when the iron hoof of Napoleon trampled upon vineyard and cornfield, his lips were silent. 'How can one write songs of hatred without hating?' he said to Eckerman, 'and how could I, to whom culture and barbarism are alone of importance, hate a nation which is among the most cultivated of the earth, and to which I owe so great a part of my own cultivation?' This note, sounded in the modern world by Goethe first, will become, I think, the starting point for the cosmopolitanism of the future. Criticism will annihilate race-prejudices, by insisting upon the unity of the human mind in the variety of its forms. If we are tempted to make war upon another nation, we shall remember that we are seeking to destroy an element of our own culture, and possibly its most important element. As long as war is regarded as wicked, it will always have its fascination. When it is looked upon as vulgar, it will cease to be popular. The change will, of course, be slow, and people will not be conscious of it. They will not say 'We will not war against France because her prose is perfect,' but because the prose of France is perfect, they will not hate the land. Intellectual criticism will bind Europe together in bonds far closer than those that can be forged by shopman or sentimentalist. It will give us the peace that springs from understanding.

Nor is this all. It is Criticism that, recognizing no position as final, and refusing to bind itself by the shallow shibboleths of any sect or school, creates that serene philosophic temper which loves truth for its own sake, and loves it not the less because it knows it to be unattainable. How little we have of this temper in England, and how much we need it! The English mind is always in a rage. The intellect of the race is wasted in the sordid and stupid quarrels of second-rate politicians or third-rate theologians. It was reserved for a man of science to show us the supreme example of that 'sweet reasonableness' of which Arnold[1] spoke so wisely, and alas! to so little effect. The author of the *Origin of Species*[2] had, at any rate, the philosophic temper. If one contemplates the ordinary pulpits and platforms of England, one can but feel the contempt of Julian,[3] or the indifference of Montaigne.[4] We are dominated by the fanatic, whose worst vice is his sincerity. Anything approaching to the free play of the mind is practically unknown amongst us. People cry out against the sinner, yet it is not the sinful, but the stupid, who are our shame. There is no sin except stupidity.

*Ernest.* Ah! what an antinomian you are!

*Gilbert.* The artistic critic, like the mystic, is an antinomian always. To be good, according to the vulgar standard of goodness, is obviously quite easy. It merely requires a certain amount of sordid terror, a certain lack of imaginative thought, and a certain low passion for middle-class respectability. Aesthetics are higher than ethics. They belong to a more spiritual sphere. To discern the beauty of a thing is the finest point to which we can arrive. Even a colour-sense is more important, in the development of the individual, than a sense of right and wrong. Aesthetics, in fact, are to Ethics in the sphere of conscious civilization, what, in the sphere of the external world, sexual is to natural selection. Ethics, like natural selection, make existence possible. Aesthetics, like sexual selection, make life lovely and wonderful, fill it with new forms, and give it progress, and variety and change. And when we reach the true

---

1 In *Culture and Anarchy.*   2 i.e. Charles Darwin.

3 I take this to be a reference to Julius the Apostate, the Roman emperor.

4 Michel Montaigne (1533–92), the French essayist.

culture that is our aim, we attain to that perfection of which the saints have dreamed, the perfection of those to whom sin is impossible, not because they make the renunciations of the ascetic, but because they can do everything they wish without hurt to the soul, and can wish for nothing that can do the soul harm, the soul being an entity so divine that it is able to transform into elements of a richer experience, or a finer susceptibility, or a newer mode of thought, acts or passions that with the common would be commonplace, or with the uneducated ignoble, or with the shameful vile. Is this dangerous? Yes; it is dangerous – all ideas, as I told you, are so. But the night wearies, and the light flickers in the lamp. One more thing I cannot help saying to you. You have spoken against Criticism as being a sterile thing. The nineteenth century is a turning point in history simply on account of the work of two men, Darwin and Renan, the one the critic of the Book of Nature, the other the critic of the books of God. Not to recognize this is to miss the meaning of one of the most important eras in the progress of the world. Creation is always behind the age. It is Criticism that leads us. The Critical Spirit and the World-Spirit are one.

*Ernest.* And he who is in possession of this spirit or whom this spirit possesses, will, I suppose, do nothing?

*Gilbert.* Like the Persephone of whom Landor tells us, the sweet pensive Persephone around whose white feet the asphodel and amaranth are blooming, he will sit contented 'in that deep, motionless, quiet which mortals pity, and which the gods enjoy.' He will look out upon the world and know its secret. By contact with divine things, he will become divine. His will be the perfect life, and his only.

*Ernest.* You have told me many strange things tonight, Gilbert. You have told me that it is more difficult to talk about a thing than to do it, and that to do nothing at all is the most difficult thing in the world; you have told me that all Art is immoral, and all thought dangerous; that criticism is more creative than creation, and that the highest criticism is that which reveals in the work of Art what the artist had not put there; that it is exactly because a man cannot do a thing that he is the proper judge of it; and that the true critic is unfair, insincere, not rational. My friend, you are a dreamer.

*Gilbert.* Yes: I am a dreamer. For a dreamer is one who can only find his way by moonlight, and his punishment is that he sees the dawn before the rest of the world.

*Ernest.* His punishment?

*Gilbert.* And his reward. But see, it is dawn already. Draw back the curtains and open the windows wide. How cool the morning air is! Piccadilly lies at our feet like a long riband of silver. A faint purple mist hangs over the Park, and the shadows of the white houses are purple. It is too late to sleep. Let us go down to Covent Garden and look at the roses. Come! I am tired of thought.

# OSCAR WILDE

## The Preface to *The Picture of Dorian Gray* (1891)

The artist is the creator of beautiful things.

To reveal art and conceal the artist is art's aim.

The critic is he who can translate into another manner or a new material his impression of beautiful things.

The highest, as the lowest, form of criticism is a mode of auto-biography.

Those who find ugly meanings in beautiful things are corrupt without being charming. This is a fault.

Those who find beautiful meanings in beautiful things are the cultivated. For these there is hope.

They are the elect to whom beautiful things mean only Beauty.

There is no such thing as a moral or an immoral book. Books are well written, or badly written. That is all.

The nineteenth-century dislike of Realism is the rage of Caliban seeing his own face in a glass.

The nineteenth-century dislike of Romanticism is the rage of Caliban not seeing his own face in a glass.

The moral life of man forms part of the subject-matter of the artist, but the morality of art consists in the perfect use of an imperfect medium. No artist desires to prove anything. Even things that are true can be proved.

No artist has ethical sympathies. An ethical sympathy in an artist is an unpardonable mannerism of style.

No artist is ever morbid. The artist can express everything.

100

Thought and language are to the artist instruments of an art.

Vice and virtue are to the artist materials for an art.

From the point of view of form, the type of all the arts is the art of the musician. From the point of view of feeling, the actor's craft is the type.

All art is at once surface and symbol.

Those who go beneath the surface do so at their peril.

Those who read the symbol do so at their peril.

It is the spectator, and not life, that art really mirrors.

Diversity of opinion about a work of art shows that the work is new, complex, and vital.

When critics disagree the artist is in accord with himself.

We can forgive a man for making a useful thing as long as he does not admire it. The only excuse for making a useless thing is that one admires it intensely.

All art is quite useless.

# PART II

# WORKS OF AESTHETICISM

# ALGERNON SWINBURNE

## From *Poems and Ballads* (1866)

### A LEAVE-TAKING

Let us go hence, my songs; she will not hear.
Let us go hence together without fear;
Keep silence now, for singing-time is over,
And over all old things and all things dear.
She loves not you nor me as all we love her.
Yea, though we sang as angels in her ear,
    She would not hear.

Let us rise up and part; she will not know.
Let us go seaward as the great winds go,
Full of blown sand and foam; what help is here?
There is no help, for all these things are so,
And all the world is bitter as a tear.
And how these things are, though ye strove to show,
    She would not know.

Let us go home and hence; she will not weep.
We gave love many dreams and days to keep,
Flowers without scent, and fruits that would not grow,
Saying 'If thou wilt, thrust in thy sickle and reap.'
All is reaped now; no grass is left to mow;
And we that sowed, though all we fell on sleep,
    She would not weep.

Let us go hence and rest; she will not love.
She shall not hear us if we sing hereof,
Nor see love's ways, how sore they are and steep.
Come hence, let be, lie still; it is enough.
Love is a barren sea, bitter and deep;
And though she saw all heaven in flower above,
    She would not love.

Let us give up, go down; she will not care.
Though all the stars made gold of all the air,
And the sea moving saw before it move
One moon-flower making all the foam-flowers fair;
Though all those waves went over us, and drove
Deep down the stifling lips and drowning hair,
    She would not care.

Let us go hence, go hence; she will not see.
Sing all once more together; surely she,
She too, remembering days and words that were,
Will turn a little toward us, sighing; but we,
We are hence, we are gone, as though we had not been there.
Nay, and though all men seeing had pity on me,
    She would not see.

## ANACTORIA

τίνος αὖ τὺ πειθοῖ
μὰψ σαγηνεύσας φιλότατα;[1]
        Sappho

My life is bitter with thy love; thine eyes
Blind me, thy tresses burn me, thy sharp sighs
Divide my flesh and spirit with soft sound,
And my blood strengthens, and my veins abound.
I pray thee sigh not, speak not, draw not breath;
Let life burn down, and dream it is not death.
I would the sea had hidden us, the fire
(Wilt thou fear that, and fear not my desire?)
Severed the bones that bleach, the flesh that cleaves,
And let our sifted ashes drop like leaves.
I feel thy blood against my blood: my pain
Pains thee, and lips bruise lips, and vein stings vein.
Let fruit be crushed on fruit, let flower on flower,
Breast kindle breast, and either burn one hour.
Why wilt thou follow lesser loves? are thine
Too weak to bear these hands and lips of mine?
I charge thee for my life's sake, O too sweet
To crush love with thy cruel faultless feet,

[1] 'From whom have you by persuasion caught love in vain': a corrupt
version of Sappho's 'Ode to Aphrodite'.

I charge thee keep thy lips from hers or his,
Sweetest, till theirs be sweeter than my kiss:
Lest I too lure, a swallow for a dove,
Erotion or Erinna[1] to my love.
I would my love could kill thee; I am satiated
With seeing thee live, and fain would have thee dead.
I would earth had thy body as fruit to eat,
And no mouth but some serpent's found thee sweet.
I would find grievous ways to have thee slain,
Intense device, and superflux of pain;
Vex thee with amorous agonies, and shake
Life at thy lips, and leave it there to ache;
Strain out thy soul with pangs too soft to kill,
Intolerable interludes, and infinite ill;
Relapse and reluctation of the breath,
Dumb tunes and shuddering semitones of death.
I am weary of all thy words and soft strange ways,
Of all love's fiery nights and all his days,
And all the broken kisses salt as brine
That shuddering lips make moist with waterish wine,
And eyes the bluer for all those hidden hours
That pleasure fills with tears and feeds from flowers,
Fierce at the heart with fire that half comes through,
But all the flowerlike white stained round with blue;
The fervent underlid, and that above
Lifted with laughter or abashed with love;
Thine amorous girdle, full of thee and fair,
And leavings of the lilies in thine hair.
Yea, all sweet words of thine and all thy ways,
And all the fruit of nights and flower of days,
And stinging lips wherein the hot sweet brine
That Love was born of burns and foams like wine,
And eyes insatiable of amorous hours,
Fervent as fire and delicate as flowers,
Coloured like night at heart, but cloven through
Like night with flame, dyed round like night with blue,
Clothed with deep eyelids under and above –
Yea, all thy beauty sickens me with love;

1 Erotion (male) and Erinna (female): lovers of Sappho; as was Anactoria.

Thy girdle empty of thee and now not fair,
And ruinous lilies in thy languid hair.
Ah, take no thought for Love's sake; shall this be,
And she who loves thy lover not love thee?
Sweet soul, sweet mouth of all that laughs and lives,
Mine is she, very mine; and she forgives.
For I beheld in sleep the light that is
In her high place in Paphos,[1] heard the kiss
Of body and soul that mix with eager tears
And laughter stinging through the eyes and ears;
Saw Love, as burning flame from crown to feet,
Imperishable, upon her storied seat;
Clear eyelids lifted toward the north and south,
A mind of many colours, and a mouth
Of many tunes and kisses; and she bowed,
With all her subtle face laughing aloud,
Bowed down upon me, saying, 'Who doth thee wrong,
Sappho?' but thou – thy body is the song,
Thy mouth the music; thou art more than I,
Though my voice die not till the whole world die;
Though men that hear it madden; though love weep,
Though nature change, though shame be charmed to sleep.
Ah, wilt thou slay me lest I kiss thee dead?
Yet the queen laughed from her sweet heart and said:
'Even she that flies shall follow for thy sake,
And she shall give thee gifts that would not take,
Shall kiss that would not kiss thee' (yea, kiss me)
'When thou wouldst not' – when I would not kiss thee!
Ah, more to me than all men as thou art,
Shall not my songs assuage her at the heart?
Ah, sweet to me as life seems sweet to death,
Why should her wrath fill thee with fearful breath?
Nay, sweet, for is she God alone? hath she
Made earth and all the centuries of the sea,
Taught the sun ways to travel, woven most fine
The moonbeams, shed the starbeams forth as wine,
Bound with her myrtles, beaten with her rods,
The young men and the maidens and the gods?

1 i.e. Cyprus.

108

Have we not lips to love with, eyes for tears,
And summer and flower of women and of years?
Stars for the foot of morning, and for noon
Sunlight, and exaltation of the moon;
Waters that answer waters, fields that wear
Lilies, and languor of the Lesbian air?
Beyond those flying feet of fluttered doves,
Are there not other gods for other loves?
Yea, though she scourge thee, sweetest, for my sake,
Blossom not thorns and flowers not blood should break.
Ah that my lips were tuneless lips, but pressed
To the bruised blossom of thy scourged white breast!
Ah that my mouth for Muses' milk were fed
On the sweet blood thy sweet small wounds had bled!
That with my tongue I felt them, and could taste
The faint flakes from thy bosom to the waist!
That I could drink thy veins as wine, and eat
Thy breasts like honey! that from face to feet
Thy body were abolished and consumed,
And in my flesh thy very flesh entombed!
Ah, ah, thy beauty! like a beast it bites,
Stings like an adder, like an arrow smites.
Ah sweet, and sweet again, and seven times sweet,
The paces and the pauses of thy feet!
Ah sweeter than all sleep or summer air
The fallen fillets fragrant from thine hair!
Yea, though their alien kisses do me wrong,
Sweeter thy lips than mine with all their song;
Thy shoulders whiter than a fleece of white,
And flower-sweet fingers, good to bruise or bite
As honeycomb of the inmost honey-cells,
With almond-shaped and roseleaf-coloured shells
And blood like purple blossom at the tips
Quivering; and pain made perfect in thy lips
For my sake when I hurt thee; O that I
Durst crush thee out of life with love, and die,
Die of thy pain and my delight, and be
Mixed with thy blood and molten into thee!
Would I not plague thee dying overmuch?
Would I not hurt thee perfectly? not touch

Thy pores of sense with torture, and make bright
Thine eyes with bloodlike tears and grievous light?
Strike pang from pang as note is struck from note,
Catch the sob's middle music in thy throat,
Take thy limbs living, and new-mould with these
A lyre of many faultless agonies?
Feed thee with fever and famine and fine drouth,
With perfect pangs convulse thy perfect mouth,
Make thy life shudder in thee and burn afresh,
And wring thy very spirit through the flesh?
Cruel? but love makes all that love him well
As wise as heaven and crueller than hell.
Me hath love made more bitter toward thee
Than death toward man; but were I made as he
Who hath made all things to break them one by one,
If my feet trod upon the stars and sun
And souls of men as his have alway trod,
God knows I might be crueller than God.
For who shall change with prayers or thanksgivings
The mystery of the cruelty of things?
Or say what God above all gods and years
With offering and blood-sacrifice of tears,
With lamentation from strange lands, from graves
Where the snake pastures, from scarred mouths of slaves,
From prison, and from plunging prows of ships
Through flamelike foam of the sea's closing lips –
With thwartings of strange signs, and wind-blown hair
Of comets, desolating the dim air,
When darkness is made fast with seals and bars,
And fierce reluctance of disastrous stars,
Eclipse, and sound of shaken hills, and wings
Darkening, and blind inexpiable things –
With sorrow of labouring moons, and altering light
And travail of the planets of the night,
And weeping of the weary Pleiads seven,
Feeds the mute melancholy lust of heaven?
Is not his incense bitterness, his meat
Murder? his hidden face and iron feet
Hath not man known, and felt them on their way
Threaten and trample all things and every day?

110

Hath he not sent us hunger? who hath cursed
Spirit and flesh with longing? filled with thirst
Their lips who cried unto him? who bade exceed
The fervid will, fall short the feeble deed,
Bade sink the spirit and the flesh aspire,
Pain animate the dust of dead desire,
And life yield up her flower to violent fate?
Him would I reach, him smite, him desecrate,
Pierce the cold lips of God with human breath,
And mix his immortality with death.
Why hath he made us? what had all we done
That we should live and loathe the sterile sun,
And with the moon wax paler as she wanes,
And pulse by pulse feel time grow through our veins?
Thee too the years shall cover; thou shalt be
As the rose born of one same blood with thee,
As a song sung, as a word said, and fall
Flower-wise, and be not any more at all,
Nor any memory of thee anywhere;
For never Muse has bound above thine hair
The high Pierian flower[1] whose graft outgrows
All summer kinship of the mortal rose
And colour of deciduous days, nor shed
Reflex and flush of heaven about thine head,
Nor reddened brows made pale by floral grief
With splendid shadow from that lordlier leaf.
Yea, thou shalt be forgotten like spilt wine,
Except these kisses of my lips on thine
Brand them with immortality; but me –
Men shall not see bright fire nor hear the sea,
Nor mix their hearts with music, nor behold
Cast forth of heaven, with feet of awful gold
And plumeless wings that make the bright air blind,
Lightning, with thunder for a hound behind
Hunting through fields unfurrowed and unsown,
But in the light and laughter, in the moan
And music, and in grasp of lip and hand
And shudder of water that makes felt on land

1 Poetry.

111

The immeasurable tremor of all the sea,
Memories shall mix and metaphors of me.
Like me shall be the shuddering calm of night,
When all the winds of the world for pure delight
Close lips that quiver and fold up wings that ache;
When nightingales are louder for love's sake,
And leaves tremble like lute-strings or like fire;
Like me the one star swooning with desire
Even at the cold lips of the sleepless moon,
As I at thine; like me the waste white noon,
Burnt through with barren sunlight; and like me
The land-stream and the tide-stream in the sea.
I am sick with time as these with ebb and flow,
And by the yearning in my veins I know
The yearning sound of waters; and mine eyes
Burn as that beamless fire which fills the skies
With troubled stars and travailing things of flame;
And in my heart the grief consuming them
Labours, and in my veins the thirst of these,
And all the summer travail of the trees
And all the winter sickness; and the earth,
Filled full with deadly works of death and birth,
Sore spent with hungry lusts of birth and death,
Has pain like mine in her divided breath;
Her spring of leaves is barren, and her fruit
Ashes; her boughs are burdened, and her root
Fibrous and gnarled with poison; underneath
Serpents have gnawn it through with tortuous teeth
Made sharp upon the bones of all the dead,
And wild birds rend her branches overhead.
These, woven as raiment for his word and thought,
These hath God made, and me as these, and wrought
Song, and hath lit it at my lips; and me
Earth shall not gather though she feed on thee.
As a shed tear shalt thou be shed; but I –
Lo, earth may labour, men live long and die,
Years change and stars, and the high God devise
New things, and old things wane before his eyes
Who wields and wrecks them, being more strong than they –
But, having made me, me he shall not slay.

112

Nor slay nor satiate, like those herds of his
Who laugh and live a little, and their kiss
Contents them, and their loves are swift and sweet,
And sure death grasps and gains them with slow feet,
Love they or hate they, strive or bow their knees –
And all these end; he hath his will of these.
Yea, but albeit he slay me, hating me –
Albeit he hide me in the deep dear sea
And cover me with cool wan foam, and ease
This soul of mine as any soul of these,
And give me water and great sweet waves, and make
The very sea's name lordlier for my sake,
The whole sea sweeter – albeit I die indeed
And hide myself and sleep and no man heed,
Of me the high God hath not all his will.
Blossom of branches, and on each high hill
Clear air and wind, and under in clamorous vales
Fierce noises of the fiery nightingales,
Buds burning in the sudden spring like fire,
The wan washed sand and the waves' vain desire,
Sails seen like blown white flowers at sea, and words
That bring tears swiftest, and long notes of birds
Violently singing till the whole world sings –
I Sappho shall be one with all these things,
With all high things for ever; and my face
Seen once, my songs once heard in a strange place,
Cleave to men's lives, and waste the days thereof
With gladness and much sadness and long love.
Yea, they shall say, earth's womb has borne in vain
New things, and never this best thing again;
Borne days and men, borne fruits and wars and wine,
Seasons and songs, but no song more like mine.
And they shall know me as ye who have known me here,
Last year when I loved Atthis, and this year
When I love thee; and they shall praise me, and say
'She hath all time as all we have our day,
Shall she not live and have her will' – even I?
Yea, though thou diest, I say I shall not die.
For these shall give me of their souls, shall give
Life, and the days and loves wherewith I live,

Shall quicken me with loving, fill with breath,
Save me and serve me, strive for me with death.
Alas, that neither moon nor snow nor dew
Nor all cold things can purge me wholly through,
Assuage me nor allay me nor appease,
Till supreme sleep shall bring me bloodless ease;
Till time wax faint in all his periods;
Till fate undo the bondage of the gods,
And lay, to slake and satiate me all through,
Lotus and Lethe[1] on my lips like dew,
And shed around and over and under me
Thick darkness and the insuperable sea.

### IN THE ORCHARD
#### (Provençal Burden)

Leave go my hands, let me catch breath and see;
Let the dew-fall drench either side of me;
   Clear apple-leaves are soft upon that moon
Seen sidelong like a blossom in the tree;
   Ah God, ah God, that day should be so soon.

The grass is thick and cool, it lets us lie.
Kissed upon either cheek and either eye,
   I turn to thee as some green afternoon
Turns toward sunset, and is loth to die;
   Ah God, ah God, that day should be so soon.

Lie closer, lean your face upon my side,
Feel where the dew fell that has hardly dried,
   Hear how the blood beats that went nigh to swoon;
The pleasure lives there when the sense has died;
   Ah God, ah God, that day should be so soon.

O my fair lord, I charge you leave me this:
Is it not sweeter than a foolish kiss?
   Nay take it then, my flower, my first in June,
My rose, so like a tender mouth it is:
   Ah God, ah God, that day should be so soon.

1 The flower and river of forgetfulness.

Love, till dawn sunder night from day with fire,
Dividing my delight and my desire,
   The crescent life and love the plenilune,
Love me though dusk begin and dark retire;
   Ah God, ah God, that day should be so soon.

Ah, my heart fails, my blood draws back; I know,
When life runs over, life is near to go;
   And with the slain of love love's ways are strewn,
And with their blood, if love will have it so;
   Ah God, ah God, that day should be so soon.

Ah, do thy will now; slay me if thou wilt;
There is no building now the walls are built,
   No quarrying now the corner-stone is hewn,
No drinking now the vine's whole blood is spilt;
   Ah God, ah God, that day should be so soon.

Nay, slay me now; nay, for I will be slain;
Pluck thy red pleasure from the teeth of pain,
   Break down thy vine ere yet grape-gatherers prune,
Slay me ere day can slay desire again;
   Ah God, ah God, that day should be so soon.

Yea, with thy sweet lips, with thy sweet sword; yea,
Take life and all, for I will die, I say;
   Love, I gave love, is life a better boon?
For sweet night's sake I will not live till day;
   Ah God, ah God, that day should be so soon.

Nay, I will sleep then only; nay, but go.
Ah sweet, too sweet to me, my sweet, I know
   Love, sleep, and death go to the sweet same tune;
Hold my hair fast, and kiss me through it so.
   Ah God, ah God, that day should be so soon.

### THE LEPER

   Nothing is better, I well think,
      Than love; the hidden well-water
   Is not so delicate to drink:
      This was well seen of me and her.

I served her in a royal house;
　I served her wine and curious meat.
For will to kiss between her brows,
　I had no heart to sleep or eat.

Mere scorn God knows she had of me,
　A poor scribe, nowise great or fair,
Who plucked his clerk's hood back to see
　Her curled-up lips and amorous hair.

I vex my head with thinking this.
　Yea, though God always hated me,
And hates me now that I can kiss
　Her eyes, plait up her hair to see

How she then wore it on the brows,
　Yet am I glad to have her dead
Here in this wretched wattled house
　Where I can kiss her eyes and head.

Nothing is better, I well know,
　Than love; no amber in cold sea
Or gathered berries under snow:
　That is well seen of her and me.

Three thoughts I make my pleasure of:
　First I take heart and think of this:
That knight's gold hair she chose to love,
　His mouth she had such will to kiss.

Then I remember that sundawn
　I brought him by a privy way
Out at her lattice, and thereon
　What gracious words she found to say.

(Cold rushes for such little feet –
　Both feet could lie into my hand.
A marvel was it of my sweet
　Her upright body could so stand.)

'Sweet friend, God give you thank and grace;
　Now am I clean and whole of shame,
Nor shall men burn me in the face
　For my sweet fault that scandals them.'

116

I tell you over word by word.
　She, sitting edgewise on her bed,
Holding her feet, said thus. The third,
　A sweeter thing than these, I said.

God, that makes time and ruins it
　And alters not, abiding God,
Changed with disease her body sweet,
　The body of love wherein she abode.

Love is more sweet and comelier
　Than a dove's throat strained out to sing.
All they spat out and cursed at her
　And cast her forth for a base thing.

They cursed her, seeing how God had wrought
　This curse to plague her, a curse of his.
Fools were they surely, seeing not
　How sweeter than all sweet she is.

He that had held her by the hair,
　With kissing lips blinding her eyes,
Felt her bright bosom, strained and bare,
　Sigh under him, with short mad cries

Out of her throat and sobbing mouth
　And body broken up with love,
With sweet hot tears his lips were loth
　Her own should taste the savour of,

Yea, he inside whose grasp all night
　Her fervent body leapt or lay,
Stained with sharp kisses red and white,
　Found her a plague to spurn away.

I hid her in this wattled house,
　I served her water and poor bread.
For joy to kiss between her brows
　Time upon time I was nigh dead.

Bread failed; we got but well-water
　And gathered grass with dropping seed.
I had such joy of kissing her,
　I had small care to sleep or feed.

Sometimes when service made me glad
　The sharp tears leapt between my lids,
Falling on her, such joy I had
　To do the service God forbids.

'I pray you let me be at peace,
　Get hence, make room for me to die.'
She said that: her poor lip would cease,
　Put up to mine, and turn to cry.

I said, 'Bethink yourself how love
　Fared in us twain, what either did;
Shall I unclothe my soul thereof?
　That I should do this, God forbid.'

Yea, though God hateth us, he knows
　That hardly in a little thing
Love faileth of the work it does
　Till it grow ripe for gathering.

Six months, and now my sweet is dead
　A trouble takes me; I know not
If all were done well, all well said,
　No word or tender deed forgot.

Too sweet, for the least part in her,
　To have shed life out by fragments; yet,
Could the close mouth catch breath and stir,
　I might see something I forget.

Six months, and I sit still and hold
　In two cold palms her cold two feet.
Her hair, half grey half ruined gold,
　Thrills me and burns me in kissing it.

Love bites and stings me through, to see
　Her keen face made of sunken bones.
Her worn-off eyelids madden me,
　That were shot through with purple once.

She said, 'Be good with me; I grow
　So tired for shame's sake, I shall die
If you say nothing:' even so.
　And she is dead now, and shame put by.

118

Yea, and the scorn she had of me
  In the old time, doubtless vexed her then.
I never should have kissed her. See
  What fools God's anger makes of men!

She might have loved me a little too,
  Had I been humbler for her sake.
But that new shame could make love new
  She saw not – yet her shame did make.

I took too much upon my love,
  Having for such mean service done
Her beauty and all the ways thereof,
  Her face and all the sweet thereon.

Yea, all this while I tended her,
  I know the old love held fast his part:
I know the old scorn waxed heavier,
  Mixed with sad wonder, in her heart.

It may be all my love went wrong –
  A scribe's work writ awry and blurred,
Scrawled after the blind evensong –
  Spoilt music with no perfect word.

But surely I would fain have done
  All things the best I could. Perchance
Because I failed, came short of one,
  She kept at heart that other man's.

I am grown blind with all these things:
  It may be now she hath in sight
Some better knowledge; still there clings
  The old question. Will not God do right?

### RONDEL

Kissing her hair I sat against her feet,
Wove and unwove it, wound and found it sweet;
Made fast therewith her hands, drew down her eyes,
Deep as deep flowers and dreamy like dim skies;
With her own tresses bound and found her fair,
  Kissing her hair.

Sleep were no sweeter than her face to me,
Sleep of cold sea-bloom under the cold sea;
What pain could get between my face and hers?
What new sweet thing would love not relish worse?
Unless, perhaps, white death had kissed me there,
  Kissing her hair?

### BEFORE PARTING

A month or twain to live on honeycomb
Is pleasant; but one tires of scented time,
Cold sweet recurrence of accepted rhyme,
And that strong purple under juice and foam
Where the wine's heart has burst;
Nor feel the latter kisses like the first.

Once yet, this poor one time; I will not pray
Even to change the bitterness of it,
The bitter taste ensuing on the sweet,
To make your tears fall where your soft hair lay
All blurred and heavy in some perfumed wise
Over my face and eyes.

And yet who knows what end the scythèd wheat
Makes of its foolish poppies' mouths of red?
These were not sown, these are not harvested,
They grow a month and are cast under feet
And none has care thereof,
As none has care of a divided love.

I know each shadow of your lips by rote,
Each change of love in eyelids and eyebrows;
The fashion of fair temples tremulous
With tender blood, and colour of your throat;
I know not how love is gone out of this,
Seeing that all was his.

Love's likeness there endures upon all these:
But out of these one shall not gather love.
Day hath not strength nor the night shade enough
To make love whole and fill his lips with ease,
As some bee-builded cell
Feels at filled lips the heavy honey swell.

I know not how this last month leaves your hair
Less full of purple colour and hid spice,
And that luxurious trouble of closed eyes
Is mixed with meaner shadow and waste care;
And love, kissed out by pleasure, seems not yet
Worth patience to regret.

## THE SUNDEW

A little marsh-plant, yellow green,
And pricked at lip with tender red.
Tread close, and either way you tread
Some faint black water jets between
Lest you should bruise the curious head.

A live thing maybe; who shall know?
The summer knows and suffers it;
For the cool moss is thick and sweet
Each side, and saves the blossom so
That it lives out the long June heat.

The deep scent of the heather burns
About it; breathless though it be,
Bow down and worship; more than we
Is the least flower whose life returns,
Least weed renascent in the sea.

We are vexed and cumbered in earth's sight
With wants, with many memories;
These see their mother what she is,
Glad-growing, till August leave more bright
The apple-coloured cranberries.

Wind blows and bleaches the strong grass,
Blown all one way to shelter it
From trample of strayed kine, with feet
Felt heavier than the moorhen was,
Strayed up past patches of wild wheat.

You call it sundew: how it grows,
If with its colour it have breath,
If life taste sweet to it, if death
Pain its soft petal, no man knows:
Man has no sight or sense that saith.

My sundew, grown of gentle days,
In these green miles the spring begun
Thy growth ere April had half done
With the soft secret of her ways
Or June made ready for the sun.

O red-lipped mouth of marsh-flower,
I have a secret halved with thee.
The name that is love's name to me
Thou knowest, and the face of her
Who is my festival to see.

The hard sun, as thy petals knew,
Coloured the heavy moss-water:
Thou wert not worth green midsummer
Nor fit to live to August blue,
O sundew, not remembering her.

## SAPPHICS

All the night sleep came not upon my eyelids,
Shed not dew, nor shook nor unclosed a feather,
Yet with lips shut close and with eyes of iron
    Stood and beheld me.

Then to me so lying awake a vision
Came without sleep over the seas and touched me,
Softly touched mine eyelids and lips; and I too,
    Full of the vision,

Saw the white implacable Aphrodite,
Saw the hair unbound and the feet unsandalled
Shine as fire of sunset on western waters;
    Saw the reluctant

Feet, the straining plumes of the doves that drew her,
Looking always, looking with necks reverted,
Back to Lesbos, back to the hills whereunder
    Shone Mitylene;[1]

Heard the flying feet of the Loves behind her
Make a sudden thunder upon the waters,
As the thunder flung from the strong unclosing
    Wings of a great wind.

1 Birthplace of Sappho.

So the goddess fled from her place, with awful
Sound of feet and thunder of wings around her;
While behind a clamour of singing women
   Severed the twilight.

Ah the singing, ah the delight, the passion!
All the Loves wept, listening; sick with anguish,
Stood the crowned nine Muses about Apollo;
   Fear was upon them,

While the tenth sang wonderful things they knew not.
Ah the tenth, the Lesbian! the nine were silent,
None endured the sound of her song for weeping;
   Laurel by laurel,

Faded all their crowns; but about her forehead,
Round her woven tresses and ashen temples
White as dead snow, paler than grass in summer,
   Ravaged with kisses,

Shone a light of fire as a crown for ever.
Yea, almost the implacable Aphrodite
Paused, and almost wept; such a song was that song.
   Yea, by her name too

Called her, saying, 'Turn to me, O my Sappho;'
Yet she turned her face from the Loves, she saw not
Tears for laughter darken immortal eyelids,
   Heard not about her

Fearful fitful wings of the doves departing,
Saw not how the bosom of Aphrodite
Shook with weeping, saw not her shaken raiment,
   Saw not her hands wrung;

Saw the Lesbians kissing across their smitten
Lutes with lips more sweet than the sound of lute-strings,
Mouth to mouth and hand upon hand, her chosen,
   Fairer than all men;

Only saw the beautiful lips and fingers,
Full of songs and kisses and little whispers,
Full of music; only beheld among them
   Soar, as a bird soars

Newly fledged, her visible song, a marvel,
Made of perfect sound and exceeding passion,
Sweetly shapen, terrible, full of thunders,
   Clothed with the wind's wings.

Then rejoiced she, laughing with love, and scattered
Roses, awful roses of holy blossom;
Then the Loves thronged sadly with hidden faces
   Round Aphrodite,

Then the Muses, stricken at heart, were silent;
Yea, the gods waxed pale; such a song was that song.
All reluctant, all with a fresh repulsion,
   Fled from before her.

All withdrew long since, and the land was barren,
Full of fruitless women and music only.
Now perchance, when winds are assuaged at sunset,
   Lulled at the dewfall,

By the grey sea-side, unassuaged, unheard of,
Unbeloved, unseen in the ebb of twilight,
Ghosts of outcast women return lamenting,
   Purged not in Lethe,

Clothed about with flame and with tears, and singing
Songs that move the heart of the shaken heaven,
Songs that break the heart of the earth with pity,
   Hearing, to hear them.

# OSCAR WILDE

## From *Poems* (1881)

### HELAS!

To drift with every passion till my soul
Is a stringed lute on which all winds can play,
Is it for this that I have given away
Mine ancient wisdom, and austere control?

Methinks my life is a twice-written scroll
Scrawled over on some boyish holiday
With idle songs for pipe and virelay,
Which do but mar the secret of the whole.
Surely there was a time I might have trod
The sunlit heights, and from life's dissonance
Struck one clear chord to reach the ears of God:
Is that time dead? lo! with a little rod
I did but touch the honey of romance –
And must I lose a soul's inheritance?


IMPRESSION DU MATIN

The Thames nocturne of blue and gold
    Changed to a Harmony in grey:
    A barge with ochre-coloured hay
Dropt from the wharf: and chill and cold

The yellow fog came creeping down
    The bridges, till the houses' walls
    Seemed changed to shadows, and S. Paul's
Loomed like a bubble o'er the town.

Then suddenly arose the clang
    Of waking life; the streets were stirred
    With country waggons: and a bird
Flew to the glistening roofs and sang.

But one pale woman all alone,
    The daylight kissing her wan hair,
    Loitered beneath the gas lamps' flare,
With lips of flame and heart of stone.


ATHANASIA

To that gaunt House of Art which lacks for naught
    Of all the great things men have saved from Time,
The withered body of a girl was brought
    Dead ere the world's glad youth had touched its prime,
And seen by lonely Arabs lying hid
In the dim womb of some black pyramid.

But when they had unloosed the linen band
   Which swathed the Egyptian's body, – lo! was found
Closed in the wasted hollow of her hand
   A little seed, which sown in English ground
Did wondrous snow of starry blossoms bear,
And spread rich odours through our springtide air.

With such strange arts this flower did allure
   That all forgotten was the asphodel,
And the brown bee, the lily's paramour,
   Forsook the cup where he was wont to dwell,
For not a thing of earth it seemed to be,
But stolen from some heavenly Arcady.[1]

In vain the sad narcissus, wan and white
   At its own beauty, hung across the stream,
The purple dragon-fly had no delight
   With its gold dust to make his wings a-gleam,
Ah! no delight the jasmine-bloom to kiss,
Or brush the rain-pearls from the eucharis.

For love of it the passionate nightingale
   Forgot the hills of Thrace, the cruel king,
And the pale dove no longer cared to sail
   Through the wet woods at time of blossoming,
But round this flower of Egypt sought to float,
With silvered wing and amethystine throat.

While the hot sun blazed in his tower of blue
   A cooling wind crept from the land of snows,
And the warm south with tender tears of dew
   Drenched its white leaves when Hesperos[2] uprose
Amid those sea-green meadows of the sky
On which the scarlet bars of sunset lie.

But when o'er wastes of lily-haunted field
   The tired birds had stayed their amorous tune,
And broad and glittering like an argent shield
   High in the sapphire heavens hung the moon,
Did no strange dream or evil memory make
Each tremulous petal of its blossoms shake?

1 See note to p. 23.    2 The evening star.

Ah no! to this bright flower a thousand years
  Seemed but the lingering of a summer's day,
It never knew the tide of cankering fears
  Which turn a boy's gold hair to withered grey,
The dread desire of death it never knew,
Or how all folk that they were born must rue.

For we to death with pipe and dancing go,
  Nor would we pass the ivory gate again,
As some sad river wearied of its flow
  Through the dull plains, the haunts of common men,
Leaps lover-like into the terrible sea!
And counts it gain to die so gloriously.

We mar our lordly strength in barren strife
  With the world's legions led by clamorous care,
It never feels decay but gathers life
  From the pure sunlight and the supreme air,
We live beneath Time's wasting sovereignty,
It is the child of all eternity.

### IMPRESSIONS

#### I *Les Silhouettes*

  The sea is flecked with bars of grey,
  The dull dead wind is out of tune,
  And like a withered leaf the moon
Is blown across the stormy bay.

  Etched clear upon the pallid sand
  The black boat lies: a sailor boy
  Clambers aboard in careless joy
With laughing face and gleaming hand.

  And overhead the curlews cry,
  Where through the dusky upland grass
  The young brown-throated reapers pass,
Like silhouettes against the sky.

#### II *La Fuite de la Lune*

  To outer senses there is peace,
  A dreamy peace on either hand,
  Deep silence in the shadowy land,
Deep silence where the shadows cease.

Save for a cry that echoes shrill
From some lone bird disconsolate;
A corncrake calling to its mate;
The answer from the misty hill.

And suddenly the moon withdraws
Her sickle from the lightening skies,
And to her sombre cavern flies,
Wrapped in a veil of yellow gauze.


THEOCRITUS

*A Villanelle*

O Singer of Persephone!
  In the dim meadows desolate
Dost thou remember Sicily?

Still through the ivy flits the bee
  Where Amaryllis lies in state;
O Singer of Persephone!

Simaetha[1] calls on Hecate[2]
  And hears the wild dogs at the gate;
Dost thou remember Sicily?

Still by the light and laughing sea
  Poor Polypheme bemoans his fate:
O Singer of Persephone!

And still in boyish rivalry
  Young Daphnis challenges his mate:
Dost thou remember Sicily?

Slim Lacon[3] keeps a goat for thee,
  For thee the jocund shepherds wait,
O Singer of Persephone!
Dost thou remember Sicily?

1 Simaetha was beloved by Polyphemus, the Cyclops whose fate
  was to be blinded by Odysseus.
2 The chief goddess of magic.
3 Speakers in Theocritus's fifth, eighth and ninth *Idylls*.

## IN THE GOLD ROOM

### *A Harmony*

Her ivory hands on the ivory keys
   Strayed in a fitful fantasy,
Like the silver gleam when the poplar trees
   Rustle their pale leaves listlessly,
   Or the drifting foam of a restless sea
When the waves show their teeth in the flying breeze.

Her gold hair fell on the wall of gold
   Like the delicate gossamer tangles spun
On the burnished disk of the marigold,
   Or the sun-flower turning to meet the sun
   When the gloom of the jealous night is done,
And the spear of the lily is aureoled.

And her sweet red lips on these lips of mine
   Burned like the ruby fire set
In the swinging lamp of a crimson shrine,
   Or the bleeding wounds of the pomegranate,
   Or the heart of the lotus drenched and wet
With the spilt-out blood of the rose-red wine.

## SANTA DECCA

The Gods are dead: no longer do we bring
   To grey-eyed Pallas[1] crowns of olive-leaves!
   Demeter's[2] child no more hath tithe of sheaves,
And in the noon the careless shepherds sing,
For Pan is dead, and all the wantoning
   By secret glade and devious haunt is o'er:
   Young Hylas[3] seeks the water-springs no more;
Great Pan is dead, and Mary's Son is King.

---

1 i.e. Pallas Athene, the Greek goddess of war.
2 i.e. Persephone.
3 The story of Hylas, a favourite of Heracles, carried off by nymphs as he
   went to draw water, dates from Theocritus.

And yet – perchance in this sea-trancèd isle,
　　Chewing the bitter fruit of memory,
　　Some God lies hidden in the asphodel.
Ah Love! if such there be then it were well
　　For us to fly his anger: nay, but see
　　The leaves are stirring: let us watch a-while.


## TAEDIUM VITAE

To stab my youth with desperate knives, to wear
This paltry age's gaudy livery,
To let each base hand filch my treasury,
To mesh my soul within a woman's hair,
And be mere Fortune's lackeyed groom, – I swear
I love it not! these things are less to me
Than the thin foam that frets upon the sea,
Less than the thistle-down of summer air
Which hath no seed: better to stand aloof
Far from these slanderous fools who mock my life
Knowing me not, better the lowliest roof
Fit for the meanest hind to sojourn in,
Than to go back to that hoarse cave of strife
Where my white soul first kissed the mouth of sin.


## PANTHEA

Nay, let us walk from fire unto fire,
　　From passionate pain to deadlier delight, –
I am too young to live without desire,
　　Too young art thou to waste this summer night
Asking those idle questions which of old
Man sought of seer and oracle, and no reply was told.

For, sweet, to feel is better than to know,
　　And wisdom is a childless heritage,
One pulse of passion – youth's first fiery glow, –
　　Are worth the hoarded proverbs of the sage:
Vex not thy soul with dead philosophy,
Have we not lips to kiss with, hearts to love and eyes to see!

130

Dost thou not hear the murmuring nightingale,
  Like water bubbling from a silver jar,
So soft she sings the envious moon is pale,
  That high in heaven she is hung so far
She cannot hear that love-enraptured tune, –
Mark how she wreathes each horn with mist, yon late and
    labouring moon.

White lilies, in whose cups the gold bees dream,
  The fallen snow of petals where the breeze
Scatters the chestnut blossom, or the gleam
  Of boyish limbs in water, – are not these
Enough for thee, dost thou desire more?
Alas! the Gods will give nought else from their eternal store.

For our high Gods have sick and wearied grown
  Of all our endless sins, our vain endeavour
For wasted days of youth to make atone
  By pain or prayer or priest, and never, never,
Hearken they now to either good or ill,
But send their rain upon the just and the unjust at will.

They sit at ease, our Gods they sit at ease,
  Strewing with leaves of rose their scented wine,
They sleep, they sleep, beneath the rocking trees
  Where asphodel and yellow lotus twine,
Mourning the old glad days before they knew
What evil things the heart of man could dream, and dreaming do.

And far beneath the brazen floor they see
  Like swarming flies the crowd of little men,
The bustle of small lives, then wearily
  Back to their lotus-haunts they turn again
Kissing each others' mouths, and mix more deep
The poppy-seeded draught which brings soft purple-lidded sleep.

There all day long the golden-vestured sun,
  Their torch-bearer, stands with his torch ablaze,
And, when the gaudy web of noon is spun
  By its twelve maidens, through the crimson haze
Fresh from Endymion's[1] arms comes forth the moon,
And the immortal Gods in toils of mortal passions swoon.

1 A beautiful young shepherd whom the moon (Selene) visited each night.

There walks Queen Juno[1] through some dewy mead,
  Her grand white feet flecked with the saffron dust
Of wind-stirred lilies, while young Ganymede[2]
  Leaps in the hot and amber-foaming must,
His curls all tossed, as when the eagle bare
The frightened boy from Ida through the blue Ionian air.

There in the green heart of some garden close
  Queen Venus with the shepherd at her side,
Her warm soft body like the briar rose
  Which would be white yet blushes at its pride,
Laughs low for love, till jealous Salmacis[3]
Peers through the myrtle-leaves and sighs for pain of lonely
    bliss.

There never does that dreary north-wind blow
  Which leaves our English forests bleak and bare,
Nor ever falls the swift white-feathered snow,
  Nor ever doth the red-toothed lightning dare
To wake them in the silver-fretted night
When we lie weeping for some sweet sad sin, some dead delight.

Alas! they know the far Lethaean[4] spring,
  The violet-hidden waters well they know,
Where one whose feet with tired wandering
  Are faint and broken may take heart and go,
And from those dark depths cool and crystalline
Drink, and draw balm, and sleep for sleepless souls, and
    anodyne.

But we oppress our natures, God or Fate
  Is our enemy, we starve and feed
On vain repentance – O we are born too late!
  What balm for us in bruisèd poppy seed
Who crowd into one finite pulse of time
The joy of infinite love and the fierce pain of infinite crime.

1 Wife of Jupiter in Roman mythology.
2 Who, because of his beauty, was carried off to be Zeus's cup-bearer.
3 A naiad, who fell in love with the youth Hermaphroditus, the son of
  Venus (Aphrodite) and Mercury.
4 The river of oblivion in the Greek underworld.

132

O we are wearied of this sense of guilt,
  Wearied of pleasure's paramour despair,
Wearied of every temple we have built,
  Wearied of every right, unanswered prayer,
For man is weak; God sleeps; and heaven is high;
One fiery-coloured moment: one great love; and lo! we die.

Ah! but no ferry-man with labouring pole
  Nears his black shallop to the flowerless strand,
No little coin of bronze can bring the soul
  Over Death's river to the sunless land,
Victim and wine and vow are all in vain,
The tomb is sealed; the soldiers watch; the dead rise not again.

We are resolved into the supreme air,
  We are made one with what we touch and see,
With our heart's blood each crimson sun is fair,
  With our young lives each spring-impassioned tree
Flames into green, the wildest beasts that range
The moor our kinsmen are, all life is one, and all is change.

With beat of systole and of diastole
  One grand great life throbs through earth's giant heart,
And mighty waves of single Being roll
  From nerveless germ to man, for we are part
Of every rock and bird and beast and hill,
One with the things that prey on us, and one with what we kill.

From lower cells of waking life we pass
  To full perfection; thus the world grows old:
We who are godlike now were once a mass
  Of quivering purple flecked with bars of gold,
Unsentient or of joy or misery,
And tossed in terrible tangles of some wild and wind-swept sea.

This hot hard flame with which our bodies burn
  Will make some meadow blaze with daffodil,
Ay! and those argent breasts of thine will turn
  To water-lilies; the brown fields men till
Will be more fruitful for our love to-night,
Nothing is lost in nature, all things live in Death's despite.

133

The boy's first kiss, the hyacinth's first bell,
　　The man's last passion, and the last red spear
That from the lily leaps, the asphodel
　　Which will not let its blossoms blow for fear
Of too much beauty, and the timid shame
Of the young bridegroom at his lover's eyes, – these with the
　　　　same

One sacrament are consecrate, the earth
　　Not we alone hath passions hymeneal,
The yellow buttercups that shake for mirth
　　At daybreak know a pleasure not less real
Than we do, when in some fresh-blossoming wood,
We draw the spring into our hearts, and feel that life is good.

So when men bury us beneath the yew
　　Thy crimson-stainèd mouth a rose will be,
And thy soft eyes lush bluebells dimmed with dew,
　　And when the white narcissus wantonly
Kisses the wind its playmate some faint joy
Will thrill our dust, and we will be again fond maid and boy.

And thus without life's conscious torturing pain
　　In some sweet flower we will feel the sun,
And from the linnet's throat will sing again,
　　And as two gorgeous-mailèd snakes will run
Over our graves, or as two tigers creep
Through the hot jungle where the yellow-eyed huge lions sleep

And give them battle! How my heart leaps up
　　To think of that grand living after death
In beast and bird and flower, when this cup,
　　Being filled too full of spirit, bursts for breath,
And with the pale leaves of some autumn day
The soul earth's earliest conqueror becomes earth's last great
　　　　prey.

O think of it! We shall inform ourselves
　　Into all sensuous life, the goat-foot Faun,
The Centaur, or the merry bright-eyed Elves
　　That leave their dancing rings to spite the dawn
Upon the meadows, shall not be more near
Than you and I to nature's mysteries, for we shall hear

The thrush's heart beat, and the daisies grow,
  And the wan snowdrop sighing for the sun
On sunless days in winter, we shall know
  By whom the silver gossamer is spun,
Who paints the diapered fritillaries,
On what wide wings from shivering pine to pine the eagle flies.

Ay! had we never loved at all, who knows
  If yonder daffodil had lured the bee
Into its gilded womb, or any rose
  Had hung with crimson lamps its little tree!
Methinks no leaf would ever bud in spring,
But for the lovers' lips that kiss, the poets' lips that sing.

Is the light vanished from our golden sun,
  Or is this dacdal-fashioned earth less fair,
That we are nature's heritors, and one
  With every pulse of life that beats the air?
Rather new suns across the sky shall pass,
New splendour come unto the flower, new glory to the grass.

And we two lovers shall not sit afar,
  Critics of nature, but the joyous sea
Shall be our raiment, and the bearded star
  Shoot arrows at our pleasure! We shall be
Part of the mighty universal whole,
And through all aeons mix and mingle with the Kosmic Soul!

We shall be notes in that great Symphony
  Whose cadence circles through the rhythmic spheres,
And all the live World's throbbing heart shall be
  One with our heart; the stealthy creeping years
Have lost their terrors now, we shall not die,
The Universe itself shall be our Immortality.

# WALTER PATER

## From *Marius the Epicurean* (1885)

### CHAPTER II – WHITE-NIGHTS

[ ... ] The traveller, descending from the slopes of Luna, even as he got his first view of the *Port-of-Venus*, would pause by the way, to read the face, as it were, of so beautiful a dwelling-place, lying away from the white road, at the point where it began to decline somewhat steeply to the marsh-land below. The building of pale red and yellow marble, mellowed by age, which he saw beyond the gates, was indeed but the exquisite fragment of a once large and sumptuous villa. Two centuries of the play of the sea-wind were in the velvet of the mosses which lay along its inaccessible ledges and angles. Here and there the marble plates had slipped from their places, where the delicate weeds had forced their way. The graceful wildness which prevailed in garden and farm gave place to a singular nicety about the actual habitation, and a still more scrupulous sweetness and order reigned within. The old Roman architects seem to have well understood the decorative value of the floor – the real economy there was, in the production of rich interior effect, of a somewhat lavish expenditure upon the surface they trod on. The pavement of the hall had lost something of its evenness; but, though a little rough to the foot, polished and cared for like a piece of silver, looked, as mosaic-work is apt to do, its best in old age. Most noticeable among the ancestral masks, each in its little cedarn chest below the cornice, was that of the wasteful but elegant Marcellus, with the quaint resemblance in its yellow waxen features to Marius, just then so full of animation and country colour. A chamber, curved ingeniously into oval form, which he had added to the mansion, still contained his collection of works of art; above all, that head of Medusa, for which the villa was famous. The spoilers of one of the old Greek towns on the coast had flung away or lost the thing, as it seemed, in some rapid flight across the river below, from the sands of which it was drawn up in a fisherman's net, with the fine golden

136

*laminæ*[1] still clinging here and there to the bronze. It was Marcellus also who had contrived the prospect-tower of two storeys with the white pigeon-house above, so characteristic of the place. The little glazed windows in the uppermost chamber framed each its dainty landscape – the pallid crags of Carrara, like wildly twisted snow-drifts above the purple heath; the distant harbour with its freight of white marble going to sea; the lighthouse temple of *Venus Speciosa* on its dark headland, amid the long-drawn curves of white breakers. Even on summer nights the air there had always a motion in it, and drove the scent of the new-mown hay along all the passages of the house.

Something pensive, spell-bound, and but half real, something cloistral or monastic, as we should say, united to this exquisite order, made the whole place seem to Marius, as it were, *sacellum*,[2] the peculiar sanctuary, of his mother, who, still in real widowhood, provided the deceased Marius the elder with that secondary sort of life which we can give to the dead, in our intensely realised memory of them – the 'subjective immortality,' to use a modern phrase, for which many a Roman epitaph cries out plaintively to widow or sister or daughter, still in the land of the living. Certainly, if any such considerations regarding them do reach the shadowy people, he enjoyed that secondary existence, that warm place still left, in thought at least, beside the living, the desire for which is actually, in various forms, so great a motive with most of us. And Marius the younger, even thus early, came to think of women's tears, of women's hands to lay one to rest, in death as in the sleep of childhood, as a sort of natural want. The soft lines of the white hands and face, set among the many folds of the veil and stole of the Roman widow, busy upon her needlework, or with music sometimes, defined them-selves for him as the typical expression of maternity. Helping her with her white and purple wools, and caring for her musical instruments, he won, as if from the handling of such things, an urbane and feminine refinement, qualifying duly his country-grown habits – the sense of a certain delicate blandness, which he relished, above all, on returning to the 'chapel' of his mother, after long days of open-air exercise, in winter or stormy summer. For poetic souls in old Italy felt, hardly less strongly than the English, the pleasures of winter, of the hearth, with the very dead warm in its generous

---

1 Thin plates of metal.    2 A little sanctuary or chapel.

heat, keeping the young myrtles in flower, though the hail is beating hard without. One important principle, of fruit afterwards in his Roman life, that relish for the country fixed deeply in him; in the winters especially, when the sufferings of the animal world became so palpable even to the least observant. It fixed in him a sympathy for all creatures, for the almost human troubles and sicknesses of the flocks, for instance. It was a feeling which had in it something of religious veneration for life as such – for that mysterious essence which man is powerless to create in even the feeblest degree. One by one, at the desire of his mother, the lad broke down his cherished traps and springes for the hungry wild birds on the salt marsh. A white bird, she told him once, looking at him gravely, a bird which he must carry in his bosom across a crowded public place – his own soul was like that! Would it reach the hands of his good genius on the opposite side, unruffled and unsoiled? And as his mother became to him the very type of maternity in things, its unfailing pity and protectiveness, and maternity itself the central type of all love; – so, that beautiful dwelling-place lent the reality of concrete outline to a peculiar ideal of home, which throughout the rest of his life he seemed, amid many distractions of spirit, to be ever seeking to regain.

And a certain vague fear of evil, constitutional in him, enhanced still further this sentiment of home as a place of tried security. His religion, that old Italian religion, in contrast with the really light-hearted religion of Greece, had its deep undercurrent of gloom, its sad, haunting imageries, not exclusively confined to the walls of Etruscan tombs. The function of the conscience, not always as the prompter of gratitude for benefits received, but oftenest as his accuser before those angry heavenly masters, had a large part in it; and the sense of some unexplored evil, ever dogging his footsteps, made him oddly suspicious of particular places and persons. Though his liking for animals was so strong, yet one fierce day in early summer, as he walked along a narrow road, he had seen the snakes breeding, and ever afterwards avoided that place and its ugly associations, for there was something in the incident which made food distasteful and his sleep uneasy for many days after-wards. The memory of it however had almost passed away, when at the corner of a street in Pisa, he came upon an African showman exhibiting a great serpent: once more, as the reptile writhed, the former painful impression revived: it was like a peep into the lower side of the real world, and again for many days took all sweetness from food and sleep. He wondered at himself indeed, trying to puzzle out the secret of that repugnance, having no particular dread of a snake's bite, like one of his companions, who had put his hand into the mouth of an old garden-god and roused there a sluggish viper. A kind of pity even mingled with his aversion, and he could hardly have killed or injured the animals, which seemed already to suffer by the very circumstance of their life, being what they were. It was something like a fear of the supernatural, or perhaps rather a moral feeling, for the face of a great serpent, with no grace of fur or feathers, so different from quadruped or bird, has a sort of humanity of aspect in its spotted and clouded nakedness. There was a humanity, dusty and sordid and as if far gone in corruption, in the sluggish coil, as it awoke suddenly into one metallic spring of pure enmity against him. Long afterwards, when it happened that at Rome he saw, a second time, a showman with his serpents, he remembered the night which had then followed, thinking, in Saint Augustine's vein, on the real greatness of those little troubles of children, of which older people make light; but with a sudden gratitude also, as he reflected how richly possessed his life had actually been by beautiful aspects and imageries, seeing how greatly what was repugnant to the eye disturbed his peace.

Thus the boyhood of Marius passed; on the whole, more given to contemplation than to action. Less prosperous in fortune than at an earlier day there had been reason to expect, and animating his solitude, as he read eagerly and intelligently, with the traditions of the past, already he lived much in the realm of the imagination, and became betimes, as he was to continue all through life, something of an idealist, constructing the world for himself in great measure from within, by the exercise of meditative power. A vein of subjective philosophy, with the individual for its standard of all things, there would be always in his intellectual scheme of the world and of conduct, with a certain incapacity wholly to accept other men's valuations. And the generation of this peculiar element in his temper he could trace up to the days when his life had been so like the reading of a romance to him. Had the Romans a word for *unworldly*? The beautiful word *umbratilis* perhaps comes nearest to it; and, with that precise sense, might describe the spirit in which he prepared himself for the sacerdotal function hereditary in his family – the sort of mystic enjoyment he had in the abstinence, the strenuous self-control and *ascêsis*, which such preparation involved. Like the young Ion in the beautiful opening of the play of Euripides, who every morning sweeps the temple floor with such a fund of cheerfulness in his service, he was apt to be happy in sacred places, with a susceptibility to their peculiar influences which he never outgrew; so that often in after-times, quite unexpectedly, this feeling would revive in him with undiminished freshness. That first, early, boyish ideal of priesthood, the sense of dedication, survived through all the distractions of the world, and when all thought of such vocation had finally passed from him, as a ministry, in spirit at least, towards a sort of hieratic beauty and order in the conduct of life.

And now what relieved in part this over-tension of soul was the lad's pleasure in the country and the open air; above all, the ramble to the coast, over the marsh with its dwarf roses and wild lavender, and delightful signs, one after another – the abandoned boat, the ruined flood-gates, the flock of wild birds – that one was approaching the sea; the long summer-day of idleness among its vague scents and sounds. And it was characteristic of him that he relished especially the grave, subdued, northern notes in all that – the charm of the French or English notes, as we might term them – in the luxuriant Italian landscape.

CHAPTER IX – NEW CYRENAICISM

Such were the practical conclusions drawn for himself by Marius, when somewhat later he had outgrown the mastery of others, from the principle that 'all is vanity.' If he could but count upon the present, if a life brief at best could not certainly be shown to conduct one anywhere beyond itself, if men's highest curiosity was indeed so persistently baffled – then, with the Cyrenaics of all ages, he would at least fill up the measure of that present with vivid sensations, and such intellectual apprehensions, as, in strength and directness and their immediately realised values at the bar of an actual experience, are most like sensations. So some have spoken in every age; for, like all theories which really express a strong natural tendency of the human mind or even one of its characteristic modes of weakness, this vein of reflection is a constant tradition in philosophy. Every age of European thought has had its Cyrenaics or Epicureans, under many disguises: even under the hood of the monk. But – *Let us eat and drink, for to-morrow we die!* – is a proposal, the real import of which differs immensely, according to the natural taste, and the acquired judgment, of the guests who sit at the table. It may express nothing better than the instinct of Dante's Ciacco, the accomplished glutton, in the mud of the *Inferno*; or, since on no hypothesis does man 'live by bread alone,' may come to be identical with – 'My meat is to do what is just and kind;' while the the soul, which can make no sincere claim to have apprehended anything beyond the veil of immediate experience, yet never loses a sense of happiness in conforming to the highest moral ideal it can clearly define for itself; and actually, though but with so faint hope, does the 'Father's business.'

In that age of Marcus Aurelius, so completely disabused of the metaphysical ambition to pass beyond 'the flaming ramparts of the world,' but, on the other hand, possessed of so vast an accumulation of intellectual treasure, with so wide a view before it over all varieties of what is powerful or attractive in man and his works, the thoughts of Marius did but follow the line taken by the majority of educated persons, though to a different issue. Pitched to a really high and serious key, the precept – *Be perfect in regard to what is here and now*: the precept of 'culture,' as it is called, or of a complete education – might at least save him from the vulgarity and heaviness of a generation, certainly of no general fineness of temper, though with a material well-being abundant enough. Conceded that what is secure in our existence is but the sharp apex of the present moment between two hypothetical eternities, and all that is real in our experience but a series of fleeting impressions: – so Marius continued the sceptical argument he had condensed, as the matter to hold by, from his various philosophical reading: – given, that we are never to get beyond the walls of the closely shut cell of one's own personality; that the ideas we are somehow impelled to form of an outer world, and of other minds akin to our own, are, it may be, but a day-dream, and the thought of any world beyond, a day-dream perhaps idler still: then, he, at least, in whom those fleeting impressions – faces, voices, material sunshine – were very real and imperious, might well set himself to the consideration, how such actual moments as they passed might be made to yield their utmost, by the most dexterous training of capacity. Amid abstract metaphysical doubts, as to what might lie one step only beyond that experience, reinforcing the deep original materialism or earthliness of human nature itself, bound so intimately to the sensuous world, let him at least make the most of what was 'here and now.' In the actual dimness of ways from means to ends – ends in themselves desirable, yet for the most part distant and for him, certainly, below the visible horizon – he would at all events be sure that the means, to use the well-worn terminology, should have something of finality or perfection about them, and themselves partake, in a measure, of the more excellent nature of ends – that the means should justify the end.

With this view he would demand culture, παιδεία,[1] as the Cyrenaics said, or, in other words, a wide, a complete, education – an education partly negative, as ascertaining the true limits of man's capacities, but for the most part positive, and directed especially to the expansion and refinement of the power of reception; of those powers, above all, which are immediately relative to fleeting phenomena, the powers of emotion and sense. In such an education, an 'aesthetic' education, as it might now be termed, and certainly occupied very largely with those aspects of things which affect us pleasurably through sensation, art, of course, including all the finer sorts of literature, would have a great part to play. The study of music, in that wider Platonic sense, according to which, *music* comprehends all those matters over which the Muses of Greek mythology preside, would conduct one to an exquisite appreciation of all the finer traits of nature and of man. Nay! the products of the imagination must themselves be held to present the most perfect forms of life – spirit and matter alike under their purest and most perfect conditions – the most strictly appropriate objects of that impassioned contemplation, which, in the world of intellectual discipline, as in the highest forms of morality and religion, must be held to be the essential function of the 'perfect.' Such manner of life might come even to seem a kind of religion – an inward, visionary, mystic piety, or religion, by virtue of its effort to live days 'lovely and pleasant' in themselves, here and now, and with an all-sufficiency of well-being in the immediate sense of the object contemplated, independently of any faith, or hope that might be entertained as to their ulterior tendency. In this way, the true aesthetic culture would be realisable as a new form of the contemplative life, founding its claim on the intrinsic 'blessedness' of 'vision' –

---

[1] Education or training.

the vision of perfect men and things. One's human nature, indeed, would fain reckon on an assured and endless future, pleasing itself with the dream of a final home, to be attained at some still remote date, yet with a conscious, delightful home-coming at last, as depicted in many an old poetic Elysium. On the other hand, the world of perfected sensation, intelligence, emotion, is so close to us, and so attractive, that the most visionary of spirits must needs represent the world unseen in colours, and under a form really borrowed from it. Let me be sure then – might he not plausibly say? – that I miss no detail of this life of realised consciousness in the present! Here at least is a vision, a theory, θεωρία,[1] which reposes on no basis of unverified hypothesis, which makes no call upon a future after all somewhat problematic; as it would be unaffected by any discovery of an Empedocles (improving on the old story of Prometheus) as to what had really been the origin, and course of development of man's actually attained faculties and that seemingly divine particle of reason or spirit in him. Such a doctrine, at more leisurable moments, would of course have its precepts to deliver on the embellishment, generally, of what is near at hand, on the adornment of life, till, in a not impracticable rule of conduct, one's existence, from day to day, came to be like a well-executed piece of music; that 'perpetual motion' in things (so Marius figured the matter to himself, under the old Greek imageries) according itself to a kind of cadence or harmony.

It was intelligible that this 'aesthetic' philosophy might find itself (theoretically, at least, and by way of a curious question in casuistry, legitimate from its own point of view) weighing the claims of that eager, concentrated, impassioned realisation of experience, against those of the received morality. Conceiving its own function in a somewhat desperate temper, and becoming, as every high-strung form of sentiment, as the religious sentiment itself, may become, somewhat antinomian, when, in its effort towards the order of experiences it prefers, it is confronted with the traditional and popular morality, at points where that morality may look very like a convention, or a mere stage-property of the world, it would be found, from time to time, breaking beyond the limits of the actual moral order; perhaps not without some pleasurable excitement in so bold a venture.

1 Theoria.

With the possibility of some such hazard as this, in thought or even in practice – that it might be, though refining, or tonic even, in the case of those strong and in health, yet, as Pascal says of the kindly and temperate wisdom of Montaigne, 'pernicious for those who have any natural tendency to impiety or vice,' the line of reflection traced out above, was fairly chargeable. – Not, however, with 'hedonism' and its supposed consequences. The blood, the heart, of Marius were still pure. He knew that his carefully considered theory of practice braced him, with the effect of a moral principle duly recurring to mind every morning, towards the work of a student, for which he might seem intended. Yet there were some among his acquaintance who jumped to the conclusion that, with the 'Epicurean stye,' he was making pleasure – pleasure, as they so poorly conceived it – the sole motive of life; and they precluded any exacter estimate of the situation by covering it with a high-sounding general term, through the vagueness of which they were enabled to see the severe and laborious youth in the vulgar company of Lais. Words like 'hedonism' – terms of large and vague comprehension – above all when used for a purpose avowedly controversial, have ever been the worst examples of what are called 'question-begging terms;' and in that late age in which Marius lived, amid the dust of so many centuries of philosophical debate, the air was full of them. Yet those who used that reproachful Greek term for the philosophy of pleasure, were hardly more likely than the old Greeks themselves (on whom regarding this very subject of the theory of pleasure, their masters in the art of thinking had so emphatically to impress the necessity of 'making distinctions') to come to any very delicately correct ethical conclusions by a reasoning, which began with a general term, comprehensive enough to cover pleasures so different in quality, in their causes and effects, as the pleasures of wine and love, of art and science, of religious enthusiasm and political enterprise, and of that taste or curiosity which satisfied itself with long days of serious study. Yet, in truth, each of those pleasurable modes of activity, may, in its turn, fairly become the ideal of the 'hedonistic' doctrine. Really, to the phase of reflection through which Marius was then passing, the charge of 'hedonism,' whatever its true weight might be, was not properly applicable at all. Not pleasure, but fulness of life, and 'insight' as conducting to that fulness – energy, variety, and choice of experience, including noble pain and sorrow even, loves such as those in

144

the exquisite old story of Apuleius,[1] sincere and strenuous forms of the moral life, such as Seneca and Epictetus[2] – whatever form of human life, in short, might be heroic, impassioned, ideal: from these the 'new Cyrenaicism' of Marius took its criterion of values. It was a theory, indeed, which might properly be regarded as in great degree coincident with the main principle of the Stoics themselves, and an older version of the precept 'Whatsoever thy hand findeth to do, do it with thy might' – a doctrine so widely acceptable among the nobler spirits of that time. And, as with that, its mistaken tendency would lie in the direction of a kind of idolatry of mere life, or natural gift, or strength – *l'idolâtrie des talents*.[3]

To understand the various forms of ancient art and thought, the various forms of actual human feeling (the only new thing, in a world almost too opulent in what was old) to satisfy, with a kind of scrupulous equity, the claims of these concrete and actual objects on his sympathy, his intelligence, his senses – to 'pluck out the heart of their mystery,' and in turn become the interpreter of them to others: this had now defined itself for Marius as a very narrowly practical design: it determined his choice of a vocation to live by. It was the era of the *rhetoricians*, or *sophists*, as they were sometimes called; of men who came in some instances to great fame and fortune, by way of a literary cultivation of 'science.' That science, it has been often said, must have been wholly an affair of words. But in a world, confessedly so opulent in what was old, the work, even of genius, must necessarily consist very much in criticism; and, in the case of the more excellent specimens of his class, the rhetorician was, after all, the eloquent and effective interpreter, for the delighted ears of others, of what understanding he himself had come by, in years of travel and study, of the beautiful house of art and thought which was the inheritance of the age. The emperor Marcus Aurelius, to whose service Marius had now been called, was himself, more or less openly, a 'lecturer'. That late world, amid many curiously vivid modern traits, had this spectacle, so familiar to ourselves, of the public lecturer or essayist; in some cases adding to his other gifts that of the Christian preacher, who knows how to touch people's sensibilities on behalf of the suffering. To follow in

1 i.e. *The Golden Ass.*      2 Roman and Greek Stoic philosophers.
3 Literally, 'the idolatry of talents'.

the way of these successes, was the natural instinct of youthful ambition; and it was with no vulgar egotism that Marius, at the age of nineteen, determined, like many another young man of parts, to enter as a student of rhetoric at Rome.

Though the manner of his work was changed formally from poetry to prose, he remained, and must always be, of the poetic temper: by which, I mean, among other things, that quite independ-entry of the general habit of that pensive age he lived much, and as it were by system, in reminiscence. Amid his eager grasping at the sensation, the consciousness, of the present, he had come to see that, after all, the main point of economy in the conduct of the present, was the question: – How will it look to me, at what shall I value it, this day next year? – that in any given day or month one's main concern was its impression for the memory. A strange trick memory sometimes played him; for, with no natural gradation, what was of last month, or of yesterday, of to-day even, would seem as far off, as entirely detached from him, as things of ten years ago. Detached from him, yet very real, there lay certain spaces of his life, in delicate perspective, under a favourable light; and, somehow, all the less fortunate detail and circumstance had parted from them. Such hours were oftenest those in which he had been helped by work of others to the pleasurable apprehension of art, of nature, or of life. 'Not what I do, but what I am, under the power of this vision' – he would say to himself – 'is what were indeed pleasing to the gods!'

And yet, with a kind of inconsistency in one who had taken for his philosophic ideal the μονόχρονος ἡδονή[1] of Aristippus – the pleasure of the ideal present, of the mystic *now* – there would come, together with that precipitate sinking of things into the past, a desire, after all, to retain 'what was so transitive.' Could he but arrest, for others also, certain clauses of experience, as the imaginative memory presented them to himself! In those grand, hot summers, he would have imprisoned the very perfume of the flowers. To create, to live, perhaps, a little while beyond the allotted hours, if it were but in a fragment of perfect expression: – it was thus his longing defined itself for something to hold by amid the 'perpetual flux.' With men of his vocation, people were apt to say, words were things. Well! with him, words should be indeed things, – the word, the phrase,

---

1 Undivided pleasure.

valuable in exact proportion to the transparency with which it conveyed to others the apprehension, the emotion, the mood, so vividly real within himself. *Verbaque provisam rem non invita sequentur*:[1] Virile apprehension of the true nature of things, of the true nature of one's own impression, first of all! – words would follow that naturally, a true understanding of one's self being ever the first condition of genuine style. Language delicate and measured, the delicate Attic phrase, for instance, in which the eminent Aristeides could speak, was then a power to which people's hearts, and sometimes even their purses, readily responded. And there were many points, as Marius thought, on which the heart of that age greatly needed to be touched. He hardly knew how strong that old religious sense of responsibility, the conscience, as we call it, still was within him – a body of inward impressions, as real as those so highly valued outward ones – to offend against which, brought with it a strange feeling of disloyalty, as to a person. And the determination, adhered to with no misgiving, to add nothing, not so much as a transient sigh, to the great total of men's unhappiness, in his way through the world: – that too was something to rest on, in the drift of mere 'appearances.'

All this would involve a life of industry, of industrious study, only possible through healthy rule, keeping clear the eye alike of body and soul. For the male element, the logical conscience asserted itself now, with opening manhood – asserted itself, even in his literary style, by a certain firmness of outline, that touch of the worker in metal, amid its richness. Already he blamed instinctively alike in his work and in himself, as youth so seldom does, all that had not passed a long and liberal process of erasure. The happy phrase or sentence was really modelled upon a cleanly finished structure of scrupulous thought. The suggestive force of the one master of his development, who had battled so hard with imaginative prose; the utterance, the golden utterance, of the other, so content with its living power of persuasion that he had never written at all, – in the commixture of these two qualities he set up his literary ideal, and this rare blending of grace with an intellectual rigour or astringency, was the secret of a singular expressiveness in it.

He acquired at this time a certain bookish air, the somewhat

---

1 Literally, 'words will not unwillingly follow your well-considered subject'. Horace, *Ars Poetica*, 311.

sombre habitude of the avowed scholar, which though it never interfered with the perfect tone, 'fresh and serenely disposed,' of the Roman gentleman, yet qualified it as by an interesting oblique trait, and frightened away some of his equals in age and rank. The sober discretion of his thoughts, his sustained habit of meditation, the sense of those negative conclusions enabling him to concentrate himself, with an absorption so entire, upon what is immediately *here* and *now*, gave him a peculiar manner of intellectual confidence, as of one who had indeed been initiated into a great secret. – Though with an air so disengaged, he seemed to be living so intently in the visible world! And now, in revolt against that pre-occupation with other persons, which had so often perturbed his spirit, his wistful speculations as to what the real, the greater, experience might be, determined in him, not as the longing for love – to be with Cynthia, or Aspasia – but as a thirst for existence in exquisite places. The veil that was to be lifted for him lay over the works of the old masters of art, in places where nature also had used her mastery. And it was just at this moment that a summons to Rome reached him.

# WALTER PATER

## 'Denys l'Auxerrois' from *Imaginary Portraits* (1887)

Almost every people, as we know, has had its legend of a 'golden age' and of its return – legends which will hardly be forgotten, however prosaic the world may become, while man himself remains the aspiring, never quite contented being he is. And yet in truth, since we are no longer children, we might well question the advantage of the return to us of a condition of life in which, by the nature of the case, the values of things would, so to speak, lie wholly on their surfaces, unless we could regain also the childish consciousness, or rather unconsciousness, in ourselves, to take all that adroitly and with the appropriate lightness of heart. The dream, however, has been left for the most part in the usual vagueness of dreams: in their waking hours people have been too busy to furnish it forth with details. What follows is a quaint legend, with detail enough, of such a return of a golden or poetically-gilded age (a denizen of old Greece itself actually finding his way back again among men) as it happened in an ancient town of medieval France.

Of the French town, properly so called, in which the products of successive ages, not without lively touches of the present, are blended together harmoniously, with a beauty *specific* – a beauty cisalpine and northern, yet at the same time quite distinct from the massive German picturesque of Ulm, or Freiburg, or Augsburg, and of which Turner has found the ideal in certain of his studies of the rivers of France, a perfectly happy conjunction of river and town being of the essence of its physiognomy – the town of Auxerre is perhaps the most complete realisation to be found by the actual wanderer. Certainly, for picturesque expression it is the most memorable of a distinguished group of three in these parts, – Auxerre, Sens, Troyes, – each gathered, as if with deliberate aim at such effect, about the central mass of a huge grey cathedral.

Around Troyes the natural picturesque is to be sought only in the rich, almost coarse, summer colouring of the Champagne country, of which the very tiles, the plaster and brickwork of its tiny villages and great, straggling, village-like farms have caught the warmth. The cathedral, visible far and wide over the fields seemingly of loose wild-flowers, itself a rich mixture of all the varieties of the Pointed style down to the latest *Flamboyant*,[1] may be noticed among the greater French churches for breadth of proportions internally, and is famous for its almost unrivalled treasure of stained glass, chiefly of a florid, elaborate, later type, with much highly conscious artistic contrivance in design as well as in colour. In one of the richest of its windows, for instance, certain lines of pearly white run hither and thither, with delightful distant effect, upon ruby and dark blue. Approaching nearer you find it to be a Travellers' window, and those odd lines of white the long walking-staves in the hands of Abraham, Raphael, the Magi, and the other saintly patrons of journeys. The appropriate provincial character of the *bourgeoisie* of Champagne is still to be seen, it would appear, among the citizens of Troyes. Its streets, for the most part in timber and pargeting, present more than one unaltered specimen of the ancient *hôtel* or town-house, with forecourt and garden in the rear;

---

1 An architectural term: 'characterised by waved lines of contrary flexure in flame-like forms' (*OED*).

and its more devout citizens would seem even in their church-building to have sought chiefly to please the eyes of those occupied with mundane affairs and out of doors, for they have finished, with abundant outlay, only the vast, useless portals of their parish churches, of surprising height and lightness, in a kind of wildly elegant Gothic-on-stilts, giving to the streets of Troyes a peculiar air of the grotesque, as if in some quaint nightmare of the Middle Age.

At Sens, thirty miles away to the west, a place of far graver aspect, the name of Jean Cousin denotes a more chastened temper, even in these sumptuous decorations. Here all is cool and composed, with an almost English austerity. The first growth of the Pointed style in England – the hard 'early English' of Canterbury – is indeed the creation of William, a master reared in the architectural school of Sens; and the severity of his taste might seem to have acted as a restraining power on all the subsequent changes of manner in this place – changes in themselves for the most part towards luxuriance. In harmony with the atmosphere of its great church is the cleanly quiet of the town, kept fresh by little channels of clear water circulating through its streets, derivatives of the rapid Vanne which falls just below into the Yonne. The Yonne, bending gracefully, link after link, through a never-ending rustle of poplar trees, beneath lowly vine-clad hills, with relics of delicate woodland here and there, sometimes close at hand, sometimes leaving an interval of broad meadow, has all the lightsome characteristics of French river-side scenery on a smaller scale than usual, and might pass for the child's fancy of a river, like the rivers of the old miniature-painters, blue, and full to a fair green margin. One notices along its course a greater proportion than elsewhere of still untouched old seignorial residences, larger or smaller. The range of old gibbous towns along its banks, expanding their gay quays upon the water-side, have a common character – Joigny, Villeneuve, Saint Julien-du-Sault – yet tempt us to tarry at each and examine its relics, old glass and the like, of the Renaissance or the Middle Age, for the acquisition of real though minor lessons on the various arts which have left themselves a central monument at Auxerre. – Auxerre! A slight ascent in the winding road! and you have before you the prettiest town in France – the broad framework of vineyard sloping upwards gently to the horizon, with distant white cottages inviting one to walk: the quiet curve of river below, with all the river-side details: the three great purple-tiled masses of Saint Germain, Saint Pierre, and the cathedral of Saint Étienne, rising out of the crowded houses with more than the usual abruptness and irregularity of French building. Here, that rare artist, the susceptible painter of architecture, if he understands the value alike of line and mass of broad masses and delicate lines, has 'a subject made to his hand.'

A veritable country of the vine, it presents nevertheless an expression peaceful rather than radiant. Perfect type of that happy mean between northern earnestness and the luxury of the south, for which we prize midland France, its physiognomy is not quite happy – attractive in part for its melancholy. Its most characteristic atmosphere is to be seen when the tide of light and distant cloud is travelling quickly over it, when rain is not far off, and every touch of art or of time on its old building is defined in clear grey. A fine summer ripens its grapes into a valuable wine; but in spite of that it seems always longing for a larger and more continuous allowance of the sunshine which is so much to its taste. You might fancy something querulous or plaintive in that rustling movement of the vine-leaves, as blue-frocked Jacques Bonhomme finishes his day's labour among them.

To beguile one such afternoon when the rain set in early and walking was impossible, I found my way to the shop of an old dealer in *bric-à-brac*. It was not a monotonous display, after the manner of the Parisian dealer, of a stock-in-trade the like of which one has seen many times over, but a discriminate collection of real curiosities. One seemed to recognise a provincial school of taste in various relics of the housekeeping of the last century, with many a gem of earlier times from the old churches and religious houses of the neighbourhood. Among them was a large and brilliant fragment of stained glass which might have come from the cathedral itself. Of the very finest quality in colour and design, it presented a figure not exactly conformable to any recognised ecclesiastical type; and it was clearly part of a series. On my eager inquiry for the remainder, the old man replied that no more of it was known, but added that the priest of a neighbouring village was the possessor of an entire set of tapestries, apparently intended for suspension in church, and designed to portray the whole subject of which the figure in the stained glass was a portion.

Next afternoon accordingly I repaired to the priest's house, in reality a little Gothic building, part perhaps of an ancient manor-house close to the village church. In the front garden, flower-garden

and *potager*[1] in one, the bees were busy among the autumn growths –
many-coloured asters, bignonias, scarlet-beans, and the old-
fashioned parsonage flowers. The courteous owner readily showed
me his tapestries, some of which hung on the walls of his parlour
and staircase by way of a background for the display of the other
curiosities of which he was a collector. Certainly, those tapestries
and the stained glass dealt with the same theme. In both were the
same musical instruments – pipes, cymbals, long reed-like trumpets.
The story, indeed, included the building of an organ, just such an
instrument, only on a larger scale, as was standing in the old
priest's library, though almost soundless now, whereas in certain
of the woven pictures the hearers appear as if transported, some of
them shouting rapturously to the organ music. A sort of mad
vehemence prevails, indeed, throughout the delicate bewilderments
of the whole series – giddy dances, wild animals leaping, above all
perpetual wreathings of the vine, connecting, like some mazy
arabesque, the various presentations of one oft-repeated figure,
translated here out of the clear-coloured glass into the sadder,
somewhat opaque and earthen hues of the silken threads. The
figure was that of the organ-builder himself, a flaxen and flowery
creature, sometimes wellnigh naked among the vine-leaves, sometimes muffled in skins against the cold, sometimes in the dress of a
monk, but always with a strong impress of real character and
incident from the veritable streets of Auxerre. What is it? Certainly,
notwithstanding its grace, and wealth of graceful accessories, a
suffering, tortured figure. With all the regular beauty of a pagan
god, he has suffered after a manner of which we must suppose
pagan gods incapable. It was as if one of those fair, triumphant
beings had cast in his lot with the creatures of an age later than
his own, people of larger spiritual capacity and assuredly of a
larger capacity for melancholy. With this fancy in my mind, by
the help of certain notes, which lay in the priest's curious library,
upon the history of the works at the cathedral during the period
of its finishing, and in repeated examination of the old tapestried
designs, the story shaped itself at last.

Towards the middle of the thirteenth century the cathedral of
Saint Étienne was complete in its main outlines: what remained
was the building of the great tower, and all that various labour of

1 Kitchen-garden.

final decoration which it would take more than one generation to accomplish. Certain circumstances, however, not wholly explained, led to a somewhat rapid finishing, as it were out of hand, yet with a marvellous fulness at once and grace. Of the result much has perished, or been transferred elsewhere; a portion is still visible in sumptuous relics of stained windows, and, above all, in the reliefs which adorn the western portals, very delicately carved in a fine, firm stone from Tonnerre, of which time has only browned the surface, and which, for early mastery in art, may be compared with the contemporary work of Italy. They come nearer than the art of that age was used to do to the expression of life; with a feeling for reality, in no ignoble form, caught, it might seem, from the ardent and full-veined existence then current in these actual streets and houses. Just then Auxerre had its turn in that political movement which broke out sympathetically, first in one, then in another of the towns of France, turning their narrow, feudal institutions into a free, communistic life – a movement of which those great centres of popular devotion, the French cathedrals, are in many instances the monument. Closely connected always with the assertion of individual freedom, alike in mind and manners, at Auxerre this political stir was associated also, as cause or effect, with the figure and character of a particular personage, long remembered. He was the very genius, it would appear, of that new, free, generous manner in art, active and potent as a living creature.

As the most skilful of the band of carvers worked there one day, with a labour he could never quite make equal to the vision within him, a finely-sculptured Greek coffin of stone, which had been made to serve for some later Roman funeral, was unearthed by the masons. Here, it might seem, the thing was indeed done, and art achieved, as far as regards those final graces, and harmonies of execution, which were precisely what lay beyond the hand of the medieval workman, who for his part had largely at command a seriousness of conception lacking in the old Greek. Within the coffin lay an object of a fresh and brilliant clearness among the ashes of the dead – a flask of lively green glass, like a great emerald. It might have been 'the wondrous vessel of the Grail.' Only, this object seemed to bring back no ineffable purity, but rather the riotous and earthy heat of old paganism itself. Coated within, and, as some were persuaded, still redolent with the tawny sediment of the Roman wine it had held so long ago, it was set aside for use at the supper which was shortly to celebrate the completion of the masons' work. Amid much talk of the great age of gold, and some random expressions of hope that it might return again, fine old wine of Auxerre was sipped in small glasses from the precious flask as supper ended. And, whether or not the opening of the buried vessel had anything to do with it, from that time a sort of golden age seemed indeed to be reigning there for a while, and the triumphant completion of the great church was contemporary with a series of remarkable wine seasons. The vintage of those years was long remembered. Fine and abundant wine was to be found stored up even in poor men's cottages; while a new beauty, a gaiety, was abroad, as all the conjoint arts branched out exuberantly in a reign of quiet, delighted labour, at the prompting, as it seemed, of the singular being who came suddenly and oddly to Auxerre to be the centre of so pleasant a period, though in truth he made but a sad ending.

A peculiar usage long perpetuated itself at Auxerre. On Easter Day the canons, in the very centre of the great church, played solemnly at ball. Vespers being sung, instead of conducting the bishop to his palace, they proceeded in order into the nave, the people standing in two long rows to watch. Girding up their skirts a little way, the whole body of clerics awaited their turn in silence, while the captain of the singing-boys cast the ball into the air, as high as he might, along the vaulted roof of the central aisle to be caught by any boy who could, and tossed again with hand or foot till it passed on to the portly chanters, the chaplains, the canons themselves, who finally played out the game with all the decorum of an ecclesiastical ceremony. It was just then, just as the canons took the ball to themselves so gravely, that Denys – Denys l'Auxerrois, as he was afterwards called – appeared for the first time. Leaping in among the timid children, he made the thing really a game. The boys played like boys, the men almost like madmen, and all with a delightful glee which became contagious, first in the clerical body, and then among the spectators. The aged Dean of the Chapter, Protonotary of his Holiness, held up his purple skirt a little higher, and stepping from the ranks with an amazing levity, as if suddenly relieved of his burden of eighty years, tossed the ball with his foot to the venerable capitular Homilist, equal to the occasion. And then, unable to stand inactive any longer, the laity carried on the game among themselves, with shouts of not too boisterous amusement; the sport continuing till the flight of the ball could no longer be traced along the dusky aisles.

Though the home of his childhood was but a humble one – one of those little cliff-houses cut out in the low chalky hillside, such as are still to be found with inhabitants in certain districts of France – there were some who connected his birth with the story of a beautiful country girl, who, about eighteen years before, had been taken from her own people, not unwillingly, for the pleasure of the Count of Auxerre. She had wished indeed to see the great lord, who had sought her privately, in the glory of his own house; but, terrified by the strange splendours of her new abode and manner of life, and the anger of the true wife, she had fled suddenly from the place during the confusion of a violent storm, and in her flight given birth prematurely to a child. The child, a singularly fair one, was found alive, but the mother dead, by lightning-stroke as it seemed, not far from her lord's chamber-door, under the shelter of a ruined ivy-clad tower. Denys himself certainly was a joyous lad enough. At the cliff-side cottage, nestling actually beneath the vineyards, he came to be an unrivalled gardener, and, grown to manhood, brought his produce to market, keeping a stall in the great cathedral square for the sale of melons and pomegranates, all manner of seeds and flowers (*omnia speciosa camporum*),[1] honey also, wax tapers, sweetmeats hot from the frying-pan, rough home-made pots and pans from the little pottery in the wood, loaves baked by the aged woman in whose house he lived. On that Easter Day he had entered the great church for the first time, for the purpose of seeing the game.

And from the very first, the women who saw him at his business, or watering his plants in the cool of the evening, idled for him. The men who noticed the crowd of women at his stall, and how even fresh young girls from the country, seeing him for the first time, always loitered there, suspected – who could tell what kind of powers? hidden under the white veil of that youthful form; and pausing to ponder the matter, found themselves also fallen into the snare. The sight of him made old people feel young again. Even the sage monk Hermes, devoted to study and experiment, was unable to keep the fruit-seller out of his mind, and would fain have discovered the secret of his charm, partly for the friendly purpose

1 All the beautiful things of the fields.

of explaining to the lad himself his perhaps more than natural gifts with a view to their profitable cultivation.

It was a period, as older men took note, of young men and their influence. They took fire, no one could quite explain how, as if at his presence, and asserted a wonderful amount of volition, of insolence, yet as if with the consent of their elders, who would themselves sometimes lose their balance, a little comically. That revolution in the temper and manner of individuals concurred with the movement then on foot at Auxerre, as in other French towns, for the liberation of the *commune* from its old feudal superiors. Denys they called *Frank*, among many other nicknames. Young lords prided themselves on saying that labour should have its ease, and were almost prepared to take freedom, plebeian freedom (of course duly decorated, at least with wild-flowers) for a bride. For in truth Denys at his stall was turning the grave, slow movement of politic heads into a wild social license, which for a while made life like a stage-play. He first led those long processions, through which by and by 'the little people,' the discontented, the despairing, would utter their minds. One man engaged with another in talk in the market-place; a new influence came forth at the contact; another and then another adhered; at last a new spirit was abroad everywhere. The hot nights were noisy with swarming troops of dishevelled women and youths with red-stained limbs and faces, carrying their lighted torches over the vine-clad hills, or rushing down the streets, to the horror of timid watchers, towards the cool spaces by the river. A shrill music, a laughter at all things, was everywhere. And the new spirit repaired even to church to take part in the novel offices of the Feast of Fools. Heads flung back in ecstasy – the morning sleep among the vines, when the fatigue of the night was over – dew-drenched garments – the serf lying at his ease at last: the artists, then so numerous at the place, caught what they could, something, at least, of the richness, the flexibility of the visible aspects of life, from all this. With them the life of seeming idleness, to which Denys was conducting the youth of Auxerre so pleasantly, counted but as the cultivation, for their due service to man, of delightful natural things. And the powers of nature concurred. It seemed there would be winter no more. The planet Mars drew nearer to the earth than usual, hanging in the low sky like a fiery red lamp. A massive but wellnigh lifeless vine on the wall of the cloister, allowed to remain there only as a curiosity on account of its immense age, in that *great* season, as it was long after called, clothed itself with fruit once more. The culture of the grape greatly increased. The sunlight fell for the first time on many a spot of deep woodland cleared for vine-growing; though Denys, a lover of trees, was careful to leave a stately specimen of forest growth here and there.

When his troubles came, one characteristic that had seemed most amiable in his prosperity was turned against him – a fondness for oddly grown or even misshapen, yet potentially happy, children; for odd animals also: he sympathised with them all, was skilful in healing their maladies, saved the hare in the chase, and sold his mantle to redeem a lamb from the butcher. He taught the people not to be afraid of the strange, ugly creatures which the light of the moving torches drew from their hiding-places, nor think it a bad omen that they approached. He tamed a veritable wolf to keep him company like a dog. It was the first of many ambiguous circumstances about him, from which, in the minds of an increasing number of people, a deep suspicion and hatred began to define itself. The rich *bestiary*, then compiling in the library of the great church, became, through his assistance, nothing less than a garden of Eden – the garden of Eden grown wild. The owl alone he abhorred. A little later, almost as if in revenge, alone of all animals it clung to him, haunting him persistently among the dusky stone towers, when grown gentler than ever he dared not kill it. He moved unhurt in the famous *ménagerie* of the castle, of which the common people were so much afraid, and let out the lions, themselves timid prisoners enough, through the streets during the fair. The incident suggested to the somewhat barren pen-men of the day a 'morality' adapted from the old pagan books – a stage-play in which the God of Wine should return in triumph from the East. In the cathedral square the pageant was presented, amid an intolerable noise of every kind of pipe-music, with Denys in the chief part, upon a gaily-painted chariot, in soft silken raiment, and, for headdress, a strange elephant-scalp with gilded tusks.

And that unrivalled fairness and freshness of aspect: – how did he alone preserve it untouched, through the wind and heat? In truth, it was not by magic, as some said, but by a natural simplicity in his living. When that dark season of his troubles arrived he was heard begging querulously one wintry night, 'Give me wine, meat; dark wine and brown meat!' – come back to the rude door of his old

157

home in the cliff-side. Till that time the great vine-dresser himself drank only water; he had lived on spring-water and fruit. A lover of fertility in all its forms, in what did but suggest it, he was curious and penetrative concerning the habits of water, and had the secret of the divining-rod. Long before it came he could detect the scent of rain from afar, and would climb with delight to the great scaffolding on the unfinished tower to watch its coming over the thirsty vine-land, till it rattled on the great tiled roof of the church below; and then, throwing off his mantle, allow it to bathe his limbs freely, clinging firmly against the tempestuous wind among the carved imageries of dark stone.

It was on his sudden return after a long journey (one of many inexplicable disappearances), coming back changed somewhat, that he ate flesh for the first time, tearing the hot, red morsels with his delicate fingers in a kind of wild greed. He had fled to the south from the first forbidding days of a hard winter which came at last. At the great seaport of Marseilles he had trafficked with sailors from all parts of the world, from Arabia and India, and bought their wares, exposed now for sale, to the wonder of all, at the Easter fair – richer wines and incense than had been known in Auxerre, seeds of marvellous new flowers, creatures wild and tame, new pottery painted in raw gaudy tints, the skins of animals, meats fried with unheard-of condiments. His stall formed a strange, unwonted patch of colour, found suddenly displayed in the hot morning.

The artists were more delighted than ever, and frequented his company in the little manorial habitation, deserted long since by its owners and haunted, so that the eyes of many looked evil upon it, where he had taken up his abode, attracted, in the first instance, by its rich though neglected garden, a tangle of every kind of creeping, vine-like plant. Here, surrounded in abundance by the pleasant materials of his trade, the vine-dresser as it were turned pedant and kept school for the various artists, who learned here an art supplementary to their own, – that gay magic, namely (art or trick) of his existence, till they found themselves grown into a kind of aristocracy, like veritable *gens fleur-de-lisés*, as they worked together for the decoration of the great church and a hundred other places beside. And yet a darkness had grown upon him. The kind creature had lost something of his gentleness. Strange motiveless misdeeds had happened; and, at a loss for other causes, not the envious only would fain have traced the blame to Denys. He was making the

158

younger world mad. Would he make himself Count of Auxerre?
The lady Ariane, deserted by her former lover, had looked kindly
upon him; was ready to make him son-in-law to the old count her
father, old and not long for this world. The wise monk Hermes
bethought him of certain old readings in which the Wine-god,
whose part Denys had played so well, had his contrast, his dark or
antipathetic side; was like a double creature, of two natures,
difficult or impossible to harmonise. And in truth the much-prized
wine of Auxerre has itself but a fugitive charm, being apt to sicken
and turn gross long before the bottle is empty, however carefully
sealed; as it goes indeed, at its best, by hard names, among those
who grow it, such as *Chainette* and *Migraine*.

A kind of degeneration, of coarseness – the coarseness of satiety,
and shapeless, battered-out appetite – with an almost savage taste
for carnivorous diet, had come over the company. A rumour went
abroad of certain women who had drowned, in mere wantonness,
their newborn babes. A girl with child was found hanged by her
own act in a dark cellar. Ah! if Denys also had not felt himself mad!
But when the guilt of a murder, committed with a great vine-axe
far out among the vineyards, was attributed vaguely to him, he
could but wonder whether it had been indeed thus, and the shadow
of a fancied crime abode with him. People turned against their
favourite, whose former charms must now be counted only as the
fascinations of witchcraft. It was as if the wine poured out for them
had soured in the cup. The golden age had indeed come back for
a while: – golden was it, or gilded only, after all? and they were
too sick, or at least too serious, to carry through their parts in it.
The monk Hermes was whimsically reminded of that *after-thought*
in pagan poetry, of a Wine-god who had been in hell. Denys
certainly, with all his flaxen fairness about him, was manifestly a
sufferer. At first he thought of departing secretly to some other
place. Alas! his wits were too far gone for certainty of success in
the attempt. He feared to be brought back a prisoner. Those fat
years were over. It was a time of scarcity. The working people
might not eat and drink of the good things they had helped to store
away. Tears rose in the eyes of needy children, of old or weak
people like children, as they woke up again and again to sunless,
frost-bound, ruinous mornings; and the little hungry creatures went
prowling after scattered hedge-nuts or dried vine-tendrils. Mysterious, dark rains prevailed throughout the summer. The great offices

of Saint John were fumbled through in a sudden darkness of unseasonable storm, which greatly damaged the carved ornaments of the church, the bishop reading his mid-day Mass by the light of the little candle at his book. And then, one night, the night which seemed literally to have swallowed up the shortest day in the year, a plot was contrived by certain persons to take Denys as he went and kill him privately for a sorcerer. He could hardly tell how he escaped, and found himself safe in his earliest home, the cottage in the cliff-side, with such a big fire as he delighted in burning upon the hearth. They made a little feast as well as they could for the beautiful hunted creature, with abundance of waxlights.

And at last the clergy bethought themselves of a remedy for this evil time. The body of one of the patron saints had lain neglected somewhere under the flagstones of the sanctuary. This must be piously exhumed, and provided with a shrine worthy of it. The goldsmiths, the jewellers and lapidaries, set diligently to work, and no long time after, the shrine, like a little cathedral with portals and tower complete, stood ready, its chiselled gold framing panels of rock crystal, on the great altar. Many bishops arrived, with King Lewis the Saint himself accompanied by his mother, to assist at the search for and disinterment of the sacred relics. In their presence, the Bishop of Auxerre, with vestments of deep red in honour of the relics, blessed the new shrine, according to the office *De benedictione capsarum pro reliquiis*. The pavement of the choir, removed amid a surging sea of lugubrious chants, all persons fasting, discovered as if it had been a battlefield of mouldering human remains. Their odour rose plainly above plentiful clouds of incense, such as was used in the king's private chapel. The search for the Saint himself continued in vain all day and far into the night. At last from a little narrow chest, into which the remains had been almost crushed together, the bishop's red-gloved hands drew the dwindled body, shrunken inconceivably, but still with every feature of the face traceable in a sudden oblique ray of ghastly dawn.

That shocking sight, after a sharp fit as though a demon were going out of him, as he rolled on the turf of the cloister to which he had fled alone from the suffocating church, where the crowd still awaited the Procession of the relics and the Mass *De reliquiis quae continentur in Ecclesiis*, seemed indeed to have cured the madness of Denys, but certainly did not restore his gaiety. He was left a subdued, silent, melancholy creature. Turning now, with an odd revulsion of feeling, to gloomy objects, he picked out a ghastly shred from the common bones on the pavement to wear about his neck, and in a little while found his way to the monks of Saint Germain, who gladly received him into their workshop, though secretly, in fear of his foes.

The busy tribe of variously gifted artists, labouring rapidly at the many works on hand for the final embellishment of the cathedral of St. Étienne, made those conventual buildings just then cheerful enough to lighten a melancholy, heavy even as that of our friend Denys. He took his place among the workmen, a conventual novice; a novice also as to whatever concerns any actual handicraft. He could but compound sweet incense for the sanctuary. And yet, again by merely visible presence, he made himself felt in all the varied exercise around him of those arts which address themselves first of all to sight. Unconsciously he defined a peculiar manner, alike of feeling and expression, to those skilful hands at work day by day with the chisel, the pencil, or the needle, in many an enduring form of exquisite fancy. In three successive phases or fashions might be traced, especially in the carved work, the humours he had determined. There was first wild gaiety, exuberant in a wreathing of life-like imageries, from which nothing really present in nature was excluded. That, as the soul of Denys darkened, had passed into obscure regions of the satiric, the grotesque and coarse. But from this time there was manifest, with no loss of power or effect, a well-assured seriousness, somewhat jealous and exclusive, not so much in the selection of the material on which the arts were to work, as in the precise sort of expression that should be induced upon it. It was as if the gay old pagan world had been *blessed* in some way; with effects to be seen most clearly in the rich miniature work of the manuscripts of the capitular library, – a marvellous Ovid especially, upon the pages of which those old loves and sorrows seemed to come to life again in medieval costume, as Denys, in cowl now and with tonsured head, leaned over the painter, and led his work, by a kind of visible sympathy, often unspoken, rather than by any formal comment.

Above all, there was a desire abroad to attain the instruments of a freer and more various sacred music than had been in use hitherto – a music that might express the whole compass of souls now grown to manhood. Auxerre, indeed, then as afterwards, was

161

famous for its liturgical music. It was Denys, at last, to whom the
thought occurred of combining in a fuller tide of music all the
instruments then in use. Like the Wine-god of old, he had been a
lover and patron especially of the music of the pipe, in all its
varieties. Here, too, there had been evident those three fashions or
'modes': – first, the simple and pastoral, the homely note of the
the pipe, like the piping of the wind itself from off the distant fields;
then, the wild, savage din, that had cost so much to quiet people,
and driven excitable people mad. Now he would compose all this
to sweeter purposes; and the building of the first organ became like
the book of his life: it expanded to the full compass of his nature,
in its sorrow and delight. In long, enjoyable days of wind and sun
by the river-side, the seemingly half-witted 'brother' sought and
found the needful varieties of reed. The carpenters, under his
instruction, set up the great wooden passages for the thunder;
while the little pipes of pasteboard simulated the sound of the
human voice singing to the victorious notes of the long metal
trumpets. At times this also, as people heard night after night
those wandering sounds, seemed like the work of a madman,
though they awoke sometimes in wonder at snatches of a new, an
unmistakable new music. It was the triumph of all the various
modes of the power of the pipe, tamed, ruled, united. Only, on
the painted shutters of the organ-case Apollo with his lyre in his
hand, as lord of the strings, seemed to look askance on the music
of the reed, in all the jealousy with which he put Marsyas to death
so cruelly.

Meantime, the people, even his enemies, seemed to have forgotten him. Enemies, in truth, they still were, ready to take his
life should the opportunity come; as he perceived when at last he
ventured forth on a day of public ceremony. The bishop was to
pronounce a blessing upon the foundations of a new bridge, designed
to take the place of the ancient Roman bridge which, repaired in a
thousand places, had hitherto served for the chief passage of the
Yonne. It was as if the disturbing of that time-worn masonry let
out the dark spectres of departed times. Deep down, at the core of
the central pile, a painful object was exposed – the skeleton of a
child, placed there alive, it was rightly surmised, in the superstitious
belief that, by way of vicarious substitution, its death would secure
the safety of all who should pass over. There were some who found
themselves, with a little surprise, looking round as if for a similar

pledge of security in their new undertaking. It was just then that Denys was seen plainly, standing, in all essential features precisely as of old, upon one of the great stones prepared for the foundation of the new building. For a moment he felt the eyes of the people upon him full of that strange humour, and with characteristic alertness, after a rapid gaze over the grey city in its broad green framework of vineyards, best seen from this spot, flung himself down into the water and disappeared from view where the stream flowed most swiftly below a row of flour-mills. Some indeed fancied they had seen him emerge again safely on the deck of one of the great boats, loaded with grapes and wreathed triumphantly with flowers like a floating garden, which were then bringing down the vintage from the country; but generally the people believed their strange enemy was now at last departed for ever. Denys in truth was at work again in peace at the cloister, upon his house of reeds and pipes. At times his fits came upon him again; and when they came, for his cure he would dig eagerly, turned sexton now, digging, by choice, graves for the dead in the various churchyards of the town. There were those who had seen him thus employed (that form seeming still to carry something of real sun-gold upon it) peering into the darkness, while his tears fell sometimes among the grim relics his mattock had disturbed.

In fact, from the day of the exhumation of the body of the Saint in the great church, he had had a wonderful curiosity for such objects, and one wintry day bethought him of removing the body of his mother from the unconsecrated ground in which it lay, that he might bury it in the cloister, near the spot where he was now used to work. At twilight he came over the frozen snow. As he passed through the stony barriers of the place the world around seemed curdled to the centre – all but himself, fighting his way across it, turning now and then right-about from the persistent wind, which dealt so roughly with his blond hair and the purple mantle whirled about him. The bones, hastily gathered, he placed, awfully but without ceremony, in a hollow space prepared secretly within the grave of another.

Meantime the winds of his organ were ready to blow; and with difficulty he obtained grace from the Chapter for a trial of its powers on a notable public occasion, as follows. A singular guest was expected at Auxerre. In recompense for some service rendered to the Chapter in times gone by, the Sire de Chastellux had the hereditary dignity of a canon of the church. On the day of his reception he presented himself at the entrance of the choir in surplice and amice, worn over the military habit. The old count of Chastellux was lately dead, and the heir had announced his coming, according to custom, to claim his ecclesiastical privilege. There had been long feud between the houses of Chastellux and Auxerre; but on this happy occasion an offer of peace came with a proposal for the hand of the Lady Ariane.

The goodly young man arrived, and, duly arrayed, was received into his stall at vespers, the bishop assisting. It was then that the people heard the music of the organ, rolling over them for the first time, with various feelings of delight. But the performer on and author of the instrument was forgotten in his work, and there was no re-instatement of the former favourite. The religious ceremony was followed by a civic festival, in which Auxerre welcomed its future lord. The festival was to end at nightfall with a somewhat rude popular pageant, in which the person of Winter would be hunted blindfold through the streets. It waɔ the sequel to that earlier stage-play of the *Return from the East* in which Denys had been the central figure. The old forgotten player saw his part before him, and, as if mechanically, fell again into the chief place, monk's dress and all. It might restore his popularity: who could tell? Hastily he donned the ashen-grey mantle, the rough haircloth about the throat, and went through the preliminary matter. And it happened that a point of the haircloth scratched his lip deeply, with a long trickling of blood upon the chin. It was as if the sight of blood transported the spectators with a kind of mad rage, and suddenly revealed to them the truth. The pretended hunting of the unholy creature became a real one, which brought out, in rapid increase, men's evil passions. The soul of Denys was already at rest, as his body, now borne along in front of the crowd, was tossed hither and thither, torn at last limb from limb. The men stuck little shreds of his flesh, or, failing that, of his torn raiment, into their caps; the women lending their long hairpins for the purpose. The monk Hermes sought in vain next day for any remains of the body of his friend. Only, at nightfall, the heart of Denys was brought to him by a stranger, still entire. It must long since have mouldered into dust under the stone, marked with a cross, where he buried it in a dark corner of the cathedral aisle.

So the figure in the stained glass explained itself. To me, Denys

164

seemed to have been a real resident at Auxerre. On days of a
certain atmosphere, when the trace of the Middle Age comes out,
like old marks in the stones in rainy weather, I seemed actually to
have seen the tortured figure there – to have met Denys l'Auxerrois
in the streets.

# LIONEL JOHNSON

## From *Poems* (1895)

### MYSTIC AND CAVALIER

Go from me: I am one of those, who fall.
What! hath no cold wind swept your heart at all,
In my sad company? Before the end,
   Go from me, dear my friend!

Yours are the victories of light: your feet
Rest from good toil, where rest is brave and sweet.
But after warfare in a mourning gloom,
   I rest in clouds of doom.

Have you not read so, looking in these eyes?
Is it the common light of the pure skies,
Lights up their shadowy depths? The end is set:
   Though the end be not yet.

When gracious music stirs, and all is bright,
And beauty triumphs through a courtly night;
When I too joy, a man like other men:
   Yet, am I like them, then?

And in the battle, when the horsemen sweep
Against a thousand deaths, and fall on sleep:
Who ever saw that sudden calm, if I
   Sought not? Yet, could not die.

Seek with thine eyes to pierce this crystal sphere:
Canst read a fate there, prosperous and clear?
Only the mists, only the weeping clouds:
   Dimness, and airy shrouds.

165

Beneath, what angels are at work? What powers
Prepare the secret of the fatal hours?
See! the mists tremble, and the clouds are stirred:
    When comes the calling word?

The clouds are breaking from the crystal ball,
Breaking and clearing: and I look to fall.
When the cold winds and airs of portent sweep,
    My spirit may have sleep.

O rich and sounding voices of the air!
Interpreters and prophets of despair:
Priests of a fearful sacrament! I come,
    To make with you mine home.

### THE DARK ANGEL

Dark Angel, with thine aching lust
To rid the world of penitence:
Malicious Angel, who still dost
My soul such subtile violence!

Because of thee, no thought, no thing,
Abides for me undesecrate:
Dark Angel, ever on the wing,
Who never reachest me too late!

When music sounds, then changest thou
Its silvery to a sultry fire:
Nor will thine envious heart allow
Delight untortured by desire.

Through thee, the gracious Muses turn
To Furies, O mine Enemy!
And all the things of beauty burn
With flames of evil ecstasy.

Because of thee, the land of dreams
Becomes a gathering place of fears:
Until tormented slumber seems
One vehemence of useless tears.

When sunlight glows upon the flowers,
Or ripples down the dancing sea:
Thou, with thy troop of passionate powers,
Beleaguerest, bewilderest, me.

166

Within the breath of autumn woods,
Within the winter silences:
Thy venomous spirit stirs and broods,
O Master of impieties!

The ardour of red flame is thine,
And thine the steely soul of ice:
Thou poisonest the fair design
Of nature, with unfair device.

Apples of ashes, golden bright;
Waters of bitterness, how sweet!
O banquet of a foul delight,
Prepared by thee, dark Paraclete!

Thou art the whisper in the gloom,
The hinting tone, the haunting laugh:
Thou art the adorner of my tomb,
The minstrel of mine epitaph.

I fight thee, in the Holy Name!
Yet, what thou dost, is what God saith:
Tempter! should I escape thy flame,
Thou wilt have helped my soul from Death:

The second Death, that never dies,
That cannot die, when time is dead:
Live Death, wherein the lost soul cries,
Eternally uncomforted.

Dark Angel, with thine aching lust!
Of two defeats, of two despairs:
Less dread, a change to drifting dust,
Than thine eternity of cares.

Do what thou wilt, thou shalt not so,
Dark Angel! triumph over me:
Lonely, unto the Lone I go;
Divine, to the Divinity.

# PART III

# REACTIONS TO AESTHETICISM

# W. H. MALLOCK

## From *The New Republic* (1877)

### BOOK I, CHAPTER III

'I rather look upon life as a chamber, which we decorate as we would decorate the chamber of the woman or the youth that we love, tinting the walls of it with symphonies of subdued colour, and filling it with works of fair form, and with flowers, and with strange scents, and with instruments of music. And this can be done now as well – better, rather – than at any former time: since we know that so many of the old aims were false, and so cease to be distracted by them. We have learned the weariness of creeds; and know that for us the grave has no secrets. We have learned that the aim of life is life; and what does successful life consist in? Simply,' said Mr. Rose,[1] speaking very slowly, and with a soft solemnity, 'in the consciousness of exquisite living – in the making our own each highest thrill of joy that the moment offers us – be it some touch of colour on the sea or on the mountains, the early dew in the crimson shadows of a rose, the shining of a woman's limbs in clear water, or ——'

Here unfortunately a sound of ''Sh' broke softly from several mouths [ . . . ].

### BOOK III, CHAPTER II

'Good,' murmured Mr. Rose; 'that is good! Yes,' he continued, 'the aim of culture, if Mr. Leslie will lend me his nice metaphor, is indeed to make the soul a musical instrument, which may yield music either to itself or to others, at any appulse from without; and the more elaborate a man's culture is, the richer and more composite can this music be. The minds of some men are like a simple pastoral reed. Only single melodies, and these unaccompanied, can be played upon them – glad or sad; whilst the minds of others, who look at things from countless points of view,

---

1 Mr Rose was a close, if caustic, portrait of Pater.

171

and realise, as Shakespeare did, their composite nature – their minds become, as Shakespeare's was, like a great orchestra. Or sometimes,' said Mr. Rose dreamily, as if his talk was lapsing into a soliloquy, 'when he is a mere passive observer of things, letting impressions from without move him as they will, I would compare the man of culture to an Aeolian harp,[1] which the winds at will play through – a beautiful face, a rainbow, a ruined temple, a death-bed, or a line of poetry, wandering in like a breath of air amongst the chords of his soul, touching note after note into soft music, and at last gently dying away into silence.'

## Book iv, chapter i

'I remember, [said Mr. Rose,] amidst the roar and clatter of our streets, and the mad noises of our own times, that there is amongst us a growing number who have deliberately turned their backs on all these things, and have thrown their whole souls and sympathies into the happier art-ages of the past. They have gone back,' said Mr. Rose, raising his voice a little, 'to Athens and to Italy, to the Italy of Leo and to the Athens of Pericles. To such men the clamour, the interests, the struggles of our own times, become as meaningless as they really are. To them the boyhood of Bathyllus[2] is of more moment than the manhood of Napoleon. Borgia[3] is a more familiar name than Bismarck.[4] I know, indeed – and I really do not blame them – several distinguished artists who, resolving to make their whole lives consistently perfect, will, on principle, never admit a newspaper into their houses that is of later date than the times of Addison; and I have good trust that the number of such men is on the increase – men I mean,' said Mr. Rose, toying tenderly with an exquisite wine-glass of Salviati's, 'who with a steady and set purpose follow art for the sake of art, beauty for the sake of beauty, love for the sake of love, life for the sake of life.'

Mr. Rose's slow gentle voice, which was apt at certain times to

---

1 A stringed instrument producing musical sounds by exposure to the air.
2 A beautiful youth of Samos, beloved by Polycrates. Homosexuality is being alluded to.
3 The Borgias were generally invoked by Aesthetic writers as the type of Renaissance depravity.
4 Otto von Bismarck (1815–98), the German statesman and architect of German national unity.

become peculiarly irritating, sounded now like the evening air grown articulate, and had secured him hitherto a tranquil hearing, as if by a kind of spell. This however seemed here in sudden danger of snapping.

'What, Mr. Rose!' exclaimed Lady Ambrose, 'do you mean to say, then, that the number of people is on the increase who won't read the newspapers?'

'Why, the men must be absolute idiots!' said Lady Grace, shaking her grey curls, and putting on her spectacles to look at Mr. Rose [ ... ].

'I will try to make my meaning clearer,' [Mr. Rose] said, in a brisker tone. 'I often figure to myself an unconscious period and a conscious one, as two women – one an untamed creature with embrowned limbs native to the air and the sea; the other marble-white and swan-soft, couched delicately on cushions before a mirror, and watching her own supple reflection gleaming in the depths of it. On the one is the sunshine and sea-spray. The wind of Heaven and her unbound hair are playmates. The light of the sky is in her eyes; on her lips is a free laughter. We look at her, and we know that she is happy. *We* know it, mark me; but *she* knows it not. Turn, however, to the other, and all is changed. Outwardly, there is no gladness there. Her dark, gleaming eyes open depth within depth upon us, like the circles of a new Inferno. There is a clear, shadowy pallor on her cheek. Only her lips are scarlet. There is a sadness – a languor, even in the grave tendrils of her heavy hair, and in each changing curve of her bosom as she breathes or sighs.'

'What a very odd man Mr. Rose is!' said Lady Ambrose in a loud whisper. 'He always seems to talk of everybody as if they had no clothes on. And does he mean by this that we ought to be always in the dumps?'

'Yes,' Mr. Rose was meanwhile proceeding, his voice again growing visionary, 'there is no eagerness, no action there; and yet all eagerness, all action is known to her as the writing on an open scroll; only, as she reads, even in the reading of it, action turns into emotion, and eagerness into a sighing memory. Yet such a woman really may stand symbolically for us as the patroness and the lady of all gladness, who makes us glad in the only way now left us. And not only in the only way, but in the best way – the way of ways. Her secret is self-consciousness. She knows that she is fair; she knows, too, that she is sad; but she sees that sadness is lovely,

173

and so sadness turns to joy. Such a woman may be taken as a symbol, not of our architecture only, but of all the aesthetic surroundings with which we shall shelter and express our life. Such a woman do I see whenever I enter a ritualistic church ——'

'I know,' said Mrs. Sinclair, 'that very peculiar people do go to such places; but, Mr. Rose,' she said with a look of appealing enquiry, 'I thought they were generally rather over-dressed than otherwise?'

# GEORGE DU MAURIER

## From *Punch*, Vol. LXXIX (25 December 1880)

The Aesthetic Young Man rose languidly from his seat, and leaning against a bookcase, with the Lily in his hand, and the Peacock's Feather in his hair, he read aloud –

### *FLEUR DES ALPES;*

#### OR, POSTLETHWAITE'S LAST LOVE

Good Philistines all, I don't carry manuscripts about me to read to the likes of you! and if I did, you couldn't understand them – and if you could, I should be Supremely disgusted, – moreover, you would have the advantage of me.

But I can speak plain English when it suits me, and make myself pretty well understood, when I like – even by such as yourselves – wherefore, since you are willing to listen, I will tell you why I am here to-night, far, far away from the CIMABUE BROWNS – remote, ah me! from the tender companionship of my MAUDLE!

You have never heard of MAUDLE and Mrs. CIMABUE BROWN? I dare say not. To know them is a Joy, and the privilege of a select and chosen few; for they are simply Perfect. Yet in their respective perfection, they differentiate from each other with a quite ineffably subtle exquisiteness.

For *She* is Supremely Consummate – whereas *He* is Consummately Supreme. I constantly tell them so, and they agree with me.

I also make a point of telling everybody else.

My modesty prevents me from revealing to you all they tell me (and everybody else) about myself, beyond the mere fact that they consider me alone to combine, in my own mind and person, Supreme Consummateness with Consummate Supremacy – and I agree with them. We get on uncommonly well together, I can tell you.

It will not surprise you, seeing that I am thus gifted, to hear that for the last year or two I have been quite a Social Celebrity. It happened in this wise.

One evening, for want of anything better to say, I told Mrs. CIMABUE BROWN, in the strictest confidence, that I could sit up all night with a *Lily*. She was holding one in her hand, as usual. She was deeply moved. Her eye moistened. She said, 'Quite so!' and wrung my fingers. And it struck her as such a beautiful thought, that she couldn't help letting it out before that blundering buffoon GRIGSBY, who always tries to poke his vulgar fun at MAUDLE and myself; and GRIGSBY went and told it to every soul he knew, *as a good joke against Me!*

Now GRIGSBY, for some reason or other that I could never make out, knows everybody worth knowing, and everybody worth knowing very naturally wanted to know a man who could sit up all night with a Lily!

A Lily! Just think of it, ye worthy Philistines! *what* a flower to have chosen! and for what a purpose! How Consummate! How Perfect! how Supreme, Precious and Blessèd! Nay, how Utter!

I became the fashion. These very adjectives of mine have grown into household words. Even GRIGSBY uses them now, and about *me* of all people; *me*, whom he pretends to hate! For does he not call me, and to my very face, too, a Supreme duffer, a Consummate ass, a Blessèd idiot, a Precious fool, a Perfect noodle, nay, an Utter Nincompoop!

Poor GRIGSBY! What an utter sell for *him*! But he lacks the real sense of humour!

I had imitators, of course. I can hardly call them rivals. PILCOX declared he could sit up all night with a Stephanotis – and actually did so, I believe, and was seedy for a month in consequence! And as for MILKINGTON SOPLEY, he swore he never went to bed without an Aloe Blossom! a thing that only happens once in a century! They overdid it. They always do. And GRIGSBY lets them alone.

175

Next season I took MAUDLE aside, and whispered to him (in the hearing of GRIGSBY) that I had sat up all night with a *Primrose*. I thought it a capital change after the Lily. So *simple*, you know! And we all went in for simplicity just then, even the little CIMABUE BROWNS! And what a sell for PILCOX and SOPLEY, with their Aloe Blossoms and Stephanotises!

A tear rolled down the Perfect cheek of MAUDLE (for his cheek is almost as consummate as mine); pressing me to his bosom he said, 'Distinctly so!' GRIGSBY let off a big D., and went forth like an indignant lamb to spread the news abroad.

It took immediately; the people worth knowing (GRIGSBY's people, Ha! Ha!) literally fought for me – GRIGSBY was nowhere.

PILCOX followed suit with a Marigold, or a Dandelion, or some such twaddling superannuated old weed. And SOPLEY, poor boy! tried it on with a Snowdrop, so he said: but it was in June, you know, and didn't do at all. They overdid it, as usual, and were out of it again! The fact is, 'they ain't got no *Tack*,' as GRIGSBY says when he wants to be funny. And as for the sense of humour, they are as badly off as GRIGSBY himself. Besides which, PILCOX gets his clothes ready-made at EPHRAIM BROTHERS, in the Strand, or some-where. And SOPLEY can't bear up against a snub from a lady of title. It upsets his stomach, and he goes home and tells his mother and sisters – and they tell everybody all round. Fatal!

Now the Lily had carried me through my first season, the Prim-rose through my second. The question arose: what Flower of Flowers is to carry me through my next? It must be simpler than Primrose, rarer than the Lily, and as consummate and all that as either; and such, moreover, as to rile GRIGSBY to madness, and leave SOPLEY and PILCOX sticking in the mud for the rest of their lives.

I sat up all night with a Botanical Dictionary, and hit upon the very flower at last – The Utter Blossom! The Perfect Thing!! Oh, my GRIGSBY! It will be the death of you! And you, Professional Beauties, look well to your laurels! For this is a stroke of Genius, and will carry me on to 1883 – or even '4!

And that is why I am here to-night.

Good Philistines, every one, you are the witnesses thereof – and when called upon to do so (by GRIGSBY, for instance), must testify to the fact that I, JELLABY POSTLETHWAITE, was actually caught, by an intelligent little quadruped answering to the name of *Toby* –

176

who informed his friend the big dog *Chang* of the fact, and *Chang* carried me hither – in a snowstorm at mid-winter, nine thousand feet above the level of the sea, Lat. 45° 52′ N., Long. 7° 12′ E., under most favourable circumstances, and at considerable personal risk and inconvenience to myself, in the very act of

SITTING UP ALL NIGHT WITH AN EDELWEISS!

Here the Aesthetic POSTLETHWAITE produced a dried specimen, smelt it passionately, and fainted away. Punch revived him. Three sniffs did it. Then *Toby* asked permission to entertain *Chang* with grilled bones and porridge before the kitchen fire. 'By all means!' said *Mr. Punch*, heartily.

'Don't twig this lingo about "Consummate,"' said 'ARRY. ROBERT the Waiter thought it had something to do with soup.

# W. S. GILBERT

————◄•••►————

## From *Patience* (1881)

### ACT I

BUNTHORNE.   Am I alone,
              And unobserved? I am!
          Then let me own
              I'm an aesthetic sham!
          This air severe
              Is but a mere
                  Veneer!
          This cynic smile
              Is but a wile
                  Of guile!
          This costume chaste
              Is but good taste
                  Misplaced!
          Let me confess!
A languid love for lilies does *not* blight me!
Lank limbs and haggard cheeks do *not* delight me!

177

I do *not* care for dirty greens
   By any means.
I do *not* long for all one sees
   That's Japanese.
I am *not* fond of uttering platitudes
   In stained-glass attitudes.
In short, my mediaevalism's affectation,
Born of a morbid love of admiration!

## SONG

If you're anxious for to shine in the high aesthetic line as a man of
   culture rare,
You must get up all the germs of the transcendental terms, and plant
   them everywhere.
You must lie upon the daisies and discourse in novel phrases of your
   complicated state of mind,
The meaning doesn't matter if it's only idle chatter of a transcendental kind.
         And every one will say,
         As you walk your mystic way,
'If this young man expresses himself in terms too deep for *me*,
Why what a very singularly deep young man this deep young man
   must be!'

Be eloquent in praise of the very dull old days which have long since
   passed away,
And convince 'em, if you can, that the reign of good Queen Anne
   was Culture's palmiest day.
Of course you will pooh-pooh whatever's fresh and new, and declare
   it's crude and mean,
For Art stopped short in the cultivated court of the Empress
   Josephine.
         And every one will say,
         As you walk your mystic way,
'If that's not good enough for him which is good enough for *me*,
Why what a very cultivated kind of youth this kind of youth must
   be!'

Then a sentimental passion of a vegetable fashion must excite your
   languid spleen,

An attachment *à la* Plato for a bashful young potato, or a not-too-
French French bean!
Though the Philistines may jostle, you will rank as an apostle in the
high aesthetic band,
If you walk down Piccadilly with a poppy or a lily in your mediaeval
hand.

> And everyone will say,
> As you walk your flowery way,

'If he's content with a vegetable love which would certainly not
suit *me*,
Why what a most particularly pure young man this pure young man
must be!'


## ACT II

DUKE, COLONEL, and MAJOR.
It's clear that mediaeval art alone retains its zest,
To charm and please its devotees we've done our little best.
We're not quite sure if all we do has the Early English ring;
But, as far as we can judge, it's something like this sort of thing:

> You hold yourself like this (*attitude*),
> You hold yourself like that (*attitude*),

By hook and crook you try to look both angular and flat (*attitude*).

> We venture to expect
> That what we recollect,

Though but a part of true High Art, will have its due effect.

If this is not exactly right, we hope you won't upbraid;
You can't get high Aesthetic tastes like trousers, ready made.
True views on Mediaevalism, Time alone will bring,
But, as far as we can judge, it's something like this sort of thing:

> You hold yourself like this (*attitude*),
> You hold yourself like that (*attitude*),

By hook and crook you try to look both angular and flat (*attitude*).

> To cultivate the trim,
> Rigidity of limb,

You ought to get a Marionette, and form your style on him (*attitude*).

COL. (*attitude*). Yes, it's quite clear that our only chance of making
a lasting impression on these young ladies is to become as aesthetic
as they are [ . . . ].

DUET – Bunthorne and Grosvenor.

Bun.    When I go out of door,
Of damozels a score,
   (All sighing and burning,
   And clinging and yearning)
Will follow me as before.
I shall, with cultured taste,
Distinguish gems from paste,
   And 'High diddle diddle'
   With rank as an idyll,
If I pronounce it chaste!
   A most intense young man,
   A soulful-eyed young man,
An ultra-poetical, super-aesthetical,
   Out of the way young man.

Both.   A most intense young man, &c.

Gros.   Conceive me, if you can,
An every-day young man:
   A commonplace type,
   With a stick and a pipe,
And a half-bred black-and-tan.
   Who thinks suburban 'hops,'
   More fun than 'Monday Pops.'
Who's fond of his dinner
   And doesn't get thinner
   On bottled beer and chops.
     A common-place young man –
     A matter-of-fact young man –
A steady and stolid-y, jolly Bank holiday
   Every-day young man!

Bun.    A Japanese young man –
   A blue and white young man –
Francesca di Rimini, miminy, piminy,
   *Je-ne-sais-quoi* young man.

Gros.   A Chancery Lane young man –
   A Somerset House young man –
A very delectable, highly respectable,
   Threepenny-bus young man!

Bun.    A pallid and thin young man –
   A haggard and lank young man –

A greenery-yallery, Grosvenor Gallery,
Foot-in-the-grave young man!

GROS.     A Sewell and Cross young man –
A Howell and James young man –
A pushing young particle – what's the next article –
Waterloo House young man!

### ENSEMBLE

| BUN. | GROS. |
|---|---|
| Conceive me, if you can, | Conceive me, if you can, |
| A crotchety, cracked young man, | A matter-of-fact young man, |
| An ultra-poetical, super aesthetical, | An alphabetical, arithmetical, |
| Out-of-the-way young man! | Every-day young man! |

# WALTER HAMILTON

From *The Aesthetic Movement in England* (1881)

### FROM THE INTRODUCTION

But the fact is, that Maudle and Company,[1] as portrayed, were not altogether imaginary individuals, but belonged to a comparatively new school, which has done, and is still doing, an immense amount of good towards the advancement of Art in this country and in America. That there are persons of Aesthetic tastes who carry them to the borders of absurdity goes without saying; every movement in intellectual, or political, life has its over-enthusiastic apostles, who damage the cause they have at heart; but that there must be *some* good in the movement is clearly shown by its having earned the abuse of a journal which never has a generous word to say for any one beyond its own immediate and narrow circle.[2] However, the so-called Aesthetic school has now been in existence some years, and is likely to survive the attacks which a portion of the press levels at it, the more so because by far the greater number of its

---

1 The names Maudle and Postlethwaite were those of Du Maurier for archetypal aesthetes.    2 i.e. *Punch*.

assailants neither study its works, understand its aims, nor appreciate the undoubted good it has wrought.

What then, is this School, – what are its aims, – and what has it achieved?

The term *Aesthetic* is derived from the Greek, *aisthesis*, signifying *perception*, or the science of the beautiful, especially in art, and the designation has long been applied by German writers to a branch of philosophical enquiry into the theory of the beautiful, or more accurately, into the philosophy of poetry and the fine arts. The term appears to have been invented, or adopted, by Baumgarten, a German Philosopher, whose work entitled *Aesthetica* was published in 1750.

A great literary controversy has been going on in Germany for a century and a-half, the chief topic in dispute being the question as to whether an object is actually beautiful in itself, or merely appears so to certain persons having faculties capable of appreciating that which is *positively* beautiful.

From this dispute came the origin of the school, and the *Aesthetes* are they who pride themselves upon having found out what is the really beautiful in nature and art, their faculties and tastes being educated up to the point necessary for the full appreciation of such qualities; whilst those who do not see the true and the beautiful – the outsiders in fact – are termed Philistines.[1]

Now up to a certain point, the theory that beauty is apparent only to some, is perfectly sound, for most persons will agree with Kant, that there can be no strict mathematical definition, or science of beauty in nature, art, poetry or music, inasmuch as beauty is not altogether a property of objects or sounds, but is relative to the tastes and faculties brought to bear upon them.

Illustrations of the truth of this axiom will occur to every one; it is founded upon the old old truism, *tastes differ*. The Aesthetes recognise this truth to the fullest extent, but having first laid down certain general principles, they have endeavoured to elevate taste into a scientific system, the correlation of the arts being a main feature of the scheme; they even go so far as to decide what shall be considered beautiful, and those who do not accept their ruling are termed Philistines, and there is no hope for them.

Hence, the essence of the movement is the union of persons of cultivated tastes to define, and to decide upon, what is to be

1 See note to p. 7.

admired, and their followers must aspire to that standard in their works and lives. Vulgarity, however wealthy it may be, can never be admitted into this exclusive brotherhood, for riches without taste are of no avail, whilst taste without money, or with very little, can always effect much. So also those who prate most of Aestheticism are often those who have least of it to show in their houses, furniture, dress, or literary culture.

It has been insinuated that the school has no existence, save in the brain of M. Du Maurier,[1] or that if it existed, it was yet merely a very insignificant clique of nobodies, whose vanity was gratified by the attention thus called to them, and to their paltry works. But the school does exist, and its leaders are men of mark, who have long been at work educating public taste.

## From 'Aesthetic Culture'

First, and above all other considerations, the leaders of the Aesthetic School in poetry have been styled fleshly[2] poets, delighting in somewhat sensually-suggestive descriptions of the passions, ornamented with hyperbolical metaphor, or told in curious archaic speech; and dressed up in quaint mediaeval garments of odd old ballad rhymes and phrases.

The strict *Aesthete* admires only what in his language is known as *intense*, and what Ruskin somewhat gushingly terms the 'blessed and precious' in art [ . . . ].

In music the Aesthetes affect Liszt, Rubinstein, and Wagner, who are all most consummately intense [ . . . ].

In painting, the Aesthetes have a great veneration for Allesandro Botticelli, a Florentine artist, who flourished about four centuries ago, and of whom Ruskin has written the praises [ . . . ].

In architecture the Queen Anne style is favoured by the Aesthetes; and on the really beautiful Bedford Park Estate, one of the chosen homes of the 'select', only houses built after this manner are permitted to be erected.

Chippendale furniture, dados, old-fashioned brass and wrought iron work, mediaeval lamps, stained glass in small squares, and old china are all held to be the outward and visible signs of an inward and spiritual grace and intensity. Let a jaded City man, if he have

1 i.e. George Du Maurier. See p. 174 and illustrations.
2 A term first used by Robert Buchanan of D. G. Rossetti in 'The Fleshly School of Poetry' in the *Contemporary Review* in 1871.

an eye for the beautiful, only walk three minutes off 'Change, and in Dashwood House, Old Broad Street, he will find a cool, shady retreat, where he can admire at his leisure one of the finest staircases in London, decorated with a charming dado, Minton's tiles, and lit by some stained-glass windows, of exquisite colouring, put in by Pitman and Son. Or, if he can only take an hour's ride, let him visit the Sanatorium, recently built, at an enormous expense, by Mr. Thomas Holloway, at Virginia Water, and there study the decorative wall paintings, by J. Moyr Smith, especially those representing *History*, *Legend*, and *Epic Poetry*, and having studied these, let him ask himself whether such work could have been produced, or would have been appreciated, forty years ago.[1]

Now, it cannot be too strongly insisted on that in much of this there is visible not only a *real love of the beautiful*, but also that the wonderful improvements which have been so eagerly seized upon by the general public during the last few years originated amongst the Aesthetes, whom the vulgar herd think it witty and clever to abuse, or to ridicule. Soft draperies of quiet, sober, yet withal delicate and harmonious tints, have replaced the heavy, gaudy curtains of yore; bevilled mirrors with black frames slightly relieved with gold, have driven out the large old plate glasses, with sham, but expensive gold frames; plain painted walls, of soft tints, show up our pictures far better than the old-fashioned papers which, pasted one over another, became the haunt of the agile flea, or still more objectionable but less lively insect abominations. But why the sunflower, the lily, and the peacock's feather have become so closely identified with the movement is not easy to explain; certain it is they appear to be as distinctively the badges of the true Aesthete as the green turban is amongst Mahommedans the sign that the wearer has accomplished a pilgrimage to the holy place [ . . . ].

Constantly yearning for the intense, the language of the Aesthetes is tinged with somewhat exaggerated metaphor, and their adjectives are usually superlative – as supreme, consummate, utter, quite too preciously sublime, etc. For some of this mannerism of speech Mr. Ruskin's writings have to answer; but the words he uses as applied to grand works of art sound ludicrous enough when debased by being applied to the petty uses of every-day small talk.

1 Hamilton is alluding to what was later to become Royal Holloway College and its gallery.

# VERNON LEE

## From *Miss Brown* (1884)

[Anne Brown] found herself being led about, passively, half unconsciously, through the mazes of aesthetic London. It was all very hazy: Anne was informed that this and that person was coming to dinner or lunch at Hammersmith; that this or that person hoped she would come and dine or take tea somewhere or other; that such or such a lady was going to take her to see some one or other's studio, or to introduce her at some other person's house. She knew that they were all either distinguished poets, or critics, or painters, or musicians, or distinguished relations and friends of the above; that they all received her as if they had heard of her from their earliest infancy; that they pressed her to have tea, and strawberries, and claret-cup, and cakes, and asked her what she thought of this picture or that poem; that they lived in grim, smut-engrained houses in Bloomsbury, or rose-grown cottages at Hampstead, with just the same sort of weird furniture, partly Japanese, partly Queen Anne, partly medieval; with blue-and-white china and embroidered chasubles stuck upon the walls if they were rich, and twopenny screens and ninepenny pots if they were poor, but with no further differences; and, finally, that they were all intimately acquainted, and spoke of each other as being, or just having missed being, the most brilliant or promising specimens of whatever they happened to be.

At first Anne felt very shy and puzzled; but after a few days the very vagueness which she felt about all these men and women, these artists, critics, poets, and relatives, who were perpetually reappearing as on a merry-go-round, – nay, the very cloudiness as to the identity of these familiar faces – the very confusion as to whether they were one, two, or three different individuals, – produced in Miss Brown an indifference, an ease, almost a familiarity, like that which we may experience towards the vague, unindividual company met on a steamer or at an hotel.

185

And little by little, out of this crowd of people who seemed to look, and to dress, and to talk very much alike, – venerable bearded men, who were the heads of great schools of painting, or poetry, or criticism, or were the papas of great offspring; elderly, quaintly dressed ladies, who were somebody's wife, or mother, or sister; youngish men, with manners at once exotically courteous, and curiously free and easy, in velveteen coats and mustard-coloured shooting-jackets or elegiac-looking dress-coats, all rising in poetry, or art, or criticism; young ladies, varying from sixteen to six-and-thirty, with hair cut like medieval pages, or tousled like moenads, or tucked away under caps like eighteenth-century housekeepers, habited in limp and stayless garments, picturesque and economical, with Japanese chintzes for brocade, and flannel instead of stamped velvets – most of which young ladies appeared at one period, past, present, or future, to own a connection with the Slade school, and all of whom, when not poets or painters themselves, were the belongings of some such, or madly in love with the great sonneteer such a one, or the great colourist such another; – out of all this confusion there began gradually to detach themselves and assume consistency in Anne's mind one or two personalities, some of whom attracted, and some of whom repelled her.

### From Book iv, chapter vi

Now that [Miss Brown] had settled down in aesthetic society, and found her place, and got to understand the main points of things, she was quite ideally happy. Her life was very full, and was surrounded by a flood of love, – on her side or on Hamlin's?[1] She scarcely knew; but she knew that she was happy. By this time the round of sight-seeing, play-going, excursions, and introductions, was over; her life had subsided into the normal. Its object, she felt, as one feels a wholesome and agreeable desire for food or sleep, was to make herself as worthy as possible of Hamlin, or rather to let him find in her the best possible bargain. She worked very hard at all the things which the school had left incomplete, – at what, living in that aesthetic society, seemed to her the solid requisites of life. She read history and biography and poetry, with the determination with which other girls, anticipating marriage, might study

---

1 A thinly disguised portrait of D. G. Rossetti; Cosmo Chough is based on Swinburne.

manuals of domestic economy; and she worked at developing her taste in art and music as others might have practised cooking or dressmaking; for these were the things which would be requisite in Hamlin's spiritual household. The people around her, the men and women of Hamlin's set, seemed to her as necessary, as inevitable, as normal as the trees and houses all round. Some of them she liked, and some she disliked; but their ideas, though sometimes absurd caricatures, and their tempers, though often intolerable, seemed to Anne quite natural and proper in the main, though rendered ridiculous or disagreeable in individuals. Indeed she got rather to believe in imperfect individuals, – being thus constantly either made cross by the touchiness, the morbidness, the disgusting fleshliness, the intolerance of the aesthetes around her, or made to laugh by their affectations, their vanity, their inconsistency, their grotesque manias of wickedness and mysticism – while unable to judge or condemn the general, intellectual, and moral condition of which these individual excrescences were the result.

Some of the people were distinctly repulsive, or distinctly boring, or distinctly annoying to her; others, like Mrs Spencer and her father and mother and sisters, decidedly lovable; others, like little Chough, decidedly amusing and amiable: and she took them as they came, but with the indifference of concentrated feeling; for what did it matter whether she cared for them, or they cared for her, as long as she was doing her best to deserve Hamlin?

Meanwhile Anne Brown read quantities of medieval and Elizabethan literature; went with Hamlin to see pictures and hear music; studied Dante and Shakespeare – the algebra and arithmetic, so to speak, of the aesthetic set – and even began, secretly, to work at a Greek grammar. Twice a-week Cosmo Chough came to practise her accompaniments with her; and twice a-week also, of an evening, friends dropped in at the house at Hammersmith, when Mrs Macgregor would leave her nephew and niece, as she called her, to entertain the guests. On other evenings Anne would usually go to the house of one of the set, where literature and art, and the faults of friends, and the wrong-headedness of the public, were largely discussed; music was made, young long-haired Germans on the loose performing; and poets, especially the inexhaustible Chough, would recite their compositions, perched on the arms of sofas, or stretched on the hearth-rug; while the ladies went to sleep, or pretended to do so, over the descriptions of the kisses of cruel, blossom-mouthed women, who sucked out their lovers' hearts, bit their lips, and strewed their apartments with coral-like drops of blood. Most of these poets, as Anne speedily discovered, were young men of harmless lives, and altogether unacquainted with the beautiful, baleful ladies they represented as sucking at their vitals; and none was more utterly harmless than Cosmo Chough. Instead of the terrible Faustinas, Messalinas, and Lucretia Borgias[1] to whom his poems were addressed, the poor little man had in his miserable home in the north of London a wife older than himself, often bed-ridden and always half crazy, who turned the house in a sort of disorderly litter, neglected her children, and vented on her husband the most jealous and perverse temper; but the victim of Venus, as he styled himself, nursed her with absolute devotion, denied himself every gratification to allow her a servant and send his children to school, and made all new-comers believe that Mrs Cosmo Chough was the most angelic invalid that the world had ever seen. People in the set had got accustomed to this fact, and treated Chough merely as an amusing little caricature of genius; but when Anne understood the real state of the case, she was deeply touched, and possessed with a violent desire to help the little man. He could not, indeed, restrain his habit of alluding in pompous language to Phryne, Pasiphaë, La Belle Heaulmière, Madame du Barry,[2] and all the most celebrated improprieties of all times and nations; nor from discussing the most striking literary obscenities, from Petronius to Walt Whitman. But although at first surprised (as every one was surprised and indeed shocked) by Anne's un-blushing and quietly resolute – 'I think you had better leave that subject alone, Mr Chough' – he became quite devoted to Anne. When he gave a set of lectures, in Mrs Spencer's house, on what was nominally Elizabethan drama, but virtually the unmentionable play of Ford, and the ladies dropped off one by one and merely laughed at poor Cosmo's eccentricities, Anne had the courage to

---

1 Faustina: wife of Roman emperor Antoninus, famous for her debauchery; Messalina: wife of Roman emperor Claudius, famous for her sexual appetite; Lucretia Borgia, see note to p. 172.
2 Phryne: a celebrated Athenian prostitute; Pasiphaë: in Greek mythology, the wife of Minos, she succumbed to a violent passion for a bull and gave birth to the Minotaur; La Belle Heaulmière: Villon's *Regrets de la Belle Heaulmière*, a lament for lost beauty addressed to prostitutes which was translated by Swinburne; Madame du Barry: Jeanne, Comtesse du Barry, mistress of Louis XV after the death of Mme de Pompadour.

sit out the performance, and to tell Chough openly that he ought to be ashamed of himself for holding forth on such subjects – a proceeding which made Hamlin's friends blame Miss Brown for want of womanly feeling and prudishness alike; and which put Hamlin just a little out of temper, until she answered his unspoken censure by remarking, with a sort of Italian bluntness and seriousness, that a woman of her age had no business not to understand the real meaning of such things, and understanding them, not to let the poets know that she would not tolerate them.

'You see, it enters into their artistic effects,' explained Mrs Spencer. 'I don't like such things personally, but of course everything is legitimate in art.'

'They may be legitimate in art,' answered Anne, sceptically, 'but they shan't be legitimate in my presence.'

To return to Chough. Anne gradually became the confidant of the domestic difficulties, though not of the domestic shame, of the little poet; and to every one's great astonishment, she obtained Hamlin's permission to have one of Chough's little girls at Hammersmith every Saturday till Monday, and tried to instil into the miserable puny imps some notion of how to behave and how to amuse themselves.

'You are not going to take that child out in the carriage with you, surely?' asked Hamlin, the first Sunday that Maggy Chough spent at Hammersmith.

'Of course I am,' answered Anne. 'She's the daughter of your most intimate friend; surely you can't grudge the poor little thing some amusement. And I want you to go with us to the Zoo, Mr Hamlin. I'm sure its much more fascinating than the Grosvenor[1] or the Elgin rooms.'[2]

Hamlin smiled; and next day made a crayon drawing of Anne, one of the dozens in his studio, with Chough's child; but he managed to make Anne look mournfully mysterious, and the child haggard and wild, so that people thought it represented Medea and one of the children of Jason.

So far Anne's acquaintance were entirely limited to the aesthetic set; but there were two exceptions. One was a couple of sisters, Mary and Marjory Leigh, who existed as it were on the borderland –

1 i.e. the recently established Grosvenor Gallery.
2 i.e. the galleries housing the Elgin marbles in the British Museum.

Mary Leigh being a sort of amateur painter with strong literary proclivities; the other was Richard Brown, who, after the meeting at Mrs Argiropoulo's, called at Hammersmith, was politely received by Hamlin, with whom he appeared quite reconciled, and talked on a variety of indifferent subjects, as if Anne Brown had never been his ward. Hamlin had apparently never appeared to him in the light of a slave-buyer and seducer, and all parties had apparently never been in any save their present position. Anne asked her cousin to one or two of their evenings: he came, seemed to know one or two people slightly, and although professing profound ignorance of art, managed to interest one or two of the aesthetic brotherhood by developing his views on the necessity of extending artistic training to the lower classes.

'He isn't at all a stupid man, that cousin of yours,' remarked little Mrs Spencer; 'and I do think he is *so* right in wishing to give poor people a taste of beauty.'

'I'm sure *we* are most of us poor people, and don't always get a taste of anything else, Edith,' cried her father, the veteran painter in tempera, who was a fearful punster.

'Oh papa, you know what I mean; and I'm sure art will gain ever so much. It's only what Mr Ruskin has said over and over again, and Mr Morris is always talking about.'[1]

'Any one is free to give the lower classes that taste of beauty, as long as *I* am not required to see or speak to the noble workmen,' said Hamlin. 'I hate all that democratic bosh.'

## FROM BOOK V, CHAPTER III

By the middle of the summer a perfect colony from aesthetic London had settled itself, to the amazed terror of the vicar and his parishioners, in Wotton Hall and the inn of the adjacent village. The Spencers came, with a perfect shipload of babies, and accompanied by Mrs Spencer's father and mother; Cosmo Chough came, bringing scarcely any luggage except MS. poems and old music; Thaddy O'Reilly came, and half-a-dozen young poets and painters, to name whom would be perfectly superfluous, and who were all the humble worshippers of Walter Hamlin. All these people had pictures to paint, poems to compose, articles to write; but the

---

1 John Ruskin and William Morris, who both emphasised the social role of the artist and the social and economic aspects of art and its production.

exciting question for the whole household was the approaching publication of Hamlin's new book.

Hamlin's acquaintance with Anne Brown had not been without a decided influence on his art. He had written a number of sonnets about her ever since the moment of their first meeting, recording various moods, real and fictitious, in connection with her, and of which he had sent or read her the greater number. Perhaps he would have written much the same sort of thing about any other woman; but Anne had influenced him at once more directly and more indirectly. The aesthetic school of poetry, of which Hamlin and Chough were the most brilliant exponents of the younger generation, was evidently running to seed. It was beginning to be obvious, to every one who was not an aesthete, that the reign of the mysterious evil passions, of the half-antique, half-medieval ladies of saturnine beauty and bloodthirsty voluptuousness, of the demigods and heroes treated like the figures in a piece of tapestry, must be coming to a close; and that a return to nature must be preparing. Anne had felt it, and had vaguely determined that the man who was to revolutionise poetry was Hamlin. Indeed, who else could it be? The elder poets were safe in their ruts; the majority of the younger ones who had already come forward were mere imitators and caricaturists, not excepting the great Chough himself. Hamlin alone was a man of genius; he alone was capable of turning over a new leaf; and one or two new departures, attempts at a new way of describing things, if not actually an attempt at describing new things, persuaded Anne that the change was beginning. She did not like telling him that she perceived it coming; for she thought that Hamlin might, did he perceive it, consider it as an apostasy from his original school, and draw back. But she encouraged him by showing a marked preference for the pieces which savoured of this new style; and she even suggested to him to write a tale, in which he should substitute, for the conventional background copied by aesthetic poetry from the borders of missals, the pictures of old masters and of their French gods, Gautier and Baudelaire, the scenery of his own home, the wide commons, the beech-woods on the downs, the solemn horizons of the fenny country which spread from Wotton to the sea. He had written it, and read it to her during that fortnight of solitude; and Anne's heart had beat at the thought of the change which was to be wrought by Hamlin's new book – of the unknown youths hitherto fumbling vainly for a new style, who were to recognise in Hamlin the leader of a new school, the prophet of a new art. When the colony of London aesthetes arrived at Wotton, the new poem was solemnly read to them. They were all seated in the old-fashioned library, the rows and rows of old novels and books of standard literature, the busts of ancient philosophers looking down upon them, – a quaint little assembly of ladies in peacock-blue and dull sage and Japanese dragoned and medieval brocaded gowns, with slashed sleeves and limp tails – of men got up to look like Frenchmen or Germans, or Renaissance creatures, in wondrous velveteens, coloured almost like the bindings of their own books. They listened with considerable attention, and obvious impatience to interrupt. The first who did so was Mrs Spencer.

'Why, Walter!' she exclaimed indignantly, 'what possesses you? are you crazy? Why, you are going in for realism; do you know that?'

'I don't see any particular realism, Edith,' answered Hamlin, testily.

'Come, now, it isn't Zola,[1] my dear,' said her father, a good-natured man, who never carried his belief in himself to the length which it was carried to by his family.

'No, it isn't Zola,' cried Miss Spencer; 'but it's worse than Zola. . . .'

('It's just the decentest thing I've heard for many a long year,' murmured the old painter.)

'It's worse than Zola, because it's poetry and not prose, because it's English poetry, because it's poetry by Walter Hamlin, who has hitherto been an apostle of beauty, and is now basely turning apostate and going over to ugliness.'

There was a slight laugh at Mrs Spencer's vehemence, in which Hamlin alone did not join.

'I don't think there's anything actually ugly in it,' put in Chough, blandly. 'Hamlin could never write anything ugly. But it is certain that there's a want of idealism in it, a want of that exotic perfume which constitutes the essence of poetry. I think it's an unfortunately chosen subject. . . .'

'I think it's perfectly disgusting,' gobbled out Dennistoun, the little rickety poet, who had to be carried up and down stairs, and

---

[1] French naturalist novels generally provoked a hostile reaction in England because of their alleged emphasis upon the sordid aspects of life.

who wrote, while slowly sinking inch by inch into the grave, about carrying off lovely girls, and throttling them in the fierceness of his love. 'Did you notice about the heroine washing the children? I call that beastly, beastly. And then, I don't know how any man can write a poem about people who are in love and get married.'

This seemed an unanswerable piece of criticism. Anne alone leaned across the table; she was very indignant. 'I think,' she said, 'that there is much more poetry in people who love each other respectably, and respectably get married, than in all the nasty situations which modern poets write about.'

Cosmo Chough looked at Dennistoun, and Dennistoun looked at Mrs Spencer's father.

'My dear young lady,' cried the old painter in his broad Scotch, 'd'ye ever know of any of these gentlemen write a poem about people who did any single respectable thing?'

'I wonder you can talk like that, papa,' silenced his daughter, whose zeal for him and his school included timely snubbings for himself.

'Well, my dear, I privately think with Miss Brown that there's nothing more poetic than a gude, bonnie lass of a wife, and I don't wonder a bit at Walter being of that opinion. But then, of course, I'm not a poet.'

'It's that washing of the children which troubles me,' reflected Chough, 'and their being married. Don't you think, now, Hamlin, that you might just alter a little, and make it appear that they *weren't* married?'

'Only put a husband of the lady in the distance,' suggested O'Reilly, laughing.

'Thank you,' said Hamlin, affecting to laugh, 'your suggestion is most happy, and most characteristic. You are always full of original ideas – all of you,' and he looked bitterly round. Chough felt the rebuke and was silent. But Dennistoun, who was gasping, propped up in his chair, was furious.

'It's not a question of an alteration here or there,' he gobbled out; 'it's the whole tone of the poem which is pestilent. It's Wordsworth pure and simple, that's what it is.'

## From Book VI, Chapter III

From Hamlin himself, and Hamlin's friends (for at Coblenz he had stipulated that Miss Brown was not to be *bored with religion*), she had heard only of the religion of beauty. Of the men and women who used to come to Hammersmith and to Wotton, some, like Chough, professed Catholicism, and wrote mystical rhapsodies to the Virgin Mary; others, like Dennistoun, called the Virgin a prostitute, and God a highway murderer: some went in for imitating the *näiveté* of medieval Christianity; yet others filled their books with hymns to the gods, clean and foul, of paganism. There was a deal of vociferating on the subject; a deal of abusive language both of the religious and the irreligious; a deal of exhortation on the part of men like Hamlin not to have the bad taste to muddle religion with poetry; and on the whole, there was an atmosphere of absolute insincerity, in which, as in abstract politics (for certain aesthetes were extreme retrogrades, and loathed civilisation; while others would pour out by the hour revolutionary tirades of the most blood-thirsty description),[1] it appeared that religion was a mere personal hobby or poetical fiction: the usual conclusion being simply that the world was too disgusting a place for a well-constituted soul; that the century was empty, and heartless, and emasculate; and that, as the people in the 'Decameron' fled from the plague, and told stories and sang songs in a pleasant villa all by themselves, so also must superior men and women fly from the sordidness, the uninterestingness, the mediocrity, and incapacity for passion of reality, and entertain one another with tales of romance and wonder in a fairy land, where the sole divinity was beauty, and where alone, among the lovely and noble things left by the past, noble natures could develop uncramped, according to the ideal of the Greeks, of medieval men, or of that most elevated genius, the late Théophile Gautier.

To meet the terrible realities which were now being revealed to her, to answer her own painful craving after usefulness, Anne had therefore only a vain negative belief – the pessimism which is at the bottom of all aestheticism, the belief in the fatal supremacy of evil and ugliness. But in Anne this purely negative creed speedily became positive; pessimism produced not a desire to abandon the

1 The allusion here is to Swinburne's espousal of Italian nationalism.

odious reality and take refuge in mere imaginary happiness, but a frightful moral tension, a constant battle of her aspirations with her belief, of her conscience with her reason, a strain of rebellion against the inevitable. So, to the weight of the knowledge of evil, to the weight of the consciousness of the deadness of soul which surrounded her, was added in Anne the terrible sense of the injustice and callousness of nature and of fate, of the groundlessness of those instincts of good which left her no peace.

But all this no one ever guessed. She despised indulging her own wretchedness. She went on, behaving as usual, goading herself to practical concerns silently, letting no one know of her misery, letting no thought of it waste a moment of her time. Her longing was to break the hateful solidarity between herself and the school of aesthetic indifferentism; her instinct was, since she (dependent as she felt herself on a man's charity) could not practically help others, at least to understand and feel about all these subjects which Hamlin and his friends tabooed. And with this haunting desire, she turned not merely to Marjory Lee and Harry Collett, but instinctively also to her cousin Dick.

'I have read the books you lent me to take into the country,' she said, giving him back the various primers and pamphlets on economical subjects. 'Thank you so much for them, Dick.'

They were sitting alone in the drawing-room at Hammersmith. Richard Brown had called only once before, ceremoniously and briefly, and he would not have come this time either, if Anne had not written expressly to beg him to fetch back the books. He looked at her in his incredulous, contemptuous way.

'Really,' he said, 'my shabby old books are very much flattered by having been permitted to sojourn so long among such an assemblage of lovely things;' and he looked round the room at the pieces of embroidery and the Eastern carpets, the pictures and drawings, the quantities of Japanese porcelain and lacquer all round. 'How much out of place they do look, and how queer they must have felt among their companions! Let me see: two volumes on artistic furniture – "Ballads of Old France" – "Rossetti" – "Contes de Gautier." I see –'

'Those are Mr Hamlin's books,' said Anne, quickly; 'he must have taken them out of the library, or brought them up from the studio. I am not reading any of them.'

'You are reading nothing but sociology and political economy;

I understand,' went on Brown, with his placid sneer, which seemed, in this frightfully masculine man, to condemn in Anne her mind, her person, her manner, her character, and even her sex. 'Ah, well, I can understand that; it must be refreshing. Who is it – Mr Pater, or some such great gun of yours – who says that the object of the wise man is to make his life consist in as many moments of thrilling impressions as possible; that the very wise people get them out of art and song, and the less wise out of vice or out of philanthropy? You must know the passage better than I. Well, I suppose you have got as many impressions out of art and song as possible, and (being far too delicate in taste to try vice) you are seeing what can be got out of philanthropy. Is that it?'

# F. H. MYERS

## From 'Rossetti and the Religion of Beauty' in *Essays: Modern* (1895)

Among those picturesque aspects of life which the advance of civilisation is tending to reduce to smoothness and uniformity we may include that hubbub and conflict which in rougher days used to salute the appearance of any markedly new influence in science, literature, or art. Prejudice – not long since so formidable and ubiquitous a giant – now shows sometimes little more vitality than Bunyan's Pope or Pagan; and the men who stone one of our modern prophets do it hurriedly, feeling that they may be interrupted at any moment by having to make arrangements for his interment in Westminster Abbey.

Now, while it would be absurd not to rejoice in this increasing receptivity of cultivated men – absurd to wish the struggle of genius sharper, or its recognition longer deferred – we may yet note one incidental advantage which belonged to the older *régime*. While victory was kept longer in doubt, and while the conflict was rougher, the advocates of a new cause felt a stronger obligation to master it in all its aspects, and to set it forth with such exposition as might best prepare a place for it in ordinary minds. The merits of Wordsworth (to take an obvious instance) were long ignored by the public; but in the meantime his admirers had explained them so often and so fully that the recognition which was at last accorded to them was given *on* those merits, and not in mere deference to the authority of any esoteric circle.

The exhibition of Dante Rossetti's pictures which now (February 1883) covers the walls of Burlington House is the visible sign of the admission of a new strain of thought and emotion within the pale of our artistic orthodoxy. And since Rossetti's poetry expresses with singular exactness the same range of ideas as his painting, and is at any rate not inferior to his painting in technical skill, we may fairly say that his poetry also has attained hereby some sort of general recognition, and that the enthusiastic notices which appeared on his decease[1] embodied a view of him to which the public is willing to some extent to defer.

Yet it hardly seems that enough has been done to make that deference spontaneous or intelligent. The students of Rossetti's poems – taking their tone from Mr. Swinburne's magnificent eulogy[2] – have for the most part rather set forth their artistic excellence than endeavoured to explain their contents, or to indicate the relation of the poet's habit of thought and feeling to the ideas which Englishmen are accustomed to trust or admire. And consequently many critics, whose ethical point of view demands respect, continue to find in Rossetti's works an enigma not worth the pains of solution, and to decry them as obscure, fantastic, or even as grossly immoral in tendency.

It will be the object of this essay – written from a point of view of by no means exclusive sympathy with the movement which Rossetti led – to show, in the first place, the great practical importance of that movement for good or evil; and, further, to trace such relations between this Religion of Art, this Worship of Beauty, and the older and more accredited manifestations of the Higher Life, as may indicate to the moralist on what points he should concentrate his efforts if, hopeless of withstanding the rising stream, he seeks at least to retain some power of deepening or modifying its channel.

From the aesthetic side such an attempt will be regarded with indifference, and from the ethical side with little hope. Even so

---

1 In 1882.

2 Probably Swinburne's 'Notes on Some Pictures of 1868' in *Essays and Studies* (1875).

bold a peacemaker as the author of *Natural Religion*[1] has shrunk from this task; for the art which he admits as an element in his Church of Civilisation is an art very different from Rossetti's. It is an art manifestly untainted by sensuousness, manifestly akin to virtue; an art which, like Wordsworth's, finds its revelation in sea and sky and mountain rather than in 'eyes which the sun-gate of the soul unbar,' or in

> Such fire as Love's soul-winnowing hands distil,
> Even from his inmost ark of light and dew.

Yet, however slight the points of contact between the ethical and the aesthetic theories of life may be, it is important that they should be noted and dwelt upon. For assuredly the 'aesthetic movement' is not a mere fashion of the day – the modish pastime of nincompoops and charlatans. The imitators who surround its leaders, and whose jargon almost disgusts us with the very mysteries of art, the very vocabulary of emotion – these men are but the straws that mark the current, the inevitable parasites of a rapidly-rising cause. We have, indeed, only to look around us to perceive that – whether or not the conditions of the modern world are favourable to artistic *excellence* – all the main forces of civilisation are tending towards artistic *activity*. The increase of wealth, the diffusion of education, the gradual decline of the military, the hieratic, the aristocratic ideals – each of these causes removes some obstacle from the artist's path or offers some fresh prize to his endeavours. Art has outlived both the Puritans and the Inquisition; she is no longer deadened by the spirit of self-mortification, nor enslaved by a jealous orthodoxy. The increased wealth of the world makes the artist's life stable and secure, while it sets free a surplus income so large that an increasing share of it must almost necessarily be diverted to some form of aesthetic expenditure.

And more than this. It is evident, especially in new countries, that a need is felt of some kind of social distinction – some new aristocracy – based on differences other than those of birth and wealth. Not, indeed, that rank and family are likely to cease to be held in honour; but, as power is gradually dissociated from them, they lose their exclusive predominance, and take their place on the same footing as other graces and dignities of life. Still less need we assume any

---

1 i.e. David Hume, *Dialogues Concerning Natural Religion* (1779).

slackening in the pursuit of riches; the fact being rather that this pursuit is so widely successful that in civilised capitals even immense opulence can now scarcely confer on its possessor all the distinction which he desires. In America, accordingly, where modern instincts find their freest field, we have before our eyes the process of the gradual distribution of the old prerogatives of birth amongst wealth, culture, and the proletariat. In Europe a class privileged by birth used to supply at once the rulers and the ideals of other men. In America the *rule* has passed to the multitude; largely swayed in subordinate matters by organised wealth, but in the last resort supreme. The *ideal* of the new community at first was Wealth; but, as its best literature and its best society plainly show, that ideal is shifting in the direction of Culture. The younger cities, the coarser classes, still bow down undisguisedly to the god Dollar; but when this Philistine deity is rejected as shaming his worshippers, aesthetic Culture seems somehow the only Power ready to install itself in the vacant shrine.

And all over the world the spread of Science, the diffusion of Morality, tend in this same direction. For the net result of Science and Morality for the mass of men is simply to give them comfort and leisure, to leave them cheerful, peaceful, and anxious for occupation. Nay, even the sexual instinct, as men become less vehement and unbridled, merges in larger and larger measure into the mere aesthetic enjoyment of beauty; till Stesichorus[1] might now maintain with more truth than of old that our modern Helen is not herself fought for by two continents, but rather her εἴδωλον or image is blamelessly diffused over the albums of two hemispheres.

It is by no means clear that these modern conditions are favourable to the development either of the highest art or of the highest virtue. It is not certain even that they are permanent – that this aesthetic paradise of the well-to-do may not sometime be convulsed by an invasion from the rough world without. Meantime, however, it exists and spreads, and its leading figures exert an influence which few men of science, and fewer theologians, can surpass. And alike to *savant*, to theologian, and to moralist, it must be important to trace the workings of a powerful mind, concerned with interests which are so different from theirs, but which for a large section of society are becoming daily more paramount and engrossing.

1 A Greek lyric poet who used mainly epic subjects.

# MAX BEERBOHM

## From '1880' in *The Yellow Book* (1894)

'History,' it has been said, 'does not repeat itself. The historians repeat one another.' Now, there are still some periods with which no historian has grappled, and, strangely enough, the period that most greatly fascinates me is one of them. The labour I set myself is therefore rather Herculean. But it is also, for me, so far a labour of love that I can quite forget or even revel in its great difficulty. I would love to have lived in those bygone days, when first society was inducted into the mysteries of art and, not losing yet its old and elegant *tenue*, babbled of blue china and white lilies, of the painter Rossetti and the poet Swinburne [ . . . ].

The period of 1880 and of the two successive years should ever be memorable, for it marks a great change in the constitution of English society. It would seem that under the quiet *régime* of the Tory Cabinet, the Upper Ten Thousand (as they were quaintly called in those days) had taken a somewhat more frigid tone. The Prince of Wales had inclined to be restful after the revels of his youth. The prolonged seclusion of Queen Victoria, who was then engaged upon that superb work of introspection and self-analysis, *More Leaves from the Highlands*, had begun to tell upon the social system. Balls and other festivities, both at Court and in the houses of the nobles, were notably fewer. The vogue of the Opera was passing. Even in the top of the season, Rotten Row, I read, was not impenetrably crowded. But in 1880 came the tragic fall of Disraeli and the triumph of the Whigs. How great a change came then upon Westminster must be known to any one who has studied the annals of Gladstone's incomparable Parliament. Gladstone himself, with a monstrous majority behind him, revelling in the old splendour of speech that not seventy summers nor six years' sulking had made less; Parnell,[1] deadly, mysterious, with his crew of wordy peasants that were to set all Saxon things at naught – the

1 i.e. Charles Stuart Parnell, the Irish nationalist politician.

activity of these two men alone would have made this Parliament supremely stimulating throughout the land. What of young Randolph Churchill,[1] who, despite his halting speech, foppish mien and rather coarse fibre of mind, was yet the greatest Parliamentarian of his day? What of Justin Huntly McCarthy, under his puerile mask a most dark, most dangerous conspirator, who, lightly swinging the sacred lamp of burlesque, irradiated with fearful clarity the wrath and sorrow of Ireland? What of Blocker Warton? What of the eloquent atheist, Charles Bradlaugh, pleading at the Bar, striding past the furious Tories to the very Mace, hustled down the stone steps with the broadcloth torn in ribands from his back? Surely such scenes will never more be witnessed at St. Stephen's.[2] Imagine the existence of God being made a party question! No wonder that at a time of such turbulence fine society also should have shown the primordia of a great change. It was felt that the aristocracy could not live by good-breeding alone. The old delights seemed vapid, waxen. Something vivid was desired. And so the sphere of fashion converged with the sphere of art, and revolution was the result.

Be it remembered that long before this time there had been in the heart of Chelsea a kind of cult for Beauty. Certain artists had settled there, deliberately refusing to work in the ordinary official way, and 'wrought,' as they were wont to asseverate, 'for the pleasure and sake of all that is fair.' Little commerce had they with the brazen world. Nothing but the light of the sun would they share with men. Quietly and unbeknown, callous to all but their craft, they wrought their poems or their pictures, gave them one to another, and wrought on. Meredith, Rossetti, Swinburne, Morris, Holman Hunt were in this band of shy artificers. In fact, Beauty had existed long before 1880. It was Mr. Oscar Wilde who managed her *début*. To study the period is to admit that to him was due no small part of the social vogue that Beauty began to enjoy. Fired by his fervid words, men and women hurled their mahogany into the streets and ransacked the curio-shops for the furniture of Annish days. Dados arose upon every wall, sunflowers and the feathers of peacocks curved in every corner, tea grew quite cold while the guests were praising the Willow Pattern of its cup. A few fashionable women even dressed themselves in sinuous draperies and unheard-of greens.

1 i.e. Lord Randolph Churchill, the Tory politician.
2 Controversial late nineteenth century politicians. Charles Bradlaugh achieved notoriety for refusing to take the oath in the House of Commons.

Into whatsoever ball-room you went, you would surely find, among the women in tiaras and the fops and the distinguished foreigners, half a score of comely ragamuffins in velveteen, murmuring sonnets, posturing, waving their hands. Beauty was sought in the most unlikely places. Young painters found her mobled in the fogs, and bank-clerks, versed in the writings of Mr. Hamerton,[1] were heard to declare as they sped home from the City, that the Underground Railway was beautiful from London Bridge to Westminster, but not from Sloane Square to Notting Hill Gate.

Aestheticism (for so they named the movement) did indeed permeate, in a manner, all classes. But it was to the *beau monde* that its primary appeal was made. The sacred emblems of Chelsea were sold in the fashionable toy-shops, its reverently chanted creeds became the patter of the *boudoirs*. The old Grosvenor Gallery, that stronghold of the few, was verily invaded. Never was such a fusion of delightful folk as at its Private Views [ . . . ].

'Private Views'. *This passage, which I found in a contemporary chronicle, is so quaint and so instinct with the spirit of its time that I am fain to quote it:*

*'There were quaint, beautiful, extraordinary costumes walking about – ultra-aesthetics, artistic-aesthetics, aesthetics that made up their minds to be daring, and suddenly gave way in some important point – put a frivolous bonnet on the top of a grave and flowing garment that Albert Durer might have designed for a mantle. There were fashionable costumes that Mrs. Mason or Madame Elise might have turned out that morning. The motley crowd mingled, forming into groups, sometimes dazzling you by the array of colours that you never thought to see in full daylight. . . . Canary-coloured garments flitted cheerily by garments of the saddest green. A hat in an agony of pokes and angles was seen in company with a bonnet that was a gay garland of flowers. A vast cape that might have enshrouded the form of a Mater Dolorosa hung by the side of a jauntily-striped Langtry-hood.'* [Beerbohm's note]

1 i.e. Philip Gilbert Hamerton (1834–94), artist and essayist.

# Further Reading

LIONEL JOHNSON

*Complete Poems* (ed. I. Fletcher), London, 1953.
*Post Liminium* (ed. T. Whittemore), London, 1912.

WALTER PATER

*The Renaissance*
*Marius the Epicurean*
*Appreciations*
*Imaginary Portraits*
*Plato and Platonism*
(Library Edition) all London, 1910.
*Letters* (ed. L. Evans), Oxford, 1970.

J. A. MCN. WHISTLER

*The Gentle Art of Making Enemies*, London, 1890.

ALGERNON SWINBURNE

*Works* (Bonchurch Edition), London, 1925–7.
*Love's Cross-Currents* and *Lesbia Brandon* in *The Novels of A. C. Swinburne* (ed. Edmund Wilson), New York, 1962.
*Letters* (ed. Cecil Y. Lang), Yale, New Haven, 1959–62.

OSCAR WILDE

There is (as yet) no standard edition of Wilde, but the following is adequate for most readers:
*The Works of Oscar Wilde* (ed. G. F. Maine), London, 1948.
*The Artist as Critic* (ed. R. Ellmann), London, 1970.
*Letters* (ed. R. Hart-Davis), London, 1963.
For the literary and social context of the Aesthetic Movement, the following works are relevant:
Théophile Gautier, *Mademoiselle de Maupin*, Paris, 1835.
William Morris, *Hopes and Fears for Art*, London, 1882.

D. G. Rossetti, 'Hand and Soul', *The Germ*, London, 1850.
John Ruskin, *The Political Economy of Art*, London, 1857.


*General*

Ian Fletcher, *Walter Pater*, London (British Council), 1959.
William Gaunt, *The Aesthetic Adventure*, London, 2nd ed., 1975.
Peter Gunn, *Vernon Lee*, London, 1964.
Graham Hough, *The Last Romantics*, London, 1949.
Holbrook Jackson, *The Eighteen-Nineties*, London, 1913.
R. V. Johnson, *Aestheticism*, London, 1969.
René Wellek, *History of Modern Criticism*, vols III and IV, London, 1955–66.